WHERE TO SEE THE BEST OF

BRITISH
STEAM TRAINS

The essential Touring Guide for every Railway Enthusiast

WHERE TO SEE THE BEST OF
BRITISH STEAM TRAINS

The essential Touring Guide for every Railway Enthusiast

David & Charles

A DAVID & CHARLES BOOK

First published in the UK in 2000

A catalogue record for this book is available
from the British Library.

ISBN 0 7153 1116 6

Designed, edited and produced by
Eaglemoss Publications Ltd, based on
the partwork *World of Trains*

Front cover photograph: John Cooper Smith
Back cover photograph: John Hunt

Printed in Spain
for David & Charles, Brunel House,
Newton Abbot, Devon

Every effort has been made to ensure the accuracy of the information
in this book. However, it is possible that timetables may change.
Also locomotives may be acquired, loaned or returned.
It is therefore advisable to check these and other details with
the specific railway in advance.

Contents

ENGLAND

The South Devon Railway

**It is more than a century since a railway
was built through the lush Dart Valley between
Totnes and Ashburton. Although it has undergone several changes
of name and ownership since then, the Primrose Line
still retains its manifest charms.**

Of the many preserved railways in Britain, the South Devon Railway (SDR), or Primrose Line, is one of the prettiest. The 22.5km (14 mile) round trip along the east bank of the meandering River Dart takes the traveller through the heart of the Devon countryside, re-creating the atmosphere of a typical Great Western Railway (GWR) branch line.

The SDR is a section of the old Totnes–Ashburton line, completed in 1872. It takes its name from the company that built the route. The line was owned by the Buckfastleigh, Totnes & South Devon Railway (BT&SDR), but it was worked by the SDR until the Great Western took over in 1876, two years before the SDR's dissolution.

As with so many other branch lines, the increasing use of motor vehicles made serious inroads into the SDR's business, and in 1958 its passenger service was closed down by the GWR's successor, the Western Region of BR. The goods service survived for a little longer, but in 1962 that, too, was withdrawn.

▼ GWR 0-6-0 No 7752, on loan from Birmingham Railway Museum until recently, pulls out of Buckfastleigh. The track has now been upgraded to 18 tonnes (tons), allowing it to run a wider range of engines.

Star attractions
Situated in the former goods shed at Buckfastleigh station is the Primrose Line's railway museum. This contains the only broad gauge locomotive still in existence – the 0-4-0VBT No 151 *Tiny*, built for the South Devon Railway in 1868, just four years after its opening.

Tiny, on loan from the National Railway Museum (NRM), was withdrawn in 1883 and used as a stationary engine at Newton Abbot works until placed on display at the station there in 1927.

Another star exhibit, also on loan from the NRM, is the former London & South Western Railway 2-4-0WT No 3298. This locomotive was built in 1874 and worked for many years on the Wenford Bridge branch, near Bodmin, hauling china clay.

After more than 90 years, the SDR seemed to have reached a dead end. However, a group of businessmen who were also railway enthusiasts announced that they would try to rescue the line. Many years of negotiation and delay followed, but on 21 May 1969 the South Devon was officially reopened by Lord Beeching, who as chairman of BR had been better known for closing lines down.

Unfortunately, the construction of the new A38 trunk road from Exeter to Plymouth put paid to plans for resurrecting the Buckfastleigh to Ashburton section of the line, with the result that Buckfastleigh became the northern terminus and headquarters of the railway.

Even so, it is worth making the short drive along the A38 to Ashburton, because the terminus building, with its over-roof designed by Brunel, still survives, though it is now used as a garage and service station. Across the road is the former Railway Hotel, aptly but rather sadly renamed the Silent Whistle.

The South Devon reborn

Following its rebirth in 1969, the line has operated under various names – the Dart Valley Railway, the Buckfast Steam & Leisure Park and the Buckfast Steam Railway. In 1991, the line was leased by the newly formed South Devon Railway Trust, since when it has operated once again as the South Devon Railway.

The most convenient starting point for a journey on the SDR is Buckfastleigh. It is easily reached from the A38 and free car parking is provided. Other facilities include a well-stocked souvenir shop, a refreshment room and a small railway museum. Nearby is the famous Buckfast

▲ Staverton Bridge typifies the GWR country station. But the South Devon, always ready for improvement, reactivated the passing loop at Staverton, using a signalbox recovered from Athelney, near Taunton, to control it.

▼ On display at the SDR's railway museum at Buckfastleigh, No 3298 was built in 1874 for the London & South Western Railway. The locomotive was later owned by the Southern Railway and appears in immaculate SR livery.

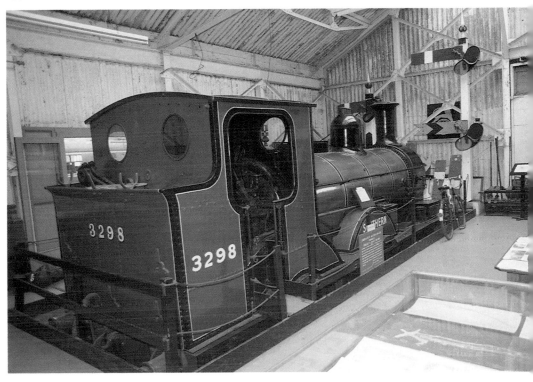

Abbey. This Norman-style building was completed by monks in 1938 and stands on the site of a ruined 10th century abbey.

The railway is still run in true Great Western fashion using, wherever possible, the type of locomotives that worked the line in its heyday. These are sometimes backed up by locomotives visiting from other lines.

As the train pulls away from the platform, you will see to your left a butterfly farm and an otter sanctuary, both of which are well worth a visit on your return. Crossing the River Mardle and then, via a small girder bridge, the River Dart, the train enters the beautiful Dart Valley.

From now on the railway shares the tranquillity of the river as it winds its way down towards Totnes. The valley is at its best in the spring and early summer, when it is bestrewn with flowers. Because of its isolation, the valley teems with wildlife, including foxes and badgers. The river itself is a magnet for swans, herons and salmon.

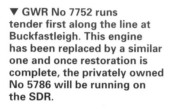

▼ **GWR No 7752 runs tender first along the line at Buckfastleigh. This engine has been replaced by a similar one and once restoration is complete, the privately owned No 5786 will be running on the SDR.**

Rounding a rather sharp bend, your train arrives at Staverton Bridge, the only intermediate station on the line. This is a typical Great Western country station, complete with level crossing and ground-level signalbox.

In days gone by, the platforms of Staverton station would have been loaded with cider barrels from the local farming communities. In recent times, the station has provided the scenes for many television and big-screen productions, including the Sherlock Holmes classic, *The Hound of the Baskervilles*.

The signalbox here has an unusual history. After the line was closed, it was purchased by a local rector for use as a garden shed. However, when the line was reopened, he agreed to return the box – in exchange for a new shed.

It is certainly worth stopping off here. Next to the station is Staverton bridge, one of the oldest

road bridges in Devon. This crosses the Dart and joins a footpath leading to Staverton village, with its ancient church and inviting hostelry. The inn dates from the 13th century and was once used as a rest home by the monks from nearby Buckfast Abbey.

After Staverton, the train continues down the valley to the town of Totnes. Under a kilometre (half a mile) from Totnes is a crossing known locally as Knapper's crossing, after Mrs Knapper, a well-loved local character who operated the crossing gates for many years.

Problems in negotiating access to the platforms of the mainline station mean that the train terminates just outside Totnes, at the stop named Totnes (Littlehempston). This small station has been constructed by the railway's volunteer workforce, using a variety of buildings and installations from other closed West Country stations. The station building, for example, came from Toller, on the Bridport branch, while the canopy originated at Axbridge, on the Yatton to Wells line.

Recently, the town of Totnes has been made accessible via a footbridge and footpath crossing over the River Dart. At Totnes connections can be made with mainline train services.

Climb back to Buckfastleigh

The engine, having run round its train, is ready to set off again. The trip to Totnes (Littlehempston) was on a falling gradient, so on the return journey the engine has to work much harder.

Back at Buckfastleigh, you should allow time for a visit to the locomotive and carriage shed. Of the many items of coaching stock to be seen here, the most spectacular is the restored ex-GWR Ocean Saloon, No 9111 *King George*. This sumptuous coach was constructed by the Great Western in 1932 for use on the Ocean Expresses between Plymouth and London.

Only eight of these carriages were ever built and they all carried names of members of the royal family. These days, *King George* is still used on certain selected services, although you don't need a luxurious carriage to enjoy a trip on the Primrose Line.

▲ The GWR 4-4-0 *City of Truro*, a former visitor from the National Railway Museum in York, heads a rake of GWR coaches towards Totnes (Littlehempston). Immediately behind the locomotive is one of the SDR's élite vehicles – the Ocean Saloon, *King George*, built in 1932 for use on the special boat trains that ran between Plymouth and London.

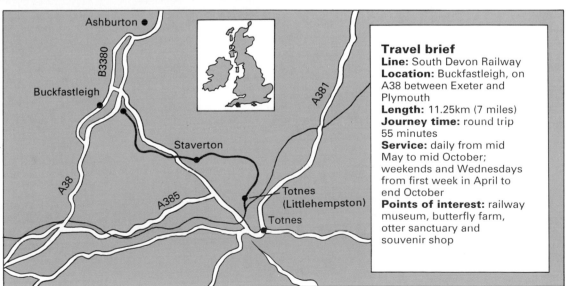

Travel brief
Line: South Devon Railway
Location: Buckfastleigh, on A38 between Exeter and Plymouth
Length: 11.25km (7 miles)
Journey time: round trip 55 minutes
Service: daily from mid May to mid October; weekends and Wednesdays from first week in April to end October
Points of interest: railway museum, butterfly farm, otter sanctuary and souvenir shop

West Somerset Railway

The West Somerset Railway, running for 32km (20 miles) through the Quantock Hills to the Bristol Channel, is Britain's longest preserved line. Operating more stations in Somerset than British Rail, it recaptures for the modern traveller the excitement of a trip to the seaside in the days of steam.

The original West Somerset Railway (WSR), designed by Brunel, opened in 1862 as a broad-gauge branch line from Norton Fitzwarren, near Taunton, to the harbour at Watchet. In 1874, it was extended to Minehead, and both parts of the line were worked by the Bristol & Exeter Railway (B&ER) until 1922, when the branch was taken over by the mighty Great Western. By that time, it had been converted to a standard-gauge line.

In 1948, after years of uneventful existence, the WSR became part of British Railways. Although escaping the wholesale closures of the 1960s, the West Somerset's receipts were badly affected by the growth in road traffic, and the last train was run by BR in 1971. Soon after this, the present West Somerset Railway Company was formed with the object of purchasing the line from BR and reopening it. In the event, it was Somerset County Council, with a shrewd eye for the potential tourist traffic, that in 1973 took over the line from BR and leased it to the new company.

After much negotiation and several delays in receiving the light railway order, the West Somerset was reopened for passenger traffic between Minehead and Blue Anchor on 28 March 1976. Passenger services were extended to Williton in August 1976, to Stogumber in April 1977 and to Bishop's Lydeard in June 1979.

At present, apart from the occasional special service, WSR trains do not run between Bishop's

▼ No 6024 *King Edward I* passes Kentsford Farm crossing near Watchet in 1997. As a popular engine, *King Edward I* has enjoyed repeated visits to the West Somerset Railway. One such visit was a gala event in 2000.

The signalbox on the down platform and passing loop has been fully reinstated following rebuilding, enabling trains to pass at this delightful rural station. Also at Crowcombe Heathfield is an exhibition of various types of track, including Brunel's broad gauge.

Hillside track

As you accelerate away from Crowcombe Heathfield, the splendour of the Somerset countryside becomes apparent. The line here runs down a valley formed by the Brendon Hills on the left and the Quantocks on the right. In fact, the track skirts along the side of one of the hills.

This is most striking at Stogumber, where the lack of space has meant that the platform is situated on the opposite side of the line to the station building.

For the last kilometre (mile) or so, the train has been travelling downhill and this continues to Williton, the halfway point of the journey. Williton, which is the headquarters of the WSR's diesel fleet, has a unique complex of Bristol & Exeter Railway architecture dating from the opening of the line. This includes the B&ER signalbox

▼ A GWR 0-6-0PT, No 6412, its sides almost touching the grassy embankment, slices through a cutting on the West Somerset Railway. Built in 1934, the locomotive was withdrawn by BR 20 years later. It came to the West Somerset in 1976.

▲ A stalwart of the West Somerset, No 53808 heads a rake of BR Western Region coaches into the beachside station of Blue Anchor. The level crossing gates are still controlled by the original mechanism inside the GWR signalbox.

Lydeard and Norton Fitzwarren, so if you are travelling from inland to the coast, you will start your journey at Bishop's Lydeard. This has a large free car park, sales and information centre, and a visitor centre, all adjacent to the station.

There are around half a dozen steam locomotives currently on the line, most of them from the GWR stable. These include No 4561, a Small Prairie 2-6-2T built in 1924; No 4160, a Large Prairie 2-6-2T built in 1948; No 7820 *Dinmore Manor* and No 7828 *Odney Manor* both built in 1950. No 88, built in 1925, spent the whole of its mainline working life at the Somerset and Dorset Railway between Bath and Bournemouth and is now undergoing a heavy general overhaul. Also under restoration are 2-8-0 No 3850 built in 1944 and rebuilt Bulleid West Country No 34046 *Braunton*.

The journey begins

Leaving Bishop's Lydeard, the train climbs for the next 6.5km (four miles) up to Crowcombe Heathfield, which, at 122m (400ft), is the highest point on the line. Crowcombe Heathfield is a typical example of a Great Western country branch station, having been splendidly restored. In 1985, it won the Association of Railway Preservation Societies' best station award and has been featured many times in films and on television.

Threat to the line

After leaving Doniford, the train steams along the cliff top towards Watchet. In 1987, there was a major landslip in this area that threatened to cut the line in half. Although this problem was solved at the time, further coastal protection work is needed in this area to secure the long-term safety of the line.

Watchet was the original north-western terminus of the WSR, which explains why the station building, unlike those you have already passed, stands at right angles to the line at the end of the platform. The views here are stunning, with the great sweep of the Bristol Channel to the right, the Brendon Hills to the left and the hazy, far-off expanse of Exmoor directly ahead.

After swinging inland for several kilometres (miles), the train pulls into Washford. Built in 1874 as part of the extension to Minehead, it is the headquarters of the Somerset & Dorset Railway Trust. The station building now houses the S&DJR museum which, together with a working replica of the former Midford signalbox, conjures up memories of the long-vanished Bath to Bournemouth line. Those with a taste for the even more distant past may care to visit nearby Cleeve Abbey, which dates from the 12th century.

Way to the beach

From Washford the train heads back to the coast again, descending for 3.25km (two miles) down to Blue Anchor. The station, which is right next to the beach, is another favourite alighting point. But sun and sand are not the only attractions. The large wheel that can be seen inside the GWR signalbox at the end of the up platform still controls the old

▲ No 53808, a Class 7F 2-8-0 built in 1925 for the Somerset & Dorset Joint Railway, heads a train along the coast near Watchet. In 1987, there was a major landslip in the area and the cliff on which the WSR ran had to be rebuilt.

– the only one still in operation. An 1889 shed, acquired for Swindon Railway Works, has been erected at Williton to accommodate repairs and overhauls of the fleet.

A short distance from Williton the train reaches the coast and halts at the recently built station of Doniford Beach. Opened in 1988, and made up of parts from other closed Great Western stations, it serves a nearby holiday complex.

▶ Passing below a stone road bridge, a Collett 2251 class 0-6-0, No 3205, heads up the track between Stogumber and Crowcombe Heathfield. The sole survivor of this 120 strong class, it was completed at Swindon in 1946 and was first allocated to Gloucester.

▲ With its careful selection of props and posters, Bishop's Lydeard exudes the atmosphere of a typical West Country branch line station in the 1930s. However, its rustic air belies the fact that it is now a terminus of one of the country's most popular preserved railways, carrying over 100,000 passengers a year.

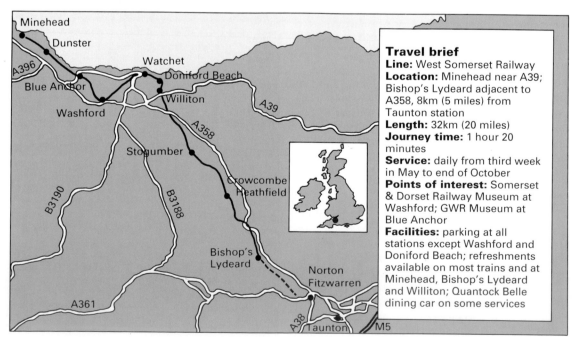

Travel brief
Line: West Somerset Railway
Location: Minehead near A39; Bishop's Lydeard adjacent to A358, 8km (5 miles) from Taunton station
Length: 32km (20 miles)
Journey time: 1 hour 20 minutes
Service: daily from third week in May to end of October
Points of interest: Somerset & Dorset Railway Museum at Washford; GWR Museum at Blue Anchor
Facilities: parking at all stations except Washford and Doniford Beach; refreshments available on most trains and at Minehead, Bishop's Lydeard and Williton; Quantock Belle dining car on some services

▲ Steaming west tender first, No 53808 hauls a train past the rolling Quantock Hills towards Minehead. Since the first section was reopened in 1976, the line's popularity has steadily increased, and the train service now clocks up more than 72,420km (45,000 miles) a year.

Mineral railway
In 1862, when the original WSR reached Watchet, the little seaport was already the terminus for the West Somerset Mineral Railway. Work on the line, which was designed to link up with the iron workings high in the Brendon Hills, started in 1856, and the first section, from Watchet to Roadwater, was opened the following year.

The run up into the Brendons, completed in 1858, was laid on a massive 1 in 4 incline that was worked by a stationary steam engine hauling wagons up and down by means of a long cable. The line, which was laid to standard gauge, finally closed in 1910 and during World War I the rails were torn up and used for scrap.

gated level crossing and is now the only working example left in the West Country. The former waiting room on the down platform houses the Great Western Railway museum. Opened in 1985, it has one of the best collections of railwayana to be found anywhere in the country.

Shortly after leaving Blue Anchor, you will see Dunster Castle looming up on your left. Built in 1070 on the site of a Saxon fortress, the Castle, now the property of the National Trust, was for 600 years the home of the Luttrell family. It was the Luttrells who provided much of the money for the extension of the line from Watchet to Minehead, and George Luttrell was the first chairman of the Minehead Railway Company, under whose auspices the new link was built. For such a small station, Dunster has an unusually elaborate entrance, a further sign of the Luttrell family's influence.

Only 10 minutes' walk from the station is the village of Dunster itself. Here there is a medieval Yarn Market, as well as a superb 18th century watermill that has recently been restored.

As the train approaches Minehead, you will see, not a castle, but the large multi-million pound Butlin's Family Entertainment Resort. The station is situated next to the promenade, and on a fine day the view of the old town and the North Hill make a fine backdrop as you leave the train. The platform here is 400m (¼ mile) long and was designed to take the longest of holiday trains during the heyday of Great Western services.

This terminus is the headquarters of the WSR, and as such it has undergone a number of additions and alterations. These have been tastefully carried out, however, and Minehead station is still as unmistakably Victorian in character as the superbly preserved drinking fountain set in the station wall.

The town is a typical West Country seaside resort with a good beach and plenty to see and do. But before you leave the station, have a look at the repair shop, where restoration and maintenance work is carried out on the WSR's collection of steam locomotives, carriages and wagons.

Paignton & Dartmouth Railway

With the crisp sharp beat of the exhaust echoing back over the chocolate and cream coaches – and perhaps with *Lydham Manor* at the head end – travel in Great Western style through 11.25km (seven miles) of glorious Devon countryside.

▼ With the ancient town of Dartmouth and the impressive naval college on the opposite hillside, No 7827 *Lydham Manor* eases the leading coach over the marina crossing as the train slides out of Kingswear. Built as an ambulance coach, the Devon Belle observation car was converted in 1921 for Pullman service.

Once, in the great days of steam, the Torbay express ran from London's Paddington station bound for Torquay, Paignton and Kingswear – and there was a GWR ferry to a station across the water at Dartmouth.

Now mainline trains terminate at Paignton, glistening Castles and Kings no longer hiss and sparkle by the platforms with their shiny green paint and polished brasswork, and the mutter of diesel engines replaces the rasping exhaust of a departing steam engine. But all is not lost. Happily, the Paignton to Kingswear section lives on. Closed and then rescued in 1972, the old Paignton to Kingswear branch is now a steam tourist line – one of Britain's best, and one of the few lines capable of regularly taking large express locomotives over its tracks.

What's more, the PDR still reflects the splendour of the Great Western Railway, with most of its engines in Brunswick green with polished brass

▲ *Lydham Manor* stands in the head shunt at Paignton. The PDR runs alongside mainline track as far as the carriage sidings at Goodrington. One of the named locomotives used regularly on the line, the Manor Class 4-6-0 tender locomotive was rescued from Barry scrapyard and later restored to full GWR livery.

nameplates, the coaches in the once so familiar chocolate and cream.

All the excitement and bustle of the world of trains are there, from the largest features – busy terminal stations, dark tunnels and lofty viaducts forging a way through surrounding countryside – to the minutiae which capture the quality of great bygone days – the guard's whistle and green flag, the sound of exhaust beats accelerating as the driver opens the regulator, shrill GWR whistles and the tang of smoke.

Starting point

After the takeover by the Dart Valley Railway, alterations were needed at Paignton to provide the new organization with a completely independent track to Goodrington, and a new station complete with run-round loop, sidings and coaling and watering facilities.

▲ With the blue of Torbay and distant views of Torquay as backdrop, 2-8-0T No 5239 *Goliath* – the most powerful preserved tank engine in Britain – storms the gradient towards Churston. These 2-8-0 tanks were built for such heavy duties as Welsh coal trains. *Goliath* was rescued from Barry scrapyard in 1973.

▶Class 45XX 2-6-2T No 4555 climbs bunker first past Goodrington Sands during the height of the summer season – there are two of these 2-6-2 tanks working the PDR line. Just ahead there's a stiff four-kilometre (2½ mile) haul up to Churston, the highest point on the line.

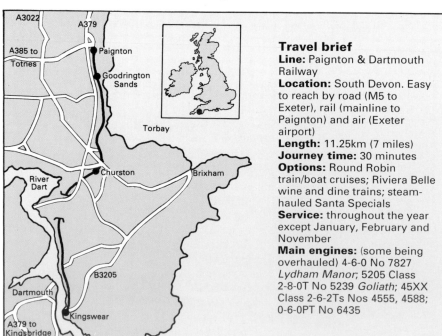

Travel brief
Line: Paignton & Dartmouth Railway
Location: South Devon. Easy to reach by road (M5 to Exeter), rail (mainline to Paignton) and air (Exeter airport)
Length: 11.25km (7 miles)
Journey time: 30 minutes
Options: Round Robin train/boat cruises; Riviera Belle wine and dine trains; steam-hauled Santa Specials
Service: throughout the year except January, February and November
Main engines: (some being overhauled) 4-6-0 No 7827 *Lydham Manor*; 5205 Class 2-8-0T No 5239 *Goliath*; 45XX Class 2-6-2Ts Nos 4555, 4588; 0-6-0PT No 6435

Paignton station now has a large concourse, shop and buffet. There is a crossover connection with South West Trains which makes it possible to run through excursions from South West Trains starting points to Kingswear with PDR locomotives taking over the train in Paignton station.

Because of the steep gradients on the line, some powerful locomotives are in use. These include two 2-6-2 tanks, a 4-6-0 tender engine and a 2-8-0 tank. Most are named to give extra personality to each train, although in Western days only the 4-6-0 No 7827 *Lydham Manor* carried nameplates.

The line is single track all the way, apart from the passing loop at Churston. During the mid 1990s the railway acquired an updated signal system with modern coloured light signals all

operated from one signalbox at Britannia level crossing near Kingswear. The line is track circuit block throughout.

Sea views

After Paignton South, the train runs parallel with the neighbouring mainline. By the time you reach Goodrington platform you have an excellent view of the sea and the golden sands. On a sunny day there will be bathers and families with picnics.

At this point the train starts to tackle the long climb up to Churston, with gradients of 1 in 70 steepening at times to 1 in 60. The crisp sharp exhaust beat of the old Western engine echoes back over the coaches as Goodrington Sands and Torbay open up on the left.

The line soars over two high viaducts – when seen from ground level, the train seems minuscule; the brick arches dwarf it. Then the summit of the line, Churston station, rolls into view. Just before you get to the station there is a carriage siding and a turntable. Because of curves on the line the

▲ Before dropping down to river level on the last stage of the journey the railway crosses Maypole Viaduct. Dense woods flanking the line sweep right down to the Dart estuary – there are spectacular views across the river upstream and down towards Dartmouth.

wheels tend to wear more on one side – to even things out, engines and coaches are turned from time to time.

Churston station was once the junction for the Brixham branch but in the late 1950s this closed and the track was removed. In busy times, trains pass at Churston, giving it the air of a lively country station reminiscent of the old days when it was part of the Great Western Railway.

From Churston on it is almost all downhill, with gradients varying from 1 in 100 to 1 in 66. You travel through steeply rolling country, much of it densely wooded, until the train is swallowed

►Trains pass at Churston during the peak season.

▼ The waterside station at Kingswear, complete with milk churns and advertisements of the era, has a special GWR charm. The PDR has often been host to TV and film companies – the railway scenes of *The French Lieutenant's Woman* were shot here.

up in the 453m (495yd) long Greenway Tunnel to emerge from the blackness in a sudden change of scenery.

Here the line winds high above thickly wooded slopes which border the Dart estuary before gradually dropping down to river level. The railway veers away from the shore past Longwood and Noss Creeks, then on to the water's edge now on the left side.

Journey's end

The vista of Dartmouth Harbour with its mass of small ships and yachts gradually opens up, with Britannia Royal Naval College on a hillside just across the water. Another kilometre (mile) or so and Kingswear station platform hoves into sight and the train comes to rest.

Over the sparkling water lies Dartmouth, no longer reached by an official railway ferry but with plenty of boats to take passengers. Return travellers from Dartmouth should allow at least half an hour in busy periods for the ferry back to Kingswear.

The Bodmin & Wenford Railway

**The Bodmin & Wenford Railway, with its
dramatic gradients and panoramic views, is Cornwall's
only preserved standard-gauge steam railway.
It was the first preserved line with a regular,
year-round commercial freight service.**

Bodmin, the county town of Cornwall, is situated on the edge of Bodmin Moor. The nearest mainline station is Bodmin Parkway, previously known as Bodmin Road, about 4.75km (three miles) to the south east. The former Great Western Railway (GWR) branch line which climbs from Bodmin Parkway up to Bodmin itself was closed by BR in 1983, only to reopen in 1990 thanks to the efforts of the Bodmin & Wenford Railway (BWR) and its volunteer workforce.

The BWR operates a service from Bodmin to Parkway and from Bodmin to Boscarne Junction, a second branch line which opened in 1996. Trains run on selected days between April and the end of October, with daily services from late May Bank Holiday to the end of September. Steam trains are the rule except for summer Saturdays, the holidaymakers' traditional changeover day, when patronage is light and diesel power is rostered instead.

The headquarters of the BWR are at the Bodmin end of the line, at the terminus known as Bodmin General. The GWR gave a number of its stations the suffix 'General'; in this case, it was to distinguish it from Bodmin Road (Parkway) and Bodmin North, the Southern Railway's station at the other end of the town, long since closed and now demolished.

Bodmin General is a brisk 10 minutes' walk up St Nicholas Street from the town centre. The station has generous parking for visitors arriving by car. The buildings and layout at Bodmin General could hardly be more typical of a country terminus – an attractive station building in local brown stone still retaining its original platform canopy; the platform itself, complete with old-fashioned seats and lamps; the train waiting on the left and well-tended gardens climbing the bank on the right.

For a short time after its closure by BR, Bodmin General was a furniture warehouse, but all traces of its temporary conversion have now been swept away. Authentic posters and piles of period luggage complete the picture of the railway scene of the 1950s. The BWR volunteers have

▼ **Double-heading by the railway's most frequently used engines – the 0-6-0 tanks *Swiftsure* and No 62 *Ugly*, with an appropriate carriage in the Great Western Railway livery of chocolate and cream.**

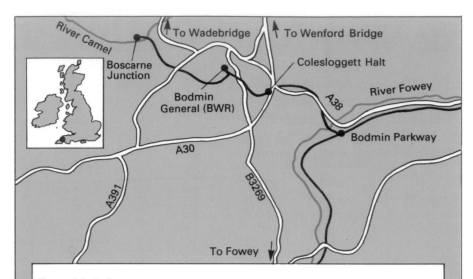

Charlie's Gate

The Royal Train was a frequent visitor on the Bodmin branch, even after closure to passenger trains in 1967. The section of line on the Bodmin side of Bodmin Road Viaduct provided a quiet and unobtrusive stabling point for the Royal Train when members of the Royal Family stayed on board overnight during visits to the West Country. The Prince of Wales regularly used the line, transferring from the Royal Train to a car on the adjoining A38. As a result, the gateway on to the road here has been dubbed Charlie's Gate.

lation of the signalling system and erection of signals. One important feature of the old Bodmin General which is unlikely to be replaced is the goods shed, a solid stone building typical of GWR branch-line practice. Sadly, it was demolished in the 1960s, and its site is now the car park.

From the far end of the platform you can look across to the engine shed, set up by the BWR, and the engine pit-road shed on the site of the original locomotive shed. You can see maintenance and restoration work being carried out in the engine shed.

In BR Western Region days, a hallmark of the line was the lightweight 2-6-2 tank engines designed by the GWR for branch-line work in the West Country. These neat and versatile locomotives were built over many years to a generally similar pattern, and photographs of them hauling trains in the Bodmin area often appeared in the railway press in steam days. So it is fitting that one of the type, No 5552 of the 4575 class, is currently being restored to working order at Bodmin General after some 30 years out of use.

Trains are usually hauled by 0-6-0 No 62 *Ugly*, built in 1950 by Robert Stephenson and Hawthorns, or 0-6-0 *Swiftsure*, an ex-National Coal Board locomotive built by Hunslet. The train is made up of three or four BR Mark I or Mark 2 coaches painted in the maroon livery of the 1950s.

Branch to Parkway

As there are no turning facilities on the line, the locomotive sets off for Parkway bunker first. The platform has barely receded before the train reaches the junction for the branch to Boscarne Junction, which curves away sharply to the right to run round the west side of Bodmin.

For the first kilometre (mile) or so towards Parkway, the train winds round the edge of the town, with good views opening up over rolling

worked hard to restore the GWR features of the station, and it has already regained the neat and cared-for air it displayed in years gone by.

A replica of the original signalbox has been constructed and a new water tower erected, both of which had disappeared in the years following closure. A major project now in hand is the instal-

▶ **BR Class 50 Co-Co No 50042** *Triumph*, built in 1968, stands with a fresh coat of paint at Bodmin General in October 1993. It had been withdrawn from Plymouth Laira exactly three years earlier.

▲ Hunslet 0-6-0ST *Swiftsure* of 1943 raises steam on the site of the old GWR engine shed at Bodmin General before hauling the first train of the day. Built for the War Department and shipped over to Belgium during World War II, *Swiftsure* later worked in coalfields in Yorkshire and Staffordshire, coming to the BWR from Cadley Hill colliery, near Burton-on-Trent, in the 1980s.

downland to the south and west. A series of sidings gives the BWR access to the Walker Lines industrial estate, and on one of these can be seen Bulleid 4-6-2 No 34007 *Wadebridge* which is being gradually refurbished.

Leaving the town behind, the line heads away eastwards, the banks on either side of the track dotted with pine trees and rhododendrons. Two bridges in quick succession take the line beneath the A30 dual carriageway. The sweeping views across open country are soon lost to sight as the train starts to plunge downhill, the gradient steepening to an impressive 1 in 40.

Trees close in over the line and foxgloves and bracken border the track on either side, while coal smoke drifts past the window. After 10 minutes' cautious progress downhill, the brakes go on for Colesloggett Halt. The short, grass-covered platform here was opened by the BWR to serve the network of footpaths in nearby Cardinham Woods, popular with walkers and birdwatchers in the summer months.

Beyond Colesloggett the downhill gradient continues as the line drops steeply into the valley of the Fowey. On the left, attractive woodland

scenery can be glimpsed between the trees, as well as traffic toiling along the A38 just below the railway. The gradient only slackens as the train runs on to the 18.25m (60ft) high Bodmin Road Viaduct, the five arches of which take the line across the river at tree-top height. From the viaduct the train enters Bodmin Parkway station.

Until BR closed the passenger service up to Bodmin General in 1967, Bodmin Road, as it then was, was a typical GWR country junction, the Bodmin train waiting beside the awning-shaded branch platform for connecting passengers from

▼ The concrete platform at Colesloggett Halt was built in early 1992 at a cost of £10,000 to provide access to the footpaths in Cardinham Woods, an attractive forest that serves as the habitat for a large variety of wildlife. Neither of the BWR's predecessors, the GWR or BR, saw fit to provide a halt here.

▲ **Bodmin General station from the overbridge at the throat of the station where the line to Boscarne Junction curves off to the west. To the right of** *Swiftsure* **are Class 10 D3452 and Class 08 D3559, both 0-6-0 diesel electric shunters, with No 50042 on the extreme right.**

Steam dinosaurs
The mineral line up to Wenford Bridge, which the BWR would like to see reopened, was always difficult to work because of its sharp curves and light axle-loading. However, the little Beattie 2-4-0 tank engines, built by the London & South Western Railway in 1874, were perfectly suited to the task. Incredibly, British Railways was still using three of these archaic veterans on the Wenford Bridge trains into the 1960s. They became great favourites with visiting enthusiasts and two have been preserved, No 30585, at the Buckinghamshire Railway Centre, and No 30587, at Buckfastleigh on the South Devon Railway.

the mainline expresses. The branch train would have been headed by a 2-6-2 tank, while services on the Plymouth–Penzance run would have been powered by a County, Castle, Grange or Hall class 4-6-0.

The platform awning has gone, as has the mainline steam, but much of the essential atmosphere of a rural junction still remains. There are sudden flurries of activity when mainline trains are due and, in between, quieter moments when birdsong is audible above the gentle hiss of the BWR locomotive waiting patiently in the bay platform for the return journey to Bodmin General.

The BWR train waits at Parkway for 10 minutes or so, usually in order to connect with one of the mainline services. A whistle from the engine is the signal to re-embark. The return journey to Bodmin General, this time mostly uphill, is much more dramatic than the outward run. Once away from the junction and over the high stone viaduct, the train begins the 1 in 40 climb.

Branch to Boscarne
As the train approaches Bodmin General, the branch to Boscarne can be seen on the left. The next departure will take passengers along this stretch of nearly six kilometres (3¾ miles).

On leaving the Bodmin General, the line turns right, passing under the Beacon Road bridge, which marks the start of a 1 in 40 gradient. The very tight curve here can be a real challenge to footplate crews on days when the rails are slippery. Once on the straight, there is an open view of Kirland and Halgavor Moor to the south of Bodmin. On the right, at the top of the Beacon, a memorial dedicated to the distinguished Victorian

soldier Sir Walter Raleigh Gilbert can be seen for some distance. After leaving the houses behind, a bridge over a minor road marks the site of the St Lawrence Platform, a small halt which was open from 1906 to 1917.

The branch is unusual for the number of 'occupational crossings' along its length – gated level crossings which provided access to the adjacent farms. Where these are still in use, the driver will sound the whistle on approaching.

Arrival at Boscarne Junction is indicated by the last bridge of the route, Bridge 25, crossing the River Camel. Once a busy junction, Boscarne dealt with passengers and freight from Bodmin North and Wenford, as well as GWR traffic from Bodmin General. To the right is the route of the old Bodmin and Wadebridge Railway to Bodmin North and Wenford Bridge. This is now a popular route designated for walkers and cyclists, called the Camel Trail.

After a 10 minute wait, the train begins the return journey. There is a real surge of steam to power the engine as it tackles both the gradient and the sharp bend, providing a dramatic approach to Bodmin General.

Promising prospects
For the future, the BWR has initiated a project to extend the railway beyond Boscarne to Wadebridge and eventually on to Padstow following the original track route. This would mean using the Camel Trail and it is recognized that an extension must combine the interests of both railway and trail. All in all, the railway looks set for some interesting and exciting developments in the years ahead.

The Swanage Railway

The Swanage Railway, which once linked Dorset's Purbeck peninsula to the rest of England, was closed in 1972. Its demise seemed final, but a few years later the Swanage was brought back to life – thanks to a vote by the local inhabitants.

In October 1884, the *Wareham and Isle of Purbeck Advertiser* proudly announced that the Dorset seaside town of Swanage was soon to be 'united with England' via a new railway. Purbeck is a peninsula, not an island, but its natural barriers of sea, uncultivated heaths and high chalk ridges still make this 155.5 square kilometre (60 square mile) area one of the most self-contained – and beautiful – corners of the English south coast.

In the Middle Ages, it was a royal hunting ground the inhabitants of which could not marry outsiders without a warrant from the Crown. Even in the industrial age, when the area's traditional resources of fine china clay and Purbeck stone were exported world-wide, the quarrymen and

their families remained a close-knit community.

Plans to build a railway to serve the mines and the growing holiday resort of Swanage were proposed as early as 1847, but almost 40 years passed before Purbeck's landowning gentry accepted the merits of a branch line connecting Swanage to Wareham on the main London–Weymouth line.

Construction of the 17.75km (11 mile) railway began in June 1883. It cost over £76,000 and was completed in two years. The line was operated by the London & South Western Railway (LSWR) until the grouping of 1923, when it came under the control of the Southern Railway (SR). By 1937, Swanage station had to be extended to cope with the traffic of 17 weekday trains, one of which,

▼ **Bulleid Light Pacific No 34072, *257 Squadron*, is seen heading out of Swanage station. Such engines were frequent visitors to the line in Southern Railway (SR) and BR days, hauling excursions and express trains from Waterloo. Note the duty number above the buffer beam – the continuation of an SR tradition.**

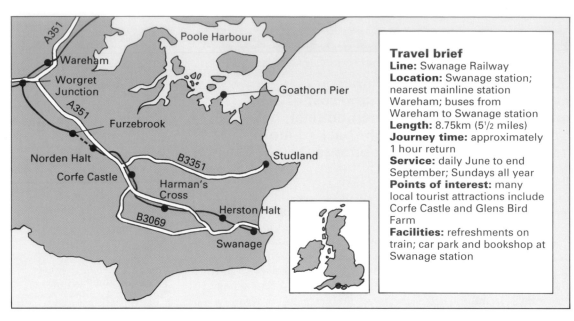

Travel brief
Line: Swanage Railway
Location: Swanage station; nearest mainline station Wareham; buses from Wareham to Swanage station
Length: 8.75km (5½ miles)
Journey time: approximately 1 hour return
Service: daily June to end September; Sundays all year
Points of interest: many local tourist attractions include Corfe Castle and Glens Bird Farm
Facilities: refreshments on train; car park and bookshop at Swanage station

▶ This view from Northbrook Road Bridge shows former visiting engine Hunslet 0-6-0T, No 47160, passing an ex-US Army 0-6-0T, No 30075. Imported from Yugoslavia before the civil war, this locomotive is now in repair. The third vehicle was used for track inspections and is now out of service.

Hauling the henhouse
At Norden, the Swanage Railway crosses the route of Fayle's Tramway, a 3ft 9in (1.14m) gauge horse railway opened in 1806. In 1868, the route was mechanized by the arrival of *Tiny*, an outside cylinder 0-4-0T. The line was closed in 1905, when its owners cut a new steam railway across the Purbeck heath to a pier on Poole Harbour's Goathorn peninsula.

From about 1920, the line provided a passenger service for about ten schoolchildren of clay workers in the Goathorn area. The children were taken to school at Corfe in an improvised carriage known as the henhouse – a clay wagon with an additional corrugated iron roof and a tiny window.

In 1939, most of the Goathorn Railway was ripped up, leaving only 3km (two miles) of track at Norden. A footpath runs along part of the old track.

equipped with a restaurant car, was a through train to Waterloo.

The flow of passengers did not last. On 1 January 1972, with its revenues fatally diminished by competition from road traffic, the railway was forced to close. Six months later, all the track was torn up except for a 4.75km (three mile) section between the mainline at Worgret Junction and the BR goods depot at Furzebrook, which is still in use to this day.

That might have been the end of the story but for the efforts of two young students who were determined to rescue the line from oblivion and formed the Swanage Railway Society in the summer of 1972.

Into battle
By then, the track was being lifted, but at a meeting in London the two campaigners persuaded the head of BR's Property Board to halt the dismantling short of Furzebrook, leaving a useful three-quarters of a kilometre (½ mile) spur, plus all the ballast, signal posts and other structures on the 10.5km (6½ mile) section to Swanage.

The society's long-term aim was to operate a tourist service, with steam locomotives running between Swanage and Furzebrook. However, Swanage District Council, which had bought Swanage station for development, had first to be persuaded to grant the society a lease on the site.

Eventually, the council put the issue to a local referendum, and by an overwhelming majority – and against the recommendation of councillors – the residents of Swanage voted for a revitalized railway. On 14 February 1976, the day after the lease was signed, jubilant volunteers moved in to restore the site.

Until 1995, the railway's steam trains ran only

the 5km (three miles) between Swanage and Harman's Cross, but now the line is open to Corfe Castle and Norden, a distance of approximately 8.75km (5½ miles). Norden has a park and ride facility for passengers who wish to leave their car there and travel by train to Swanage.

Swanage makes an ideal base from which to explore Purbeck. On the seafront, the town's horse-drawn tramway, which once carried stone from the station goods yard to the pier, has been attractively incorporated into the relaid footpaths. Located in the town centre and built of Purbeck stone, the station retains its Victorian station-master's house, but is otherwise a typical piece of 1930s railway architecture.

A 1950s atmosphere is lovingly preserved at all stations on the line – from the Southern Railway

▶ M7 0-4-4T No 30053, dating from 1905, steams east from Herston Halt. The M7s were still working the branch in BR days and this particular example actually served on the line in 1964. Bought by an American railroad enthusiast, it was later brought back to England and restored at Swanage.

repeated accidents with locomotives overrunning the turntable forced a rebuild with a straight lintel in 1959.

Shortage of space means that much of the railway's stock is not on public view. Eight engines are based at Swanage, although not all of them are there at any one time. There are also three shunting diesels, a mainline diesel and approximately 30 carriages of varying ages and build. Of these, eight Mark 1s are in regular use.

Close connections

The LSWR and SR connection is maintained with the 1880 MR Class 1F 0-6-0T, No 41708. LSWR Class M7 0-4-4T No 30053 was repatriated from the United States and has undergone restoration. A particularly impressive locomotive is Battle of Britain class 4-6-2 No 34072, *257 Squadron*, built in 1948.

Whichever engine is in service, the round trip takes just under an hour and there is much to appreciate *en route*. Close to the track, deer can often be seen grazing, but it is the great ridges on each side that draw the attention.

The escarpment to the north – superb walking country – is rich in prehistoric sites, while the ridge to the south has been quarried for thousands of years, supplying marble for the villas of Roman Britain and stone for some of the great engineering projects of the industrial age.

▼ Seen from the remains of Corfe Castle, No 30053 hauls a works train across Corfe Viaduct. The aim of the Swanage Railway is to restore the link with the mainline at Furzebrook and run trains between Wareham and Swanage. This would ease traffic congestion through Corfe village.

green livery to the old metal advertising boards and the Edmondson tickets. A well-stocked bookshop occupies the former parcels office at Swanage, and there will soon be an exhibition coach and museum at Corfe Castle goods shed.

At Swanage, the site is constricted, so the engine shed has to be approached at an angle, necessitating the use of the ex-Neasden turntable. The shed entrance was originally a stone arch, but

Purbeck trail blazer

The Swanage was not the first steam railway on Purbeck. In 1866, Pike Bros, a china clay company, opened a 2ft 8½in (0.8m) gauge line of about 8km (five miles) from near Furzebrook to the River Frome, close to Wareham. The first locomotive, *Primus*, was an 0-6-0 built by Bellis & Seekings of Birmingham.

After World War I, Pike Bros supplemented their stock with a diesel-powered Simplex. Produced in large numbers to supply the battlefront in France, many of these ex-War Department engines – some still with armour plating – ended up with industrial concerns.

In 1949, Pike Bros amalgamated with B. Fayle & Co., a rival china clay firm which had built its own steam railway system on Purbeck in 1868. Being of different gauges, the systems operated independently until they were closed in the 1950s.

Local service

A few minutes after leaving Swanage, the train steams into Herston Halt, the original western terminus of the revived railway. Opened in April 1984, this halt has undergone a full refurbishment since then, which has turned it into an attractive wayside station. It is used regularly by visitors during the summer and it is not uncommon for local residents, returning from shopping in Swanage, to get off here. As in earlier days, and as those who voted in the referendum hoped, the railway is serving those who live in the area.

Beyond Herston, there is some stiff climbing and the engine has to work hard to cope with it. During World War II, the line was used by American servicemen stationed on Purbeck, and for one GI from Illinois, the journey reminded him of his home state's Wabash, Chester & Western Railway, known as the 'Wait Charlie and Walk' because of its leisurely pace.

Harman's Cross – at 48m (157ft), the highest point on the railway – is approached up a 1 in 76 gradient. This is the mid-point of the journey, where the trains to and from Norden pass each other. In 1996, a new signalbox was contstructed of Purbeck stone.

The next stop is Corfe Castle and it would be a pity to miss the chance of alighting at this restored Victorian station to visit the ruins. Guarding a gap in the chalk escarpment, the castle is situated at one of the most dramatic sites in Britain.

Built in 1080 by William the Conqueror, and much extended by King John, the castle was a Royalist stronghold in the Civil War. It survived one siege in 1643 but fell to the Parliamentarians three years later. They systematically destroyed its defences. Below it, the town, with its steep winding road and stone-tiled cottages, is saved from picture-postcard prettiness by the grandeur of its surroundings.

From Corfe the line crosses a three-arch viaduct and descends to Norden, which marks the present limit of the line. However, track-laying operations have begun north towards Furzebrook and the mainline. Plans to run a regular service from Bournemouth to Swanage are in hand and given the dedication of the Swanage Railway's supporters, it surely will not be long before the gap is closed and a working railway once again 'unites' Purbeck with England.

▼ The Swanage branch was once part of the London & South Western Railway, and it is appropriate that two of its locomotives are found buffer to buffer by the coaling stage at Swanage station. No 120, built in 1899, is the only surviving T9 4-4-0, and is owned by the National Railway Museum in York.

Didcot Railway Centre

Once known as 'railwaymen's town', Didcot owes its growth almost entirely to the arrival of the GWR. Appropriately, with everything from pen nibs to locomotives on view, the Great Western tradition can be relived today at Didcot Railway Centre.

Seen by some as the most prestigious of the Big Four railway companies that existed prior to nationalization in 1948, the Great Western was something of a national institution. The GWR thrived for over a century, running a business that ranged from hauling coal from south Wales mines to ferrying holidaymakers to resorts in the West Country on trains that were fast and frequent – chocolate and cream carriages pulled by magnificent Brunswick green engines, each adorned with shiny copper and brass fittings.

Didcot Railway Centre is home to the Great Western Society, the members of which run the railway museum. The centre is situated next to the busy Didcot Parkway station – mainline services scream past at 201km/h (125mph) on what is still essentially the original railway laid out by Isambard Kingdom Brunel in 1841.

Starting point

You enter the centre via the station subway, tracing the footsteps of the Great Western engine drivers and firemen as they reported for duty all those years ago.

A small hut now serves as the centre's ticket office. It began life as a ground frame for controlling points in the adjacent goods yard, and is just one of many restored original buildings. Another is the concrete platform which once stood at Eynsham, Oxford, and today forms part of the

▼ **Easing the demonstration freight train into Didcot Halt is the first locomotive bought by the Great Western Society – 0-4-2T No 1466 was designed by Collett and built at Swindon in 1936. The halt – made by restoring old buildings and fittings found around the Western Region – represents a typical 1930s GWR utility station.**

Great Western Society's main demonstration line.

Take a ride if there's a train waiting at the platform – apart from refreshments, all activities are included in the admission price. The train is usually formed using three restored Great Western coaches, all dating from the 1930s and hauled by one of the Great Western engines from the society's collection.

Shovelling coal

The coal stage and water tank are only a short walk from the platform. Brute strength was – and still is – needed to operate the coal stage. Small iron tubs, which hold about half a tonne (ton) of steam coal, are filled by hand from one of the large coal wagons parked at the top of the incline and the contents tipped into the tenders or bunkers of the locomotives below.

In its heyday Didcot had an allocation of about 40 locomotives, and each needed to be stacked up with coal at least once every 24 hours. This amounted to 200–300 tonnes (tons) of coal being shovelled every day. Now, members of the volunteer workforce do it for fun. The water tank above the coaling stage holds 337,540 litres (74,250 gallons) and is these days fed from the mains.

▲ The signalbox, originally from Radstock in Somerset, controls all the signals and pointwork at the Didcot Halt end of the branch, as well as a pair of level crossing gates. The award-winning Radstock Box is fully operational and open to visitors on some of the special Steamdays.

▼ Engines are coaled by hand at Didcot. Pannier tank No 3738 receives half a tonne (ton) from one of the small tubs which in true GWR fashion are hand filled with good steam coal. In the days of steam, hundreds of tonnes (tons) of coal were shovelled each day – ten tubs for each Castle, eight for a Hall.

At Didcot

The site is a development of a former BR engine shed and is located in the triangle formed by the mainline to Bristol, the GWR line to the west Midlands and a curve joining the two (below). It is approached from Didcot Parkway station by a subway. The centre of the site is occupied by an engine shed which contains the finest collection of GWR engines remaining. Extensive restoration work is undertaken in the adjacent works and lifting shop, while a fine collection of coaches is stored in the carriage shed. A unique length of Brunel's broad-gauge line still exists beyond this shed. Short running lines are located on either side of the site to carry passengers on Steamdays.

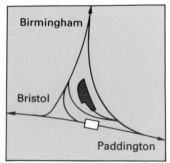

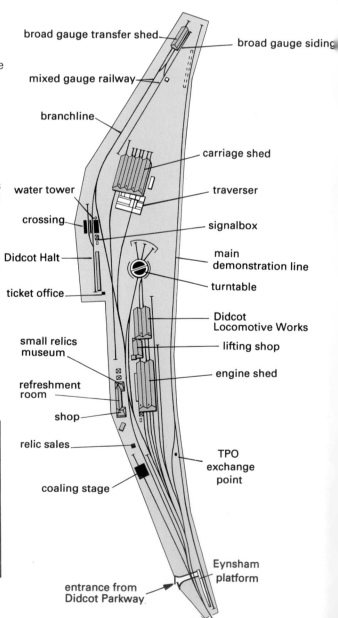

broad gauge transfer shed
broad gauge siding
mixed gauge railway
branchline
carriage shed
water tower
traverser
crossing
signalbox
Didcot Halt
main demonstration line
ticket office
turntable
Didcot Locomotive Works
small relics museum
lifting shop
refreshment room
engine shed
shop
relic sales
TPO exchange point
coaling stage
Eynsham platform
entrance from Didcot Parkway

Early days

In 1961, four schoolboys were wondering how to preserve a small ex-Great Western tank engine. The Great Western Society was formed and 0-4-2T No 1466 was reborn.

The society started buying any redundant ex-GW locomotives and coaches they could find, and in 1967 they were offered accommodation at Didcot to restore and display their growing collection. By the end of the year the engine shed was full, heralding the start of Didcot Railway Centre.

Oh, Mr Porter!

When you visit Didcot, give yourself plenty of time to wander around the museum and inspect its fine collection of artefacts, ranging from holiday posters to silverware and crockery bearing the initials GWR. Among the more obvious treasures is the enamel sign that once directed passengers to the Weston, Clevedon & Portishead Railway. There is a tale of a lady passenger who, on asking how to get to Portishead, was directed by a porter to cross the footbridge and proceed to the WC and P!

Centrepiece

The engine shed is the focal point of the centre. Erected by the Great Western Railway in 1932, it is now the largest and most complete GWR shed in existence being used for its original purpose.

The four-road shed is 61m (200ft) long and houses up to 20 locomotives. Only three of the tracks have roof smoke extractors – the fourth was lost when the roof was rebuilt in 1962. The shed was finally closed to steam traction in 1965 but continued to be used by British Rail to house diesel locomotives until 1970.

Hinderton Hall and *Cookham Manor* are on display, as well as *Earl Bathurst* and *Pendennis Castle* – recently repatriated from Australia. The latter two are famous Castle class express passenger locomotives which once pulled such famous trains as the *Cheltenham Flyer* and the *Torbay Express*.

Down the line

The small lifting shop at the back of the engine shed was constructed in 1932 and is used by the society for locomotive repairs. Look inside and you will see the original electrically operated hoist capable of lifting 50 tonnes (tons). Here, and in the new workshop built in 1988, you can see locomotives in varying states of repair and the replica broad-gauge engine *Firefly* under construction. Also being rebuilt is the King Class locomotive *King Edward II.*

Unfortunately, the original Great Western turntable was removed by BR soon after the shed closed to steam traction, but it has been replaced by a Southern Railway example rescued from Southampton Docks and installed at Didcot in 1978.

Next along the line is the large carriage shed

▲ Inside the four-road engine shed Nos 3738 and 4144 await attention. Didcot houses the largest single collection of GWR rolling stock – the soot-blackened building, manned by a volunteer workforce, is one of the few GW sheds still used for its original purpose.

▼ On parade outside the engine shed are *Drysllwyn Castle, Cookham Manor, Hinderton Hall* and Mogul No 5322. There has been an engine shed at Didcot for a century and a half. During the 1930s the shed had an allocation of 40 or so engines but by 1964 this had dwindled to 17. The depot closed to steam in 1965 – happily, Didcot survived.

built in 1977 and enlarged four years later. It accommodates all the society's coaching stock. Many of the carriages are made of wood and they need to be kept under cover if they are not to deteriorate.

The oldest in the collection is a Dean four wheeler, No 416, built in 1891. The dining saloon, No 9635 – the only one of its type in existence – was built by the GWR in 1935 to form part of the company's special centenary train.

Broad-gauge display

At the northern end of the centre is the broad-gauge display and transfer shed. When the Great Western opened its line from London to Bristol in 1841, Brunel, the Chief Engineer, built his railway using a broad track gauge of 7ft ¼in (2.13m). Unfortunately, nearly all the other railway companies used what became known as the standard-gauge of 4ft 8½in (1.44m).

Where these two gauges met, passengers and goods had to change trains. At these points transfer sheds were installed to house the trains – the one at Didcot is the only surviving example. Notice the difference in size between the two entrance arches, one for standard-gauge trains, the other for broad-gauge.

The broad-gauge track was replaced by the standard one, with the last broad-gauge train on the Great Western leaving Paddington on 20 May 1892. The original broad-gauge track at the centre was discovered near Burlescombe in Devon.

▲ The replica broad-gauge *Iron Duke* passes an ancient Great Western disc signal after leaving the historic Didcot transfer shed – the only example still in existence. A large entrance arch is for broad-gauge trains, with a smaller one for standard. Although *Iron Duke* has since been returned to the National Railway Museum, another replica broad-gauge locomotive, *Firefly*, is under construction.

Award winners

Retracing your steps and keeping to the right of the carriage shed, you come to the level crossing and Radstock signalbox. This box arrived at Didcot in 1976 and is operational. It controlled a level crossing at Radstock, just as it does at Didcot today. A member of staff will explain how it all works. In 1990, the society won a nationwide award for the best restored signalbox.

Next to Radstock Box is Didcot Halt, another national award winner. This small platform is typical of the Great Western Railway halts of the 1930s, and contains many original features.

The metal pagoda-shaped waiting room once stood at Stockcross & Bagnor Halt on the Lambourn Valley branch, and the ticket office came from Welford Park. If you are taking a ride you may be lucky enough to board a train hauled by 0-4-2T No 1466, the engine that set in motion all that you see at Didcot today.

GWR relics

A short walk from Didcot Halt takes you to the small relics museum – the jewel in the crown of the centre. This unassuming brick building houses what is arguably the finest collection of Great Western small relics and publicity material anywhere in the world.

▼ Didcot is on a mainline steam route and is host to many famous express locomotives. One famous name included the Standard 8P *Duke of Gloucester*, seen here passing the Oxford Canal in 1990.

The Bluebell Railway

Named after the swathes of bluebells in the adjoining woods, the Bluebell Railway in Sussex is one of the few independent lines to rely exclusively on steam. Its fleet of some 30 locomotives spans five generations and ranges from tiny Terrier tank engines to a giant 2-10-0.

Of nearly 100 independent steam railways operating in the UK today, the Bluebell Railway, in the heart of rural Sussex, is one of the best known. The original line was opened in 1882 by the London, Brighton & South Coast Railway (LBSCR) and ran for 29km (18 miles) between Lewes and East Grinstead. The line was finally closed by BR in 1958, but the section known as the Bluebell was resurrected in 1960.

It is not the biggest or scenically the most spectacular of the preserved railways – but it has a great deal of charm and was the first to prove that railway enthusiasts could successfully run a line which BR had abandoned. The single-track line, which leads northwards from the Bluebell's Sheffield Park headquarters, runs for 8km (five miles) through a pastoral backdrop of farms, fields and woodland to Horsted Keynes.

In May 1994, the line to the present northern terminus at Kingscote was opened, adding a further 6.5km (four miles) to the journey. Next on the agenda is an extension of the line to East Grinstead, which the company hopes to complete in due course.

Crossing the Ouse

Sheffield Park is easily accessible by road and it is from here that most passengers begin their journey. Pulling gently away from the platform, the train crosses the River Ouse and rumbles past the trackside marker denoting the Greenwich Meridian. The river may look innocuous enough, but in times of spate it has been known to flood the valley floor away to the left.

The travelling time of 33 minutes from Sheffield Park to Kingscote is governed partly by

▼ The Bluebell's insistence on authenticity is reflected in every aspect of its operations – from the provision of fire buckets outside the porters' room at Horsted Keynes station to the restoration of locomotives such as the 1875 veteran *Stepney*, seen below working in tandem with 0-6-0WT *Bellerophon*, a former visiting engine from the Keighley & Worth Valley Railway in West Yorkshire.

80064

▲ The crew of BR Standard 4MT 2-6-4T No 80064, an engine dating from 1953, wait the right away at Sheffield Park. The Bluebell employs six full-time railway staff and is served by around 100 regular volunteers, and many others who help out occasionally. No 80064 is not operating at the moment but remains on show.

Blooming Bluebell
British Railways was still building steam locomotives when it axed the 29km (18 mile) stretch of money-losing line between Lewes and East Grinstead in 1958.

A year later, the Bluebell Railway Preservation Society was launched. Its first objective was to buy the 8km (five mile) middle section between Sheffield Park and Horsted Keynes.

BR's asking price of £34,000 was too high, but pursuing the option of a five-year lease, the society was able to run its first service on 7 August, 1960. The Bluebell was about to bloom again.

the Department of Transport's 40km/h (25mph) speed limit, which applies to almost all steam railways on the standard gauge, and partly by the demands of the two 1 in 75 gradients on the line.

The first of these gradients extends for 2.5km (1½ miles) up Freshfield Bank and begins almost immediately after the train has left Sheffield Park. It is a stiff test for a small engine and crew with five fully laden coaches weighing 200 tonnes (tons) or more.

Having crested Freshfield Bank, the train pushes through the open farmland of the Sussex Weald. To the right, the land becomes noticeably more hilly as, for the next 3.25km (two miles), the railway flirts with the edges of Lindfield Wood.

It is not long before the train is digging in for the second major climb of the journey, which leads to Horsted Keynes. The exhaust note of the engine echoes back off the big red-brick Three Arch Bridge at the start of a long curve to the right, and it is here that the train crew usually whistle up to let the Horsted Keynes signalman and station staff know of their approach.

Passing the former Haywards Heath line junction, the train eases into Horsted Keynes station. Its grandiose buildings, five platforms and

▶ No 928 *Stowe*, a Southern Railway Schools class locomotive of 1934, the most powerful 4-4-0 in the country, heads a rake of matching green Bulleid and Maunsell coaches. The Bluebell is famed for its ability to run pre-nationalization engines with the appropriate rolling stock.

passenger subway are a legacy of its days as an important link in the Southern Railway network.

Several minutes later, the second leg of the journey to Kingscote starts with further 1 in 75 gradients. Halfway there, the train enters the straight 668m (731yd) long Sharpthorne tunnel, the longest on a preserved railway in Britain. A gentle descent takes the train into Kingscote.

All-steam policy

Almost alone among Britain's independent lines, the Bluebell is still a 100 per cent steam-operated railway, having resisted for 30 years the temptation to run a diesel. Even for yard shunting and works trains, the staff and volunteers still turn out at dawn to light up in the traditional way. Back in 1965, the railway was presented with a tiny petrol-engined shunter, but it serves no active role, existing merely as a relic.

The all-steam policy is part of the Bluebell Railway's obsession with authenticity – the accurate portrayal of stations, booking offices, waiting rooms, signalboxes, locomotives and coaches just as they used to be.

The line had three different operators before the preservationists took over. From 1882 to 1922 it belonged to the LBSCR. Then with the grouping of the railway companies in 1923, it came under the auspices of the Southern Railway, and with nationalization in 1948, it became a part of the British Railways empire.

Each of the railway companies had its own

individual livery and house style and the railway today reflects them all. So, while Sheffield Park is restored as an LBSCR station of the turn of the century, Horsted Keynes is the very image of a busy Southern Railway country junction of the 1930s; and Kingscote has the appearance of a BR station of the early 1950s.

Matchless collection

The Bluebell Railway today boasts a matchless collection of classic locomotives and coaching stock from the Victorian and Edwardian eras – thanks to the foresight of its first volunteers who in the winter of 1960 drew up a shopping list of vintage locomotives still in BR service but in imminent danger of being scrapped. However, cash was scarce, and some engines on the Bluebell list did go to the breaker's yard. Nevertheless, the

▲ Beribboned for a Bluebell Railway gala day, an LSWR Adams Radial 4-4-2T No 488, built in 1885, stands amid the suitably Victorian surroundings of Sheffield Park station. The locomotive, bought by the Bluebell from BR in 1961, was given a major overhaul 10 years later. It has had several changes of livery since arriving at Sheffield Park, but is shown here decked in its original colours.

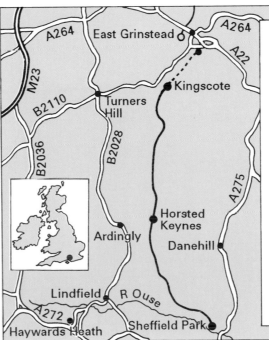

Travel brief
Line: Bluebell Railway
Location: Sheffield Park, East Sussex on the A275; nearest mainline stations East Grinstead, with dedicated bus service to Kingscote, and Haywards Heath
Length: 14.5km (9 miles)
Journey time: 33 minutes one way; 90 minutes round trip
Service: daily from mid-April to end September; weekends the rest of the year
Locomotive stock: fleet of about 30, from mainline expresses to industrial engines
Points of interest: small exhibits museum and model railway (Sheffield Park); picnic areas at all stations; riverside walk at Sheffield Park

fleet now stands at over 30 (13 are privately owned) and ranges from mainline express locomotives to humble industrial engines.

Sheffield Park locomotive shed boasts no fewer than five centenarian engines, as well as representatives from each of the three principal pre-grouping railway companies in the south – the LBSCR, the South Eastern & Chatham Railway (SECR) and the London & South Western Railway (LSWR).

The first locomotive to be bought from British Railways, in May 1960, was the diminutive LBSCR Terrier Class A1X 0-6-0T No 55 *Stepney*, dating from 1875. It was the inspiration for the Reverend W. Awdry's children's book, *Stepney, the Bluebell Engine*. Restored to its original mustard coloured livery, and carrying a face mask on the smokebox, it is the undoubted celebrity of the line.

The oldest member of the fleet is another A1X engine, No 72 *Fenchurch*, three years older than Stepney, and the first of its class to enter service. *Fenchurch* and *Stepney* both worked the Havant–Hayling Island branch at different stages in their careers.

The aesthetic favourite of the fleet is probably the LSWR Adams Radial 4-4-2T No 488, dating from 1885. It was designed for suburban passenger work but ended its days with British Railways on the Axminster–Lyme Regis run. The engine remains the elegant epitome of Victorian locomotive design.

At the other end of the spectrum for both size and power is BR Class 9 2-10-0 express freight engine No 92240, totally rebuilt after 13 years in a South Wales scrapyard.

However, the Bluebell Railway's collection of more than 60 historic passenger coaches, based at Horsted Keynes carriage depot, is not there simply for show. For despite a throughput of more than 200,000 passengers a year, the Bluebell

prides itself on running 50- and 60-year-old coaches on its normal service trains, matched wherever possible with historically appropriate locomotives.

Some of the carriages date from the 1920s, and were designed by the SECR chief mechanical engineer, Richard Maunsell, with later stock from the 1940s and '50s, produced by Southern Railway Chief Mechanical Engineer Oliver Bulleid. All of these are the envy of other independent steam railways, which started out too late to acquire much more than redundant ex-BR coaches of the 1950s and '60s.

▲ A North London Railway 0-6-0T of 1880, No 58850, its smokebox door hung with a wreath of Remembrance Day poppies, waits to couple up to a brake coach at the southern end of Horsted Keynes. No 58850 is currently on loan to another railway. The water crane, semaphore signal and platform barrow recall the rural charm of bygone days.

◄ Empty stock headed by a Southern Railway 4-6-2, No 35027 *Port Line*, of 1948 vintage, waits for No 55 *Stepney* to clear its path. No 35027 is now to be seen at Swanage. In its guise as the Bluebell Engine featured in the Rev. Wilbert Awdry's children's stories, *Stepney* has helped to impress many youngsters with the attractions of steam.

▶ Bluebells border the line as No 80064 steams through Lindfield Wood. It was not far from here that a trackman named Pope was supposedly murdered by a gamekeeper. The facts are lost in time, but in the early 1960s trains carrying school parties would sometimes spot 'Pope's ghost' – a part acted out by some long-suffering member of the Bluebell staff wearing a white sheet.

The Mid-Hants Railway

Although intended as a cross-country route, the Mid-Hants Railway or Watercress Line also once echoed to the sound of crack Southern expresses such as the Bournemouth Belle. Saved from the death sentence imposed by BR, it now offers a seductive journey back into the past.

The Mid-Hants Railway (MHR) or Watercress Line – it once carried produce from the watercress beds around Alresford – opened in 1865 and, operated by the London & South Western Railway (LSWR), ran for 27.25km (17 miles) between Alton and Winchester. Plied mainly by local trains, but also regularly used as an alternative route for mainline services between Waterloo, Southampton and Bournemouth, the line was closed by British Rail in 1973.

That seemed to be the end of the story, but in 1976 some 16km (10 miles) of the route was purchased by the enthusiasts of the Winchester & Alton Railway Co. Ltd, with the aim of operating a preserved steam railway. The plan began to bear fruit in 1977, when the first section, from Alresford to Ropley – a distance of just under 4.75km (three miles) – was opened to passenger traffic. The line was extended to Medstead and Four Marks in 1983 and finally, in 1985, to Alton, where it connects with mainline services to Aldershot and Waterloo. Unfortunately, it was not possible to save the 11.25km (seven mile) section between Alresford and Winchester.

Rolling landscape

The one and a half hour round trip gives the traveller some excellent views of the rolling

▼ The signalman at Medstead and Four Marks waits to collect the single-line token from the crew of LSWR Class T9 No 30120, formerly on loan from the National Railway Museum, York. The T9s were known as Greyhounds because of their speed, and No 30120, built in 1899, was no exception. But it lacked the necessary adhesion for the MHR's gruelling climbs and now can be found at a less demanding railway.

◀ Standard Class 5 No 73096 departs from Alton station on the mainline Daylight Railtour. Built in 1955, the engine was restored in 1993 and was launched as No 73080 *Merlin*. It regained its former number, 73096, in 1995.

Peak-time enthusiasm

At peak times, the MHR has a minimum of 40 unpaid staff, including locomotive crews, booking and information clerks, guards, porters, shunters, signalmen, ticket inspectors and catering staff.

The only essential qualification for volunteers is enthusiasm, since all departments on the MHR provide training for those without railway knowledge or experience.

And, just as in the age of steam, it is possible for MHR staff to progress from the lowliest grade to the highest.

Hampshire countryside, as well as the chance to travel by steam traction over what has now become a superbly preserved Southern Railway (SR) branch line. Passengers can start their journey either from Alresford or Alton. Both places are easily accessible by car or bus, and in addition, Alton can be reached by mainline trains.

Claim to fame

Alton was once the junction for no less than three separate lines. The first of these was the Mid-Hants route to Winchester, over which the present-day Watercress Line operates. The second was the Basingstoke & Alton Light Railway. Opened in 1901 and closed in 1932, this line's one claim to fame was that it provided the set for the famous Will Hay film, *Oh! Mister Porter*. The third route out of Alton was the Meon Valley line to Fareham, which opened in 1903 and survived up until 1955.

Mid-Hants trains now leave from platform three at Alton, and it is from here that the present journey begins. The engine on your train will be one of the Watercress Line's fleet of large steam engines, many of which would have worked on this line in steam days, hauling diverted Southern expresses or goods trains.

▶ The last 4SUB electric operating on BR, No 4732, stands beside LSWR Urie Class S15 4-6-0 No 506 at Alton station, where passengers from Waterloo can change on to the Mid-Hants. Built in 1920–21, S15s became one of the main sources of power for fast freight services on the SR network.

The time has come to depart, and sitting comfortably in your seat you will hear the familiar sound of the guard's whistle. This is quickly echoed by a whistle from the engine and, with a satisfying hiss of steam, the train slowly moves away from the platform, passing Alton signalbox on the right.

For a number of years this box served as the stationmaster's office, but is now being restored to working order by Mid-Hants volunteers. Looking to your left you will see a second track. This runs

alongside the Watercress Line for about one and a half kilometres (a mile) and once formed part of the main route from Alton to Fareham, but today it is used as a storage siding.

The train plunges into a deep cutting as it passes through the residential area of Alton, then crosses an iron bridge. This is the site of Butts Junction where the three routes from Alton diverged. There is no doubt that steam engines are at their most impressive when working hard, so sit back and listen to the exhaust as the engine climbs the 5km (three mile) 1 in 60 gradient.

Nestling in the open country to your left is the small village of Chawton, once the home of the novelist Jane Austen. The train continues its climb through the woodlands of Chawton Park, which is particularly attractive in the spring and summer, with an abundance of wild flowers.

Over the Alps

Entering yet another cutting, you reach the summit of the line, 198.75m (652ft) above sea level, before eventually drawing up at the small station at Medstead and Four Marks. In a little over 6.5km (four miles) the train has climbed nearly 103.5m (340ft). The steep gradient on either side of the summit led many generations of Southern enginemen to describe a journey on this route as going 'over the Alps'.

Medstead station was opened in 1868, some three years after the rest of the line, and was renamed Medstead and Four Marks in 1937. The buildings here are on a smaller scale than elsewhere on the route. This is because the LSWR did not incorporate the stationmaster's house into the station itself, as at Ropley and Alresford.

The small signalbox on the up platform, originally located at Wilton South, has been fully restored to working order by volunteer members

▲ A 2-6-0, No 31874, the sole survivor of 80 Maunsell N class Moguls, ambles tender first through the undulating Hampshire countryside near Ropley. The locomotive was assembled at Ashford, Kent in 1925, relying mostly on parts manufactured at Woolwich Arsenal under a government scheme to give work to the unemployed.

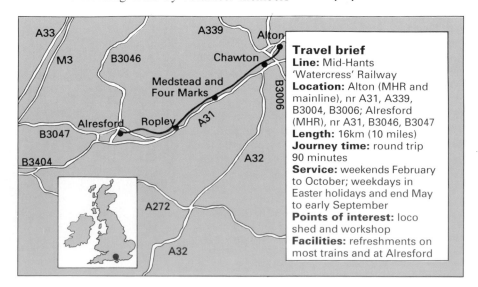

Travel brief
Line: Mid-Hants 'Watercress' Railway
Location: Alton (MHR and mainline), nr A31, A339, B3004, B3006; Alresford (MHR), nr A31, B3046, B3047
Length: 16km (10 miles)
Journey time: round trip 90 minutes
Service: weekends February to October; weekdays in Easter holidays and end May to early September
Points of interest: loco shed and workshop
Facilities: refreshments on most trains and at Alresford

of the railway. The topiary box hedge on the up platform will certainly catch your attention, for it has been trimmed into the shape of a large armchair. On your right, as the train leaves the station, is a traditional country station goods yard.

For the next 4.75km (three miles) the train runs downhill, passing over embankments and through cuttings to arrive at Ropley. On this stretch, look out for kestrels as they hover hunting for prey.

Prize winner

The station at Ropley is decorated in the green and cream SR livery similar to Alresford. The striking topiary work on both platforms has been a feature of the station for almost a century. It was an attraction for all those years before closure and the tradition is being maintained by the volunteer workforce. The signalbox, which is currently under restoration, is situated on the down platform and came from Netley, near Southampton. Signals here include some fine examples from the LSWR.

The beautifully restored footbridge, which provides an excellent vantage point from which to

▼ No 31874 enters Medstead and Four Marks. With BR's closure of the line, the station was badly vandalized, prompting the suggestion that it should be totally demolished. But the enthusiasts had other ideas, and the atmosphere is once again that of a well-tended pre-war country station.

view the station, originally stood at North Tawton on the Exeter–Barnstaple line.

Ropley is the operating centre for motive power on the line, with a large engine shed and works. It is certainly worth breaking your journey here to inspect the locomotive yard (open 10.30 a.m. to 4.30p.m. on most operating days) or to visit the delightful picnic area, where you can relax and watch the trains go by.

▲ Immaculate in the Brunswick green livery of BR's Southern Region, West Country Pacific No 34105 *Swanage* prepares for a tour of duty at Ropley shed as former visitor T9 4-4-0 No 30120 receives attention. *Swanage* is currently awaiting overhaul.

▲ West Country Pacific No 34105 *Swanage* hauls a rake of BR Mark 1 coaches under the restored footbridge at Ropley station. Although its steam fleet includes many veterans, the Mid-Hants Railway was formed too late to acquire period rolling stock, and most of it is of BR vintage.

US Army veteran

Locomotives include ex-BR Class 4 2-6-0 No 76017, built in 1954; ex-BR Standard Class 5 4-6-0 No 73096, built in 1955; and a US Army Transportation Corps Class S160 2-8-0, No 701 *Franklin D. Roosevelt*, of 1944 vintage. There are also two U-Class 2-6-0 engines, No 31625 and No 31806.

Two engines unique to the Mid-Hants are a pair of Urie S15s, Nos 30499 and 506. Built in 1920, they are the only preserved locomotives to represent the work of Robert Wallace Urie, who served as Chief Mechanical Engineer of the LSWR between 1912 and 1922. S15s were engaged mainly on freight duties, but at busy periods they were also used for hauling passenger trains, being capable of speeds of up to 112.5km/h (70mph).

The fleet is dominated by ex-Southern Railway engines. West Country Pacific No 34105

Swanage, although still at the MHR, is currently out of action. The other Bulleid Pacifics are No 34016 *Bodmin* and No 35018 *British India Line*, both completed in 1945.

Soon after leaving Ropley on the final 4km (2½ miles) to Alresford, you pass, on the left, the village of Bishops Sutton and many of the watercress beds of the river Arle. Traditionally, watercress was sold on Mid-Hants trains but sadly, this custom has been discontinued.

End of the line

Passing through a deep cutting you soon arrive at the old market town of Alresford, the end of the journey and the headquarters of the Watercress Line. Alresford was, and still is, the busiest station on the line. The brick-built station building here dates from the opening of the railway in 1865.

On the up platform stands the original 1865 signalbox. It is worth asking the signalman if you can climb the steps for a closer inspection of the many levers that control the various signals and points within the station area.

One of the additions to the original building is the all-wooden West Country buffet, which was originally the station building at Lyme Regis. It provides a fine period setting for refreshments – the ideal prelude to an exploration of Alresford itself, with its many Georgian buildings.

The Isle of Wight Steam Railway

**The Isle of Wight once had eight railways.
Today, it has just two – one operated by Island Line and the other
by the Isle of Wight Steam Railway, which continues
to attract thousands of steam enthusiasts.**

The few examples of island railways around the British mainland have always had a great attraction for enthusiasts, and none more so than the 88.5km (55 mile) network that once served the Isle of Wight. The first line on the island, the Cowes & Newport Railway, opened in 1862, and over the next 35 years this was supplemented by the lines of seven more companies.

Eventually, several of the companies amalgamated, and by 1914 the number had been reduced to three. In 1923, with the implementation of grouping, these became part of the mainland Southern Railway. Although many improvements were made, nothing was done to alter the essential character of the island's lines. The country station atmosphere survived and the collection of pre-grouping stock remained intact.

The first setbacks came after nationalization in 1948. Within four years, British Railways had begun to prune the island's network – a process that culminated in 1966 with the closure of the Ryde–Cowes line and the changeover from steam to electric trains on the only surviving line between Ryde and Shanklin.

Happily, this was not the end of steam on the island. A group of enthusiasts, formed initially to buy a locomotive for display, went on to set up the Isle of Wight Steam Railway (IoWSR). Their first success came in 1971 with the reopening of a small section of the Ryde–Cowes line. This was the 3.25km (two mile) stretch which ran between Haven Street and Wootton.

But the IoWSR had an even more ambitious aim. This was to reopen the 4.75km (three mile)

▼ The first locomotive preserved by the IoWSR, No 24 *Calbourne*, waits to couple up at Haven Street station. The only surviving Adams 02 class tank, *Calbourne* was built in 1891 and worked for almost 35 years on the mainland. It was shipped to the Isle of Wight in 1925 as part of a modernization programme carried out by the new owner of the island's railways, the Southern Railway.

▶ Decked in Army green livery, an Austerity 0-6-0ST, *Royal Engineer*, drifts its way along the line between Haven Street and Wootton. The engine, on loan from the Royal Corps of Transport, was supplied to the Army in kit form in the 1950s, but was not assembled until 1969.

▼ The Terrier tank engine, No 11 *Newport*, hauling a train to Wootton, puts in a powerful performance that belies its age. Outshopped at Brighton in 1878, it won its designer, William Stroudley, a gold medal for design and workmanship at the Paris Exhibition of 1878.

section between Haven Street and a completely new station at Smallbrook Junction, allowing interchange with mainline trains on the Ryde–Shanklin line.

Network SouthEast agreed to build the station, and the line from Haven Street was put down by gangs of IoWSR volunteers, the tracklaying being completed in just 11 days over a two-year period – an average of 400m (440yds) a day. The extension was opened in 1991, the year in which the railway carried 100,000 passengers for the first time.

Travelling by tube

From the mainland, the most convenient route to the IoWSR is by Wightlink ferry from Portsmouth Harbour, and then by Island Line train to Smallbrook Junction. The ferry crossing takes about 15 minutes, and passengers disembark alongside former London Underground carriages, dating from 1938, which operate the line to Shanklin.

The journey from Ryde to Smallbrook Junction takes about eight minutes. It was here in 1926 that the Southern Railway established the first physical connection between the Ryde–Ventnor and Ryde–Cowes lines. This took the form of a scissors crossover controlled by a new signalbox.

It proved to be an arrangement unique in Britain; the box was switched out during the winter months, the signals were removed and the lines reverted to single-line operation.

The train that draws into the IoWSR platform at Smallbrook to take you to Haven Street would be familiar to anyone who knew the local railways before nationalization. The little Terrier 0-6-0T

No 11 worked on the island between 1902 and 1947, and the carriages have been operating here for half a century or more.

A whistle from the smartly attired guard, replete with buttonhole, and your train steams out of Smallbrook. The Terrier emits crisp, staccato barks as it climbs away from the junction and swings to the west, plunging into a wood.

Bluebells carpet the woodland floor in spring, and wild flowers abound along the trackside as trees give way to open country to the south. The hedge-lined fields dotted with mature trees show little sign of the harsh farming regimes that have spoiled many a mainland landscape.

Fields ablaze with oil seed rape lead the eye to distant hills as you pass the Suffolk pink farmhouse of Whitefield Farm on the left. The Ryde to Newport road passes overhead on a bridge so oblique that it seems more like a short tunnel.

A day at the races

A brief glimpse of the station buildings at Ashey as the train passes gives little clue to the station's earlier importance. It is hard to imagine that 3,000 people a day once came here for the twice-yearly meetings at the nearby racecourse. The excursions ended in 1929 when the grandstand was destroyed by a fire.

Ashey was also a junction for a three-quarters of a kilometre (half mile) branch that went off to the left, running beside the racecourse to a chalk quarry on Ashey Down that can still be seen from the train. A reminder of the time when nearly all the island's freight traffic went by rail, the line included a 12m (40ft) tunnel and an engine shed at the quarry. Trains call at Ashey on request to the guard or signalling to the driver to stop.

Gasworks bequest

After travelling through more woodland, you can see in the distance to your right the village of Havenstreet, once the home of John Rylands whose name was given to the famous Manchester library. As an act of local benevolence, he built a gasworks beside Haven Street station, which you see on the left as the train runs into the loop and which now houses the IoWSR's offices, museum and shop. (The name of the village has been contracted into one word, but the IoWSR, like its predecessors, retains the original two-word form for the station.)

Today's activity at Haven Street belies its past as a quiet rural backwater. Groups of schoolchildren chatter excitedly as they are given a tour of the railway's busy locomotive and carriage workshops or shown the signalbox. In contrast, Haven Street used to be such a tranquil spot that several adders and a swan once found their way into the signalbox, much to the consternation of the sole porter-signalman.

Best-kept station

With so little to do between trains, the porter-signalman was able to devote most of his attention to the gardens, and Haven Street was a frequent winner of the island's best-kept station award. That tradition is maintained by the present staff, with vigorous bedding-out in spring.

As the train comes to a halt at Haven Street, the only passing place on the single line between Wootton and Smallbrook, you may catch sight of engines outside the shed on the left. All the IoWSR's locomotives are tank engines, which is wholly appropriate since no tender engines ever worked on the island.

Among these tank engines are a second Terrier, No 8 *Freshwater*, which worked on the

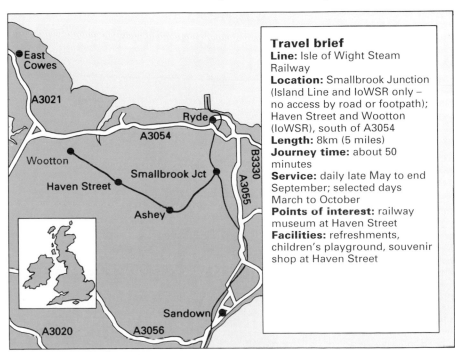

Travel brief
Line: Isle of Wight Steam Railway
Location: Smallbrook Junction (Island Line and IoWSR only – no access by road or footpath); Haven Street and Wootton (IoWSR), south of A3054
Length: 8km (5 miles)
Journey time: about 50 minutes
Service: daily late May to end September; selected days March to October
Points of interest: railway museum at Haven Street
Facilities: refreshments, children's playground, souvenir shop at Haven Street

island from 1913 to 1949, and a London & South Western Railway 0-4-4T, No 24 *Calbourne*, which was shipped to the island by the Southern in 1925 and retained by British Rail to work engineers' trains during the electrification of the Ryde–Shanklin line.

A measure of the 1 in 66 gradient out of Haven Street is soon provided as you pass carriages in the siding on the left at their roof height. The Terrier pounds past a fine LSWR signal on the right before entering an old oak wood that fringes the line for the next three-quarters of a kilometre (half mile).

End of the line

As the views open out to reveal fields of sheep and distant woods, the engine whistles for a series of gated farm crossings. A short climb brings the train to the end of its 8km (five mile) journey at the shaded station of Wootton.

It proved impossible to use the old station here because of the unstable clay subsoil, so a new station has been built, using traditional materials and a recovered signalbox from Freshwater. Its convincing appearance enables visitors to savour the authentic atmosphere of the island's railways in the days of steam.

Gasworks museum

The old gasworks beside Haven Street station is now home to the IoWSR Museum. The items, which reflect all aspects of the island's unique railway history, range from refreshment room silver to locomotive nameplates and signalling equipment.

The wooden bench that was presented by the Southern Railway to the best-kept station has finally come to rest here, after moving round the island each year from 1937 to 1974.

Among the smaller items is a pass issued to the Steward of Parkhurst, the island's prison, which entitled him to use the railways for making visits to local suppliers.

▲ Evoking the flavour of times past is this four-wheeler coach, No 4112. Built in 1898, it formed part of a two-coach push-pull set that came to the island in 1924. In 1938, the set was withdrawn, but No 4112 and its partner, No 6369, survived.

▶ The 1876 Terrier tank engine No 8 *Freshwater* pulls into Wootton station. The locomotive first arrived on the island in 1913 and returned to the mainland in 1949, where it ended up on display outside a pub. In 1979, the brewery donated *Freshwater* to the IoWSR, and it re-entered active service in 1981.

The Romney, Hythe & Dymchurch Railway

Conceived by two enthusiasts in the 1920s, the Romney, Hythe & Dymchurch Railway was once claimed to be the world's smallest public line. The route runs for almost 22.5 kilometres (14 miles) along the Kent coast and is still worked by the locomotives that first steamed along it 70 years ago.

The Romney, Hythe & Dymchurch Railway (RHDR) is unique: a mainline in miniature, built to a track gauge of 15in (381mm), it is quite without peer anywhere in the world. Ever since its opening in 1927, it has been one of Britain's best-known, best-loved small railways, and its steam and diesel-hauled trains dashing across Romney Marsh have been a perennial attraction to generations of holiday visitors and railway enthusiasts.

The RHDR runs along the south coast of Kent from the historic Cinque Port of Hythe, near Folkestone, out to the great shingle headland of Dungeness. From Hythe to Dungeness is a journey of almost 22.5km (14 miles); the line is double track as far as New Romney, 12.75km (eight miles), where the headquarters of the line is sited.

The railway's gauge is approximately one quarter the width of standard gauge. However, in all dimensions other than track gauge, the line's engines and rolling stock are around one-third full size, providing the strength needed to carry the RHDR's heavy peak-season traffic.

When the railway was built, the 15in (381mm) gauge was generally regarded as the narrowest suitable for routine railway operations, and this is why the RHDR was previously styled 'The World's Smallest Public Railway'.

Arriving at Hythe or New Romney for a day on the line, the visitor may well wonder how such an ambitious miniature system came to be built in the first place. The railway's history is an unusual one. The whole operation was the brainchild of two railway enthusiasts, Count Louis Zborowski and Captain Jack Howey.

These two friends, both heirs to considerable property fortunes, had grown up with the tradition

▼ The RHDR's only terminus is at Hythe. Here No 2 *Northern Chief*, shown before its renovation, waits to head a train down the line to Dungeness. *Northern Chief* hauled the first official train on 5 August 1926, when the Duke of York (later King George VI) visited the railway.

▲ No 10 *Dr Syn,* shown here before undergoing recent rebuilding, steams past the signal into Hythe station. Colour lights were installed on the line after World War II, but by the mid 1970s semaphore signals had been reinstated.

Front line fighter

Soon after the outbreak of war in 1939, the RHDR was taken over by the military authorities for transporting troops and equipment between Hythe and Dungeness. They also operated the world's only 15in (381mm) gauge armoured train. Powered by a Mountain class 4-8-2, No 5 *Hercules* – still active on the line – it was concealed under a fake hill just over a kilometre (nearly a mile) east of Dymchurch.

Although each of the train's two wagons was fitted with two light machine guns and an anti-tank rifle, it is unlikely that they would have had much effect on invading Germans. Its true role has been described by the local Army commander in 1940, Colonel Dale Trotter: 'At the time it was just about bow and arrow defence – without the arrows being very sharp or very many. And looking back on it, was the train worthwhile? From the point of view of *morale* it definitely was!'

of the Edwardian garden railway laid out in the grounds of country houses. In the early 1920s, mainlines worked by Pacific-hauled express trains were state-of-the-art transport technology, and Zborowski and Howey resolved to build and operate one of their own – in miniature.

Unfortunately, Zborowski was killed while motor racing at Monza in Italy before their plan could take shape. But Howey pressed on alone, and the RHDR became his life's work. He enlisted the gifted engineer, Henry Greenly, to help realize his dream. It was Greenly who surveyed the eventual route of the railway along the Kent coast, who saw to the building of the line and, more particularly, designed its steam locomotives.

The first public trains ran across Romney Marsh in 1927 and, although Captain Howey died in 1963, the RHDR still preserves his vision of a mainline in the confident high summer of railway development.

During the high season, the timetable requires four separate trains to steam up and down the line at any one time, and it is quite possible to break your journey as often as you wish and continue it on a later train.

Hythe, at the northern end of the line, is within reasonable distance of both the mainline station at Folkestone and Junction 11 of the M20 motorway.

The RHDR station, situated just off the A259, is a traditional terminus with an overall train-shed roof spanning the tracks.

The station buildings combine services for full-sized passengers with an appropriate setting for the arrival and departure of the miniature trains. The signalbox, water tower and turntable are features which contribute to the steam railway atmosphere.

Intriguing though the line-side features at Hythe certainly are, what really attracts the visitor's attention are the locomotives themselves. Captain Howey equipped the RHDR with a fleet of nine express engines. Seven of them were built to Henry Greenly's design by the Colchester firm of Davey Paxman.

Pacific inspiration

Five of these engines were 4-6-2s based on Sir Nigel Gresley's famous North Eastern Railway Pacifics, while the other two were 4-8-2s, intended for goods traffic that did not match expectations. In 1931, the Yorkshire Engine Company was asked to provide two more 4-6-2s, this time of a generally Canadian appearance. (Howey enjoyed taking railway holidays in Canada.)

The RHDR is noteworthy in retaining all its original steam locomotives in service to this day. As you watch the engines at Hythe rolling slowly back from the turntable, hissing gently along to join their trains – with the driver's head and shoulders appearing incongruously above the cab – the identity of each locomotive is immediately clear from its livery.

Trains waiting to leave for the run down the coast to New Romney and Dungeness may be made up of a dozen or more coaches, usually modern 20 seaters. Your train may even include the observation-cum-bar car, complete with attendant – an astonishing vehicle for so narrow a gauge.

With steam jetting from the cylinder cocks, the locomotives pull away from the platforms at Hythe just as purposefully as any full-sized counterpart, before heading steadily away southwards, past the back gardens of Hythe through an avenue of trees.

The clicking of the coach wheels over the rail joints tells you that speed is gradually increasing and, as the train emerges from the built-up area into the countryside, you will be travelling at around 40km/h (25mph), a scale speed for the train of about 121km/h (75mph).

The level crossing at Botolph's Bridge, 3.25km (two miles) out, is a good spot for lineside spectators to watch the trains. Here the double-track line crosses the New Cut River, and the imposing Lympne Castle rears up on its chalk ridge in the background.

The scaled-down 4-6-2s and 4-8-2s generate a real sense of excitement as they forge past, whistles sounding. The Canadian-style locomotives – Nos 9 and 10 – are fitted with genuine North American steam whistles; the deep, rasping hoots echo across the marsh with an authentic Prairie sound.

Flashing light control

Twenty minutes' brisk running across the flat countryside brings the train to Dymchurch, a traditional seaside village on the coast road. As with the dozen or so other level crossings on the railway, the one here is controlled by flashing lights to warn traffic of the train's approach.

The line continues south, with the coast road and sea wall off to the left, and pastoral Romney Marsh to the right. The next station, Jefferstone Lane, comes 1.5km (a mile) or so further on. This is where passengers bound for the sands of St Mary's Bay alight. Alongside the Hythe end of the down platform is a single-storey bungalow called The Long Boat. For several years, this was the home of E. Nesbitt, author of *The Railway Children*.

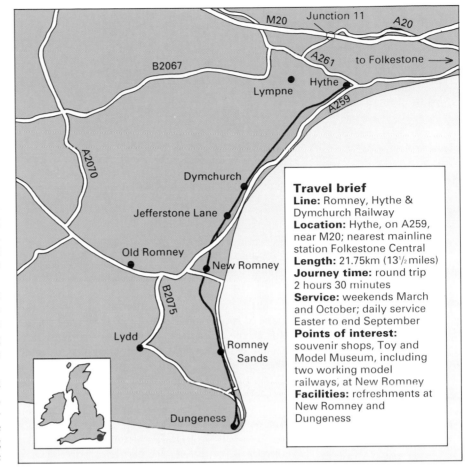

Travel brief
Line: Romney, Hythe & Dymchurch Railway
Location: Hythe, on A259, near M20; nearest mainline station Folkestone Central
Length: 21.75km (13½ miles)
Journey time: round trip 2 hours 30 minutes
Service: weekends March and October; daily service Easter to end September
Points of interest: souvenir shops, Toy and Model Museum, including two working model railways, at New Romney
Facilities: refreshments at New Romney and Dungeness

A lucky survivor
The RHDR's little shunting engine, No 4 *The Bug*, has had an unusual career. It was built by the famous firm of Krauss in Munich in 1926 and was used in the construction of the railway. Never a favourite with the line's owner, Captain Howey, it was disposed of to an amusement park in 1931.

It eventually fell into the hands of a Belfast scrap-merchant, and spent many years under a mountain of scrap metal at his yard. Rescued and restored by the head of the consortium which now owns the line, Sir William MacAlpine, *The Bug* returned to service at New Romney in 1977.

◄No 9 *Winston Churchill*, the second of the RHDR's Canadian-style Pacifics, speeds through Dymchurch with a Santa Special. Carrying the name *Dr Syn* from new in 1931, the locomotive was renamed in 1948 when it was sent to Toronto for exhibition.

▲ Overlooked by back gardens, one of the line's two 4-8-2s, No 5 *Hercules*, is revolved on the turntable at Hythe. *Hercules* was clad in steel plate during World War II to work the armoured train that patrolled the marshes. After the war, it was used principally on ballast trains, but since the late 1940s, it has shared passenger working with the RHDR's Pacifics.

School traffic

The RHDR operates two diesel locomotives to haul regular school trains during term time. The school at New Romney has a catchment area which stretches along the route of the railway as far as Dymchurch, and trains of as many as 18 coaches are run morning and evening to transport up to 200 pupils at a time.

With loadings of this size, the railway is a more economic proposition than private buses for handling the school traffic. The service began in 1977 and was worked by steam locomotives until 1983, when the RHDR acquired the first of two Bo-Bos from TMA Birmingham.

▶ No 10 *Dr Syn* heads back to New Romney from Dungeness – once known as 'The Land That God Never Finished' – an area of shingle dominated by the nuclear power station and lighthouse. The engine was originally called *Black Prince*, a name now carried by the Krupp Pacific No 11 of 1937.

Once away again, the driver puts on another burst of speed, and the chatter of the exhaust quickens as the train sprints across the flat landscape. Gentle curves to right and left bring the line under the A259 at the shallow cutting known as The Warren and round past New Romney golf course on the approach to the RHDR's headquarters.

As the brakes go on for the New Romney stop, you can catch a glimpse of the engine shed on the left. Here all the RHDR's locomotives are stabled. Here, too, overhauls are carried out in the quiet winter months. Beyond the engine shed can be seen the black-and-white gables of Red Tiles, the extensive bungalow in which Captain Howey and his family lived for many years.

Although New Romney station now sports a large pitched roof spanning four tracks, some of the buildings, including the wooden clock tower, date back to the railway's inception. Watching the trains coming and going and the locomotives moving to and from the shed is a continual source of fascination at New Romney.

On busy days, you may see an 0-4-0 tender engine called *The Bug* shunting as well. This tiny machine was built in Munich in 1926 for the construction of the Romney line. In 1976, a larger compatriot arrived in the shape of No 11 *Black Prince*, a typically German 4-6-2 design built by Krupps. In the 1980s, the steam fleet was augmented by two powerful new diesel engines which are popular with the younger visitors.

Pulling away from New Romney towards Dungeness, the railway becomes a single line. For the first few kilometres (miles), the ribbon development along the coast road screens the train from any contact with the beach. However, once past Romney Sands station, the track emerges on to the strange beachscape of the Dungeness peninsula.

This is a railway setting unlike any other in Britain. For the final kilometre (mile) or so, the train runs across shingle dunes, past timber-framed houses and wooden shacks. A lifeboat station, beached fishing boats and tiny, isolated inns can all be seen beside the line. In the background stand the two Dungeness lighthouses and the looming power station complex.

At Dungeness station, there is a balloon loop, which enables your train to continue round and return to New Romney and Hythe. However, if the weather is kind, it is well worth breaking your journey here for an hour or so to savour the unique atmosphere. The area is a naturalist's paradise, attracting thousands of visiting birds and with a great variety of unusual plants.

The Romney, Hythe and Dymchurch line has, over the years, become something of an institution among railway enthusiasts, not only in Britain, but also abroad.

While numerous improvements have been carried out, and the engine stock enlarged to include diesel, the RHDR remains much as Zborowski and Howey must have envisaged it – a working memento of the great heyday of steam.

The North Norfolk Railway

**Running within sight of the sea
along the north Norfolk coast, this picturesque
line belies the county's image of flatness by taking
a switchback route through the coastal
hills from Sheringham to Holt.**

The North Norfolk Railway (NNR) is part of the former Midland & Great Northern Joint Railway (M&GNJR) which meandered for over 193km (120 miles) from the Midlands to the Norfolk coast. Most of the line was closed in 1959 and the existence of the NNR is a tribute to a largely independent and much-loved line that contributed to the development of the resorts of Sheringham and Cromer.

Sheringham is a small, attractive seaside town with two railway stations – the three-platform NNR, formerly the BR station, and, just over 183m (200yds) away, the present mainline station, which is a one-platform halt with regular train services to Cromer and Norwich. In its latter days, famous express trains such as the *Broadsman* and *Norfolkman*, sometimes hauled by Britannia class locomotives, called there.

Although the former BR station lost most of its buildings on the island platform in the late 1950s, the North Norfolk station still retains an aura of the past when trains, packed with holidaymakers, arrived from London and the Midlands. Today, Sheringham station preserves its 1950s image; the sounds and smells of steam still linger and its museum and displays of the railway's past attract thousands of summer visitors.

Services today are modest in comparison with the past, but a variety of trains can be seen by the visitor. Trains leave Sheringham for the 8.5km (5¼ mile) journey to Holt from platform 1 or 2 – both eight-coach platforms. To start with, the train passes through Sheringham's suburbia for a few hundred metres (yards) before gaining the open country. They say East Anglia is flat and uninteresting but this is certainly not the case in north Norfolk. Straightaway the noise from the locomotive is noticeable as it tackles a 1 in 92 gradient.

▼ Framed by the arch of the stone bridge at the west end of Weybourne station, B12 No 61572 stands at the main platform with a train from Sheringham. During the early 1990s, the engine underwent an extensive refit but has been back in service since 1995.

The railway runs through an area designated as being of outstanding natural beauty, with rolling fields and forested hills, usually in sight of the sea. After a short level and downhill section, the train starts to climb again – even steeper this time, with a gradient of 1 in 80, towards the station stop at Weybourne.

The halfway point

About 5km (three miles) from Sheringham, the first impression of Weybourne station is of a delightfully typical country station, seemingly built in the middle of nowhere. The actual village is nearly 1.5km (a mile) away, close to the sea, and when the railway was first built it by-passed Weybourne completely. The station was added 13 years after the opening of the line with the aim of attracting visitors to a large Victorian hotel built in the woods nearby. The hoped-for holiday traffic never materialized; the hotel fell into disuse and was closed before World War II. It was the war, in fact, that brought Weybourne its main traffic. Thousands of servicemen were stationed at a large

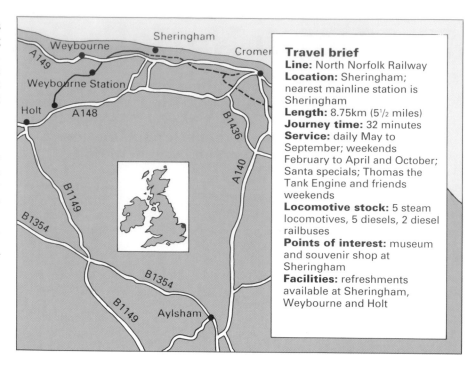

Travel brief
Line: North Norfolk Railway
Location: Sheringham; nearest mainline station is Sheringham
Length: 8.75km (5½ miles)
Journey time: 32 minutes
Service: daily May to September; weekends February to April and October; Santa specials; Thomas the Tank Engine and friends weekends
Locomotive stock: 5 steam locomotives, 5 diesels, 2 diesel railbuses
Points of interest: museum and souvenir shop at Sheringham
Facilities: refreshments available at Sheringham, Weybourne and Holt

◀ An atmosphere recalling memories of the 1950s has been re-created at Sheringham station. The museum attracts thousands of visitors a year and the station is the starting point for most journeys over the NNR.

army camp in the village and trains carrying troops, tanks and army equipment regularly called at the station.

Weybourne is rather a large station, having a luxurious booking hall and waiting room, a separate waiting room for ladies, the usual ticket and stationmaster's office and a fairly commodious luggage and parcels office – designed, no doubt, for the holiday visitors who never came.

This is the mid-point of the 8.75km (5½ mile) journey to Holt and on busy days trains pass one another, controlled from the signalbox on platform 1. Sadly, the original Weybourne box was demolished shortly after the railway had been sold to the NNR. BR demolition engineers had not been told of the sale and dismantled it 'in the interests of preventing vandalism'. There were apologies from British Rail and the NNR was able to acquire the present box from the closed Holt station.

Weybourne is the engineering headquarters of the railway and a locomotive shed has been built on its former goods yard. The steelwork for the shed was acquired from the M&GNJR station at Norwich City. It has been much altered and expanded to provide the essential facilities for the restoration and maintenance of the NNR locomotives and rolling stock.

On to Holt

The second stage of the journey to Holt was not possible until 1989. The line had lain derelict since 1964. Work on the construction of the Holt extension started in 1980 and volunteers toiled for eight years clearing vegetation and laying over 5,000 concrete sleepers, 500 tonnes (tons) of rails and 3,000 tonnes (tons) of ballast.

▲ The safety valves lift on J15 0-6-0 No 7564 as it waits to leave Sheringham. The engine has been a mainstay of passenger services for many years. From 1907 to 1914 through carriages came from London on the Norfolk Coast Express.

▼ When the summer has been warm and dry, Birmingham Railway Carriage & Wagon Co. Bo-Bo Class 27 No 5386 takes over at Weybourne for the last, and most scenic, part of the journey across Kelling Heath to Holt, where it is seen running round its train.

From Weybourne station the steam train is prepared for the gruelling 1 in 80 climb to Holt. If there has been a long spell of dry weather and there is danger of a stray spark from the chimney starting a fire on Kelling Heath, a mainline diesel locomotive will take over for the remainder of the journey. Whatever the motive power, the sound of the steam or diesel engine climbing the 1 in 80 gradient leaves a lasting impression.

This part of the line is dominated by Kelling Heath, beautifully unspoiled, with a backcloth of pine trees. There is no doubt that the section of the line between Weybourne and Holt is the prettiest in all Norfolk and one can imagine the delight of thousands of families from the industrial Midlands emerging from Kelling cutting and seeing the vast expanse of ocean – perhaps the children's very first sight of the sea.

All too soon the train arrives at Holt, a Georgian market town. Unfortunately, the station is about 1.5km (a mile) from the town centre as the last part of the trackbed was acquired by the local authority for a new bypass. A new station for Holt was created on the site of the planned, but never built, branch line to Blakeney. Although there are no station buildings at present, there are plans to build a replica of the original Holt station when funds allow.

▲ This fireless 0-6-0, built by W.G. Bagnall of Stafford in 1929, was until recently on display at the east end of Sheringham station. In front of the engine is a tablet exchange arm; a corresponding arm on a locomotive enabled single-line tablets to be exchanged at speed.

A mixed collection

Steam-hauled trains of four or five standard Mark 1 coaches are common and this rake often includes an immaculately restored Gresley buffet car. Another set includes three BR outer suburban coaches, a little more luxurious than normal, with side corridors and central toilets dividing the first- and second-class compartments. They do not, however, have corridor connections.

Although out of traffic at present, the railway often used the four-car LNER Gresley articulated quad-art set – four wooden-bodied suburban coaches that are remarkable in that the centre and end coaches share one bogie, giving a genuine articulated set. These unique survivors are undergoing a lengthy programme of restoration.

A more luxurious set operating on the line as a named train – the East Coast Pullman – comprises two Pullman cars of the famous Brighton Belle with a former full brake now converted into a full kitchen car, together with a brake suburban coach converted this time to carry a generator to provide electric power for the set.

Finally, the visitor can travel on one of two German-built, diesel railbuses which were introduced on branch lines in East Anglia in the late 1950s. A total of 22 were built, two of the bodies at the nearby Eastern Coach Works at Lowestoft.

▼ On loan from the Severn Valley Railway, LMS 0-6-0T No 47383, built by Vulcan Foundry in 1926, climbs past the Weybourne starting signal, a fine somersault example, on its way to Holt. At present there are no plans to install signalling at Holt, where a station building is a priority.

A hundred year gap
The new M&GN line from Holt to Sheringham was opened to traffic on 16 June 1887 and the first train passed through Weybourne at 12.11 p.m. Exactly a hundred years later on 16 June 1987, the first train from Holt on the North Norfolk Railway extension passed through Weybourne at 12.11 p.m.

However, they failed to save the branch lines for which they were built.

Just as the rolling stock is varied, so is the motive power. The railway owns two unique ex-British Rail steam locomotives. One is a former Great Eastern 0-6-0 Y14, No 564, a class of locomotive that first emerged from Stratford works in 1883. As the last example of its type, this one remained in service until the end of steam in East Anglia in 1961. The Y14 has given 14 consecutive years' service on the North Norfolk line.

The other former British Rail steam engine is express passenger locomotive B12 4-6-0, a member of the famous 1500 class locomotives which dominated the express passenger trains between London and East Anglia between 1908 and 1923. This engine has undergone a long and costly restoration, with the final works and assembly being undertaken in Holland and Germany.

The mainstays of the steam locomotive fleet are three industrial locomotives which have proved perfectly capable of operating the required services. These are Hunslet-built saddle tanks. One is a 16in (406.5mm) cylinder Fitzwilliam class locomotive called *Ring Haw*, named after a wood copse at the Nassington Borrowden quarries near Peterborough where it spent most of its life; the other two are larger Austerity types, No 3809 and No 8009.

In regular use from the diesel fleet is a former Scottish Region Class 27 No 5386, a Class 25 Sulzer mixed-traffic type locomotive and a Class 37 English Electric. Also from the diesel fleet and used mainly on works trains and for shunting duties is a former LMS Class 11 locomotive, No 12131, and a Class 08.

This mixed collection makes up the locomotive fleet of the railway.

▲ The former Great Eastern Railway's Y14 No 564 crosses Kelling Heath, returning from Holt to Sheringham. In the distance the village of Weybourne, with its landmark windmill, is set at the sea's edge – some way from the station which bears its name.

The East Anglian Railway Museum

Situated on the edge of picturesque Constable country, the East Anglian Railway Museum provides a close-up focus on the rural railway of Victorian times. Here it is literally only a few steps from Network SouthEast to the Great Eastern Railway.

▼ An N7 0-6-0 tank, No 69621, built by the London & North Eastern Railway in 1924, passes the Chappel North signalbox. No 69621 was the last engine built at Stratford works to a Great Eastern Railway design. As indicated by its destination board, it was used on suburban services to London's Liverpool Street station.

Nestling in the undulating Essex countryside just over 11 kilometres (seven miles) north-west of Colchester is Chappel & Wakes Colne station. This was once owned by the Great Eastern Railway (GER) and following the 1923 grouping, by the London & North Eastern Railway (LNER). Today, it is the headquarters of the East Anglian Railway Museum. Here you can unravel the mysteries of signalling, watch the repair and operation of steam locomotives and wonder at the engineering and architectural skills of the Victorians.

In its heyday, Chappel & Wakes Colne was served by the Stour Valley branch, which ran from Marks Tey to Shelford on the mainline from London to Cambridge. However, in 1965 the section beyond Sudbury was closed and the remaining stations on the branch were reduced to unstaffed halts. Five years later, the Stour Valley Railway Preservation Society began its transformation of Chappel & Wakes Colne.

▶ The boiler of an ex-British Railways Standard 4MT 2-6-4T, No 80151, is made ready for testing at Chappel & Wakes Colne station. The EARM, which carries out its refurbishments in the specially built locomotive shed, acquired No 80151 from Barry scrapyard. Built in 1957, the engine spent its 10 years of BR service on the Southern Region.

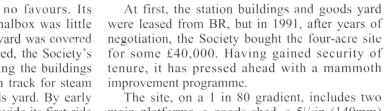

▼A Hunslet 0-6-0T, No 47160 *Cunarder*, on loan from the Swanage Railway, edges forward with a train on the EARM shuttle. In the background are the station buildings and the lattice footbridge joining the two platforms. On the right, platform 1 is used by a Network SouthEast DMU service between Sudbury, Marks Tey and Colchester.

Time had done the station no favours. Its buildings were in ruins, its signalbox was little more than a shell and its goods yard was covered with weeds and debris. Undeterred, the Society's members set to work, refurbishing the buildings and laying a short demonstration track for steam locomotives in the cleared goods yard. By early 1971, the Society was able to provide its first ride for members, the train being hauled by an Austerity class 0-6-0 saddle tank, *Gunby*.

At first, the station buildings and goods yard were leased from BR, but in 1991, after years of negotiation, the Society bought the four-acre site for some £40,000. Having gained security of tenure, it has pressed ahead with a mammoth improvement programme.

The site, on a 1 in 80 gradient, includes two main platforms, a goods shed, a 5½in (140mm) gauge miniature railway and a motley assortment of workshops. Entry is through the red-brick booking hall, dating from the 1840s, which now includes a souvenir and bookshop. The booking hall features a comprehensive map pinpointing all the lines before the cuts introduced by Lord Beeching in the 1960s.

Items of Victorian luggage, including suitcases and a trunk, help to create the right atmosphere. Inside the small, neat booking office there is a cast-iron fireplace bearing the GER insignia. The office issues tickets for normal mainline services as well as for entry to the museum.

Making room for relics

Adjoining the booking hall are the stationmaster's office, the toilets and lamp room. Extensive excavations beneath this complex have made room for a heritage centre with relics spanning a hundred years of railway history.

At the rear of the slip road behind the station are the stationmaster's house and a former railway tavern, again both in characteristic red brick and faithfully echoing the Victorian era.

Moving beyond the booking hall, you step on to platform 1. An hourly mainline diesel service still rattles through here between Sudbury, Marks Tey and Colchester. The signalbox at the end of the platform is the original and was installed by the GER around 1880. It has been handsomely restored in green and cream GER livery. Now non-operational, it is used for demonstration purposes

– the levers and telegraph equipment can be operated by visitors. The broken lever frame was found among the rubbish in the goods yard and it took the Society's volunteers three months to put the shattered pieces together again – a considerable engineering achievement.

A lattice footbridge transported from Sudbury station in Suffolk leads across the mainline metals to platform 2. This adjoins the site of the old goods yard and stands at the centre of the Museum's 400m (440yd) steam circuit.

Steam-train schedule

Steam trains operate on the first Sunday of each month from March to November and will be headed by one or other of nine locomotives, including the Museum's first engine, *Gunby*, which is still performing admirably.

Other reliable workhorses are an 0-6-0 saddle tank, No 54 *Penn Green*, and an 0-4-0 saddle tank, *Jubilee*. *Penn Green* was built in 1941 by Robert Stephenson & Co. of Leeds and spent the next 28 years hauling mineral trains at Corby in Northamptonshire. It moved to Chappel & Wakes Colne in 1973. *Jubilee* was built in 1936 by Bagnalls of Stafford and worked until 1971 at a paper mill at Sittingbourne in Kent. It was bought for restoration in 1976 and has made trips on low-loader lorries to publicize Museum events.

The pride of the Museum's fleet is an award-winning LNER N7 0-6-2 tank, No 69621. Built in 1924, it was the last of a batch of 134 ordered by the GER just prior to grouping. It was, indeed, the last GER locomotive to be outshopped at Stratford works. The N7s were used on the Liverpool Street suburban Jazz Service, so called because of the distinctively coloured stripes over the first- and second-class compartments.

No 69621 was withdrawn from Stratford (London) shed in 1962 and stored at Neville Hill shed in Leeds for 11 years before moving to Chappel & Wakes Colne. Here it underwent a complete rebuild, winning the coveted British Coal Steam Heritage Award for 1990.

The Museum possesses three diesel locomotives – a 1938 Barclay 0-4-0 AMW No 144, a 1960 Class 04 0-6-0 shunter No D2279, and a 1965 Fowler 0-4-0 No 23. There is one Metropolitan Vickers 0-4-0 electric locomotive, No 2, built in 1912. It has a top speed of just 19.25km/h (12mph) and spent its working life hauling enormous coal loads up steep gradients to

▲ Undeterred by winter cold or threatening snow clouds, visitors stand at the end of the EARM platform at Chappel & Wakes Colne station to watch the former LNER N7 0-6-2T No 69621 go through its paces. Behind stands a less exalted member of the EARM stable, an 0-6-0ST *Penn Green* built in 1941 by Robert Stephenson & Co. of Leeds.

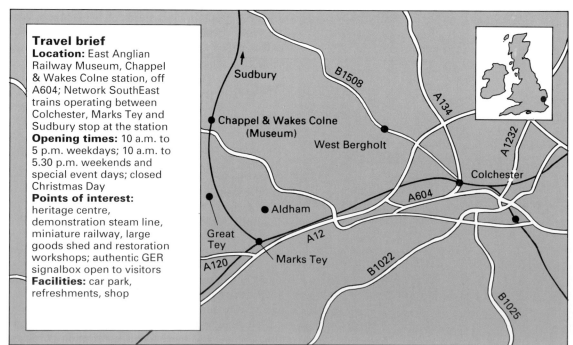

Travel brief
Location: East Anglian Railway Museum, Chappel & Wakes Colne station, off A604; Network SouthEast trains operating between Colchester, Marks Tey and Sudbury stop at the station
Opening times: 10 a.m. to 5 p.m. weekdays; 10 a.m. to 5.30 p.m. weekends and special event days; closed Christmas Day
Points of interest: heritage centre, demonstration steam line, miniature railway, large goods shed and restoration workshops; authentic GER signalbox open to visitors
Facilities: car park, refreshments, shop

▶ The 32 arch Chappel Viaduct, opened in 1849, is still part of Network SouthEast's line from Marks Tey to Sudbury, but the EARM is occasionally able to operate over it at weekends – here No 69621 steams across. Built for double track, the 325m (355yd) viaduct consumed seven million bricks and was the longest on the Great Eastern Railway.

▼ **The restored goods shed at Chappel houses a relics museum and various other EARM items. The shed is a fine example of Victorian railway architecture.**

the Foss Island Power Station at York. No 2 underwent a thorough restoration in 1987, but since there are no immediate plans to build a 500 volt overhead wire at the Museum, it seems likely to remain a static exhibit.

The Museum's collection of rolling stock includes a number of superbly restored 19th century passenger vehicles. One of these is a handsome six-wheeled third-class coach, No 373, built in 1899 for the Manchester, Sheffield & Lincolnshire Railway. It arrived at Chappel & Wakes Colne in 1971 after a chequered history including one stint as a camping coach and another as a mess van.

Even older is a four-wheeled first-class coach, No 19, built for the Great Eastern in 1878. It was one of seven coaches which the GER widened by 305mm (1ft) in 1903, thus enabling 12 passengers to be carried in each compartment instead of 10. The vehicle came to Chappel & Wakes Colne after several years as a beach chalet. The wheels, axles and W irons were obtained from a derelict chassis at Parkeston Quay (Harwich).

A more recent item is the King's Cross suburban brake (BS) No E43157, dating from 1954. An example of standard British Rail non-corridor stock, it featured in an episode of the BBC television series *Nanny*.

Among the goods vehicles is a pair of furniture containers, both more than 70 years old, presented to the Museum by the Braintree, Essex, removal firm of Henry Joscelyne. In effect, these were the

forerunners of the container trains regularly seen over parts of the rail system.

The GER four-wheeled Pooley van, No 3, was built in 1911 by the company which supplied most of the weighbridges to the Great Eastern. It was constructed as a mobile workshop and has work benches, vices and a skylight. Also on display is an LNER fish van, No 159918, equipped with vacuum brakes for running on fast goods and passenger trains.

Controlling signalbox

All main points and signals within the yard are controlled by the Chappel North signalbox, erected at the northern limit of the Museum's track. A listed 1888 structure, it came from nearby Mistley station on the Harwich branch. It has been mounted on a new brick base and the locking has been purpose-built. Any locomotive driver passing the box has to collect a token before proceeding. A small signalbox called a ground frame is used to control shunting at the southern end of the yard.

Back in the 1960s, when the fate of the Stour Valley branch was still being decided, it was the ambition of the preservationists to save at least part of the line from Sudbury to Shelford. In the event, this proved to be impossible and the move into Chappel & Wakes Colne was the only feasible alternative. The subsequent venture presents a close-up view of railway history often lacking on some of the more glamorous projects.

The Railway Age, Crewe

When a railway repair and construction works was opened at Crewe in 1843, the population was barely 200. By 1910, it had increased to 50,000 – most of it dependent on the railway. A flavour of those early days has been created by the Railway Age, Crewe.

The first station at Crewe, then a rural area surrounding the stately home of Crewe Hall, was opened in 1837 by the Grand Junction Railway (GJR), which connected Birmingham with the early lines in Lancashire. Branches from Crewe to Chester, Manchester, Stoke and Shrewsbury soon followed, making the station a major junction.

Accordingly, when the GJR was relocating its works from a cramped site at Edge Hill in Liverpool, Crewe, with plenty of land available, was an obvious choice. The first works opened in 1843 on a site between the junction of the Chester and Warrington lines, creating a new town that soon overshadowed the ancient market centre of nearby Nantwich.

Over the years Crewe works expanded enormously under the GJR's successors, principally the London & North Western Railway (LNWR).

The main site, further down the Chester line, is operated by Chrysler Daimler Benz (Adtranz), although the original Old Works was demolished as surplus to requirements.

All was not lost, however, as Crewe and Nantwich Borough Council, looking for somewhere to celebrate the 1987 sesquicentenary of both the town and the GJR, settled on this historic location. An exhibition hall was erected and on 4 July 1987, 150 years to the day since the GJR started operating, Crewe Heritage Centre opened its doors to the public.

The project, which has since changed its name to the Railway Age, Crewe, and is now run by a charitable trust rather than the local council, occupies a three-acre site bounded by Vernon Way and the lines to Chester and Preston. The first items you encounter on entering the Railway Age are the surviving cars of the Class 370 Advanced

▼ A view of the Railway Age, taken during the 1987 opening season, when the museum was known as Crewe Heritage Centre. A visiting Stanier 8F 2-8-0, No 48151, with a 5B Crewe South shedplate, gets up steam by the former demonstration line platform, while on display in the background is another visitor, No 71000 *Duke of Gloucester*, built at Crewe in 1954.

England: Midlands

Passenger Train (APT), dating from 1979, on loan from the National Railway Museum, York.

The story of the tilting, high speed APT's long development and failure in trial service is well-known, but it is interesting to be able to board the train, try out the comfortable tartan seats and see how the tilting mechanism meant that the carriage sides had to be sharply angled inwards to avoid fouling lineside obstructions.

As an ironic reminder of what might have been, the APT is located alongside the West Coast main-line, where it was to have operated. Its high-speed days are now distinctly over, however, for it is securely plumbed into mains services so that the buffet car can be used to serve refreshments.

Austere transplant

Walking the length of the APT brings you to the apex of the site and one of its key features – Crewe North Junction signalbox. The fifth box to be erected here, it was opened in 1938 and is a typically austere concrete building of the period.

On the ground floor, there are displays on the history of signalling, with plenty of hands-on exhibits for visitors to try out for themselves. These are accompanied by clear explanations of point and signal interlocking, the use of block instruments and bell codes, and the operation of colour light signals.

Also on the ground floor is the relay room, where you can see the 750 relays that ensured the safe operation of trains at this busy and complex junction. Just how busy Crewe still is can be seen by spending a few minutes sitting in front of the picture window that provides an unrivalled view straight down into the station, with its constant procession of trains to Chester, Manchester, Liverpool and the North.

Upstairs in the signalbox all the facilities, including the long miniature lever frames, remain intact. North Junction box was taken out of use in

1985, when for seven weeks the unthinkable happened and Crewe station closed almost completely for resignalling and remodelling of the track layout. The replacement signalling centre, controlling the whole area, is an undistinguished single-storey structure which can be seen on the right looking towards the station. Built on the site of Crewe North shed, it is painted red and white.

A volunteer steward is usually on hand to demonstrate the operation of North Junction box. It is possible to pull the appropriate point and signal levers as though setting up a route into Crewe station. A computer simulates the approach of a train along the illuminated track diagram above.

On leaving the box, you should look back at it to catch sight of the impressive iron eagle perched on the roof. This is one of a pair rescued from a bridge inside the works; its partner is also preserved at the centre.

Close to North Junction box is the concrete platform, where a brake van is on show. A 1926 Kerr Stuart 0-4-0ST from Etruria Gas Works near

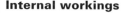

▲ Some of BR's early 25kV electric locomotives have been restored at the Railway Age, including E3003, one of the original AL1 Bo-Bos from the 1960s, here seen restored to the blue and white livery in which it first appeared.

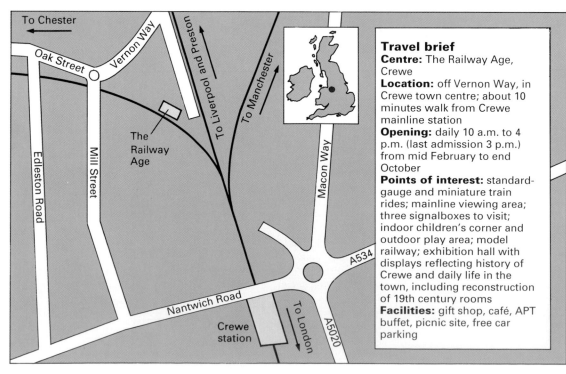

Travel brief
Centre: The Railway Age, Crewe
Location: off Vernon Way, in Crewe town centre; about 10 minutes walk from Crewe mainline station
Opening: daily 10 a.m. to 4 p.m. (last admission 3 p.m.) from mid February to end October
Points of interest: standard-gauge and miniature train rides; mainline viewing area; three signalboxes to visit; indoor children's corner and outdoor play area; model railway; exhibition hall with displays reflecting history of Crewe and daily life in the town, including reconstruction of 19th century rooms
Facilities: gift shop, café, APT buffet, picnic site, free car parking

Internal workings

In the early 1860s, the first 18in (457mm) gauge tracks were laid in Crewe works to improve internal transport. Seven 0-4-0 tank locomotives were built for it at Crewe, the first, the appropriately named *Tiny*, in 1862, and the last, *Dickie*, in 1876. After most of the steam engines had been withdrawn, Hudswell Clarke supplied a diesel, *Crewe*, in 1930. Narrow-gauge locomotive working ceased in 1932, although a hand-worked line lingered on until 1967.

A feature of the works line was a long bridge connecting the Old Works with Crewe station foot-bridge, so that spares could be easily transhipped on to the standard-gauge system. It was known as Midge Bridge, after one of the narrow-gauge locomotives. Narrow-gauge trains approached the bridge by a steep ramp, and the 1906 North Junction signalbox, predecessor of today's preserved box, was built around the line, with trains passing through the middle of its brickwork base.

◄ Once the shape of things to come on the West Coast mainline, the streamlined APT set is the largest and most striking exhibit at the Railway Age. The steps lead to the buffet car, which is sometimes used to serve refreshments. Between the APT and the boundary fence can be seen the track of the miniature railway.

Good neighbours
The Crewe Heritage Centre originally occupied all the land bounded by Vernon Way and the lines to Chester and Preston. When it was first proposed by the local council that part of the area should be sold for a supermarket development, the fear was expressed that potential customers would be scared off by the smoke and noise of steam trains.

The development went ahead anyway, and not only were customers undeterred, but the supermarket now has a preserved standard-gauge steam engine of its own. The 1922 Avonside 0-4-0ST *Elizabeth*, which worked at South Sydenham Gas Works, stands outside the store and is maintained by staff and supporters from the Railway Age.

Stoke-on-Trent used to provide motive power for a short ride in the brake van, but this locomotive is no longer at the Railway Age and the rides have been discontinued. That locomotive was clearly a larger cousin of the Talyllyn Railway's *Edward Thomas*, produced by the same builder five years earlier.

Signalboxes
Apart from the might Crewe North Junction box, the Railway Age has two other preserved signal-boxes, the small Crewe Station A box and the much larger and grander Exeter West box. The Exeter West is a wooden structure which has been painstakingly restored after its long journey north. Both boxes can be visited, but are not always open.

Diesels in demand
Sidings between the steam demonstration line and the exhibition hall house most of the stock at the Railway Age. Among the mainline diesels from the 1960s are Class 47 D1842 Co-Co and Class 15 D8233, both currently awaiting repair. Operating diesels include the 1959 Class 03 D2073, in unlined black livery. Diesel engines are regularly in demand for diesel weekends at preserved railways. Therefore, they are often on loan and not always present at Crewe.

Class 25s have been restored at Crewe, as has an AC electric 82008, while the six-wheeled diesel shunter 03073 is in full working order.

Class 45 D120 1-Co-Co-1 has been transferred to Crewe carriage shed, along with Class 25 D7523 Bo-Bo and Class 46 D172 *Ixion*. The Class 46 is occasionally used on special trains.

The Railway Age has a connection on to the main Chester line. It is hoped that, when mainline

preserved diesel operation becomes established, Crewe will be a major centre for it.

For the present, the mainline connection is used primarily for the stabling of steam engines working mainline specials in the area. Visiting locomotives, such as the handsome London Midland & Scottish Railway Stanier 4-6-2 No 6201 *Princess Elizabeth*, can often be seen at the centre awaiting their next rostered duty.

Currently undergoing restoration at the Railway Age are three Great Western Railway locomotives – a 4-6-0, No 7027 *Thornbury Castle*, a 2-8-0T No 5224, and an 0-6-2T No 6634. Also under restoration is ex-industrial locomotive *Robert*, an 0-6-0T formerly used by the Coal Board and most recently an LNWR Super D 0-8-0. The Railway Age also undertakes boiler repairs for other railways.

▼ No 6201 *Princess Elizabeth*, an LMS Stanier 4-6-2, is one of the visiting steam engines at Crewe.

◄ Pride of the 7¹/₄in (184mm) gauge railway is *Jenny*, based on the Hunslet 2-4-0STs that worked the 'mainline' of the Penrhyn Quarries in North Wales. Here *Jenny*, built in 1992 and originally known as *Card*, waits for passengers at Old Works station.

one of Crewe's major employers in the field of engineering, is not neglected.

Outside the hall on display is the former Western Region gas turbine locomotive No 18000. Behind the exhibition hall is the two-road workshop and shed.

The most recent feature of the Railway Age is a 7¹/₄in (184mm) gauge miniature railway, mainly built during 1992. On special occasions, *Jenny*, a live steam model of the Ffestiniog Railway's Hunslet 2-4-0ST locomotives *Linda* and *Blanche*, works the trains, but the more usual motive power is the battery electric No 7940, loosely based on a Santa Fé Railroad diesel prototype.

Miniature train journey

Miniature trains depart from Old Works station, just to the right of the main entrance. Crossing the approach road, they run alongside the APT back towards Vernon Way until Forge End station is reached. Here the train reverses and heads back down the other side of the APT, this time sandwiched between the high-speed set and the fence bordering the mainline.

The journey ends near North Junction signalbox at Midge Bridge station, a name that commemorates an earlier line on the site, the 18in (457mm) gauge works railway. Stock is stored in a new shed near the APT. The miniature railway also boasts a petrol hydraulic locomotive, loosely based on the former BR Hymek diesels.

The model railway enthusiast is not forgotten and there are various displays and special events held during the year.

LNWR survivor

The Railway Age's famous 2-2-2, No 3020 *Cornwall*, was built at Crewe in 1847, just a year after the London & North Western Railway, the 'Premier Line', had been formed by the amalgamation of the Grand Junction Railway with the London & Birmingham and Liverpool & Manchester railways. Because *Cornwall*'s driving wheels were so large, the engine was built with its boiler most unusually positioned beneath the driving axle. It must have presented a curious spectacle as it steamed along, apparently without a boiler.

In 1858, John Ramsbottom rebuilt *Cornwall*, this time with the boiler in the usual position above the driving axle. After working the directors' saloon for 20 years, *Cornwall* was finally withdrawn in 1927, being stored at Crewe works.

However, to see what is undoubtedly the star steam attraction at Crewe you must go inside the exhibition hall. Here you will find the splendid 2-2-2 No 3020 *Cornwall*, built at Crewe in 1847. The 2.5m (8ft 6in) diameter driving wheels of the veteran locomotive, painted in LNWR black, tower above every visitor. You can also see the driving cab from a withdrawn Class 47 diesel locomotive.

The exhibition hall also houses photographic displays on the history of Crewe, along with reconstructed rooms from typical houses and shops in the town as they would have been towards the end of the 19th century. Rolls-Royce,

▶ The Railway Age is renowned as a centre for the preservation of modern traction. Typical of the high standard of restoration work carried out is D120, one of the British Rail 1-Co-Co-1 Peak class locomotives, running on the mainline service. D120 was latterly numbered 45108 by BR.

Birmingham Railway Museum

**It is over 30 years since Tyseley steam depot
closed down. Part of Birmingham's railway heritage seemed
to have gone forever. But Tyseley is enjoying a new lease
of life – as both a museum and a locomotive repair
and restoration centre.**

▼ Young enthusiasts inspect two LMS Jubilee class 4-6-0s – No 5593 *Kolhapur* – now on loan to another railway – and No 5690 *Leander* – a former visitor to Tyseley. It was to provide accommodation for *Kolhapur* and the GWR Castle class 4-6-0 *Clun Castle,* that the Birmingham Railway Museum was founded.

A generation or so ago, when steam was still very much in evidence, the name Tyseley was synonymous with two large roundhouses that provided the passenger (mostly suburban) and freight locomotives that worked the services over the old Great Western Railway (GWR) lines in the Birmingham area. Each roundhouse had a central turntable with radiating tracks for engine storage. There was also a repair shop and coaling stage.

The Tyseley shed was opened in 1908. The works' demise began just over half a century later, in 1963, when British Rail demolished the freight roundhouse. The workshop went the following year and in 1967 the steam depot was closed. The passenger roundhouse was razed soon afterwards.

However, by then the enthusiasts were active. In 1969, they launched the Standard Gauge Steam Trust, and it was this body, with financial backing from the West Midlands County Council (no longer in existence), that took over the whole $4\frac{1}{2}$ acre site to form the Birmingham Railway Museum.

You can reach it off the A41 Warwick Road – buses pass the entrance – or by taking a train to Tyseley station, which is only a five-minute walk away. The station dates from 1907 and still retains its original buildings.

Passing a diesel unit depot an early symptom

▲ One of Tyseley's Castle 4-6-0s, No 5080 *Defiant*, heads a steam train excursion over BR metals near Cheltenham in Gloucestershire in 1988. The Museum's locomotives may not always be on show and are often seen in action elsewhere in the country, steaming over lines which offer a greater challenge.

of the steam shed's decline – you come to the Museum's entrance. The model railway display is on your left next to the driving simulator as you enter the Museum's visitor centre. This houses a large range of railway memorabilia, including some magnificent old nameplates and number-plates and cast-iron signs.

Turning right from the visitor centre, you come to what used to be the shed area. Here there is an impressive reminder of the old Tyseley – is an impressive reminder of the old Tyseley –

the 19.75m (65ft) diameter turntable from the passenger roundhouse. When BR demolished the last of the sheds, the turntable pits were partly destroyed and filled with rubble, and most of the rails were cut up and sold for scrap. However, thanks largely to help from the Manpower Services Commission, the pits were dug out and new tracks were laid.

The turntable, previously worked manually, is now power operated after being fully restored. It

Symbol of success

The locomotive most closely bound up with Tyseley's revival is No 7029 *Clun Castle*. Built at Swindon in 1950, it finished its days in BR service at Gloucester. In November 1965, just before its withdrawal, it headed the last steam train out of Paddington station.

The locomotive arrived at Tyseley in January 1966. But its active life was far from over, and during the next few months, it hauled a number of excursions over BR rails. In June 1972, however, it was involved in an event closer to home. Tyseley inaugurated its Return to Steam programme, with *Clun Castle* working a mainline excursion from Tyseley BR station to Didcot in Oxfordshire.

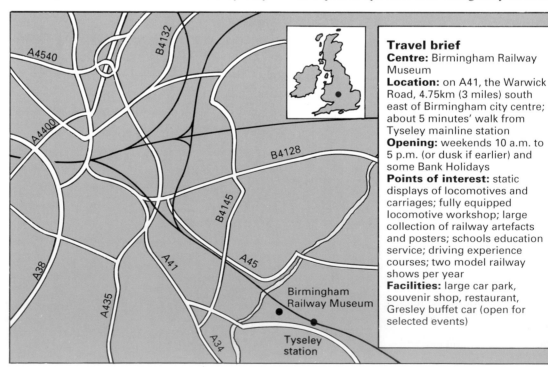

Travel brief

Centre: Birmingham Railway Museum
Location: on A41, the Warwick Road, 4.75km (3 miles) south east of Birmingham city centre; about 5 minutes' walk from Tyseley mainline station
Opening: weekends 10 a.m. to 5 p.m. (or dusk if earlier) and some Bank Holidays
Points of interest: static displays of locomotives and carriages; fully equipped locomotive workshop; large collection of railway artefacts and posters; schools education service; driving experience courses; two model railway shows per year
Facilities: large car park, souvenir shop, restaurant, Gresley buffet car (open for selected events)

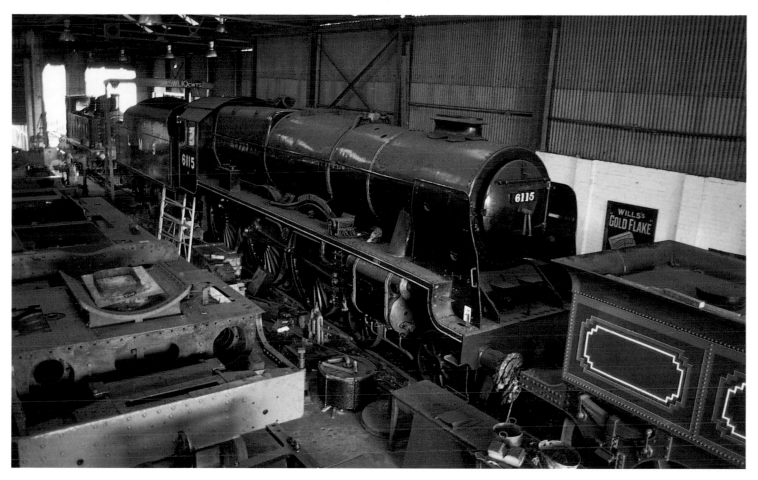

▲ The future of the LMS Royal Scot 4-6-0 *Scots Guardsman* is under debate as it would require much attention if rebuilt. The Museum has one of the best equipped steam restoration and maintenance workshops in Britain, enabling it to do extensive contract work for others.

is used for turning carriages and locomotives up to a maximum weight of 146 tonnes (tons). There are 28 display roads radiating from the turntable, together with inspection pits, some of which are occupied by diesel engines owned by Fragonset Railways Ltd.

Tyseley is home to a large collection of engines, including a London Midland & Scottish (LMS) Jubilee, a GWR Hall, three GWR Castles and three GWR Pannier tanks. There is also a range of industrial locomotives and at any one time there will be several visiting engines. Bear in mind, however, that when you visit the Museum your favourite may be out on loan to one of the preserved lines.

In addition to these locomotives, there are a number of coaches undergoing restoration for the Shakespeare Express – a regular steam-train service between Birmingham and Stratford-upon-Avon – and other mainline steam excursions.

Dream steam day

For real steam enthusiasts, there is the opportunity on most weekends to book an engine driving course at Tyseley. For up to two hours, groups of three can drive and crew No 7029 *Clun Castle*. A tour of the workshop is included and a talk on the technical aspects of driving steam trains with an opportunity to ask questions. For more information please telephone the Museum.

Gresley buffet car

A short distance from the Museum's station is a picnic area, the centrepiece of which is a GWR-style wooden platform. This is the site of a 1937 London & North Eastern Railway Gresley buffet car, No 24279. This is open for business at selected events.

Even if trains are not running, there is an excellent view up the track, with signals and points clearly in sight. The fully operative 39 lever signalbox can be seen from here, and guided visits can be arranged if advance notice is given.

Close by is the external locomotive refurbishment area, with its beguiling jumble of boilers, frames, wheels and bogies.

As you continue down the path, you will see two choices ahead – Chuffs restaurant, beneath the arches of the old coal stage, or the workshop. Chuffs is adorned with railway ephemera – maps, signs, posters, numberplates – and is well worth a visit even if you do not intend to eat there.

Workshop tour

In some ways, the word 'museum' is a misnomer. Originally founded to house two mainline steam locomotives – the GWR Castle class 4-6-0 No 7029 *Clun Castle*, and the LMS Jubilee class 4-6-0 No 5593 *Kolhapur*, currently on loan to Barrow Hill, near Chesterfield – Tyseley became more than just an exhibition centre, and now has the facilities to keep a large express locomotive in fighting trim.

The Tyseley Locomotive Works employs over 15 experienced full-time engineers and undertakes many outside engineering contracts. Its successes include the rebuilding from scrap condition of the privately owned engine, Manor class 4-6-0 No 7820 *Dinmore Manor* and Tyseley's own engines No 5080 *Defiant*, No 4965 *Rood Ashton Hall* (formerly called *Albert Hall*) and Pannier tank No 9600. An ex-Southern Railway Bulleid Pacific No 35005 *Canadian Pacific* has been repaired and now undertakes mainline rail tours.

Several projects are under way in the workshop. The privately owned GWR Hall class *Kinlet Hall* is undergoing a full restoration and once this has been completed, the engine will be used in conjunction with No 4965 *Rood Ashton Hall*.

▼ Smoke pours from its distinctive double chimney as No 7029 *Clun Castle* waits on the road leading to the Tyseley turntable in 1987. Its headboard refers to the closure of old Moor Street station, once used by commuters travelling on the GWR lines south of Birmingham.

◀ A Tyseley signalman displays his skills in the fully operative 39 lever signalbox. The box is an interesting feature at Tyseley and guided tours can be arranged in advance for those wishing to follow its workings from the inside.

▼ A pair of 60 year old Great Western Pannier tanks – Nos 7760 and 7752 – double-head a train on the old Tyseley demonstration track as part of the celebrations marking the opening of the Museum's new platforms and signalbox.

The workshop, open to the public by prior arrangement only, has a viewing gallery from which you can see the three lines that run through it. The two nearer the viewing gallery are used for locomotives under heavy repair. The other is for locomotives in service. At ground level you must be accompanied by a member of the Museum staff and this may not always be possible.

On entering, to the left is a 40 tonne (ton) Noble & Lund wheel and crank pin lathe, dating from 1947, which is capable of coping with the largest express locomotives. Next to this is a Ransome & Rapier wheel drop installation from Ipswich steam depot. Other equipment, which includes a modern electric crane, is used for removing wheels from locomotives.

The workshop also uses a combination shaper, lathe and drilling machine, which was originally installed at Bescot depot, near Birmingham, in the latter years of the LMS.

Castle restoration

Castle class locomotives represent everything that the golden age of railways gave to transport – speed, style and power.

GWR No 5043 *Earl of Mount Edgcumbe*, the seventy-first member of its class to be built, was purchased from a scrapyard in South Wales in 1973. It was originally intended to serve as a source of spare parts for the other two Castle class locomotives, No 7029 *Clun Castle* and No 5080 *Defiant*. However, the restoration of this engine which once hauled the world's fastest regular train, the Great Western's *Cheltenham Flyer* was a challenge too tempting to miss. When this project is completed, it is hoped that the engine will be the main locomotive for the regular Shakepeare Express service.

Model railway

The Museum has an active group of model railway enthusiasts. In addition to the two shows a year they put on at Tyseley, they participate in various other shows and exhibitions, taking their displays around the country.

Shop

Before leaving Tyseley, you may like to return to the visitor centre, which you have to pass on your way to the exit, to browse in the shop. It has a second-hand section as well as a wide range of magazines, books, videos and souvenirs.

Severn Valley Railway

**Covering the picturesque route between
Kidderminster and Bridgnorth, the 25.75km (16 mile) long Severn
Valley Railway has re-created the classic GWR cross-country
line, complete with wayside stations that display oil
lamps, milk churns and well-tended flower gardens.**

Rejoicing in its claim to be Britain's premier preserved railway, the Severn Valley Railway, which for most of its 25.75km (16 miles) follows the course of the River Severn through Worcestershire and into Shropshire, is one of the best equipped and most intensively operated of the UK's independent steam lines.

With a steam fleet of some 25 ex-British Railways engines, of which approximately one-third are kept serviceable at any one time, and over 60 passenger coaches, the SVR steams more

than 64,374km (40,000 miles) a year. In high season, it operates a 45 minute interval service so that up to five trains are out on the line simultaneously.

Even in off-peak periods, the line has five trains a day in each direction – which is more than it did in the old days of the Great Western Railway – and since 1989, it has carried more than 200,000 passengers annually.

The Severn Valley Railway of today takes its name from the company which in 1862 opened the original 64.25km (40 mile) SVR line between

Shrewsbury and Hartlebury (near Droitwich), via Ironbridge, Bridgnorth, Bewdley and Stourport. Of the original route, the present-day SVR comprises just the 20km (12½ miles) between Bridgnorth and Bewdley. In addition, there is the 5.5km (3½ miles) from Bewdley to Kidderminster which the Great Western Railway built in 1878 to connect Shrewsbury with the west Midlands.

Guaranteed steam

Most passengers begin their journey on the SVR at Kidderminster – the mainline station on the Birmingham–Worcester line shares the same forecourt as the SVR station – and for several years now, principal mainline stations have sold through

Former BR tank engine No 80079 hauls GWR carriages over the 61m (200ft) Victoria Bridge, spanning the River Severn (main picture). Other locomotives in the Severn Valley steam fleet include BR Class 4MT 4-6-0 No 75069 (awaiting overhaul), leaving Bewdley station (below, left) and LMS Class 5MT 4-6-0 No 45110, crossing Bewdley North viaduct (below, right). On 11 August 1968, No 45110 had the distinction of working the last section of the special run which marked the end of mainline steam services on British Railways.

tickets to Bridgnorth. But whether you start your journey at one of the two termini, or at any of the four stations in between – Bewdley (the administration headquarters of the line), Arley, Highley or Hampton Loade – allow a full day to explore the line and local landmarks.

Steam is guaranteed on all the timetabled trains – the SVR's diesels are generally used at special gala events and on some Saturdays. For most of the journey, the railway is never more than three-quarters of a kilometre (half mile) from the River Severn. It crosses the fast-flowing river in spectacular style just south of Arley, via the single-span Victoria Bridge, built by Sir John Fowler who went on to design the Forth Bridge.

The most heavily photographed point on the line, the Victoria Bridge was the largest cast-iron span in the world when built in 1861. Other key lineside landmarks to watch out for include the now disused junctions to Stourport and Tenbury Wells on either side of Bewdley, Trimpley Reservoir between Bewdley and Arley – popular with yachtsmen and anglers – and for passengers alighting at Bewdley, Wribbenhall Junction – one of the largest N gauge model railway layouts in

▲ Heading a rake of BR Mark 1 coaches in the maroon livery of the late 1950s, Class 4MT 4-6-0 No 75069 (awaiting overhaul) accelerates towards Bewdley tunnel and Foley Park. It was in 1984 that the Severn Valley Railway crowned more than a decade of expansion by acquiring the 2.5km (1½ mile) section of line between Foley Park and Kidderminster, so completing the route.

the country, which is housed inside a restored GWR bogie van.

The intermediate stations

Bewdley, Arley and Highley stations have all featured extensively in films and TV dramas, the latter two being outstanding examples of the classic wayside GWR country stations of the 19th century, rich in oil lamps (with cleverly concealed electric bulbs to boost illumination), hanging baskets and flower gardens, milk churns and suitcases, porters' trolleys and, like all SVR stations, a stationmaster and enthusiastic volunteer staff to keep everything in trim condition.

Arley appeals particularly to family parties. Apart from its period charm, Norman church, picnic site and a riverside pub, there are two walks downriver to Victoria Bridge. Highley, like Arley, a winner of the national Best Restored Station competition, also has a picnic site, flower gardens and riverside pub. Bewdley, with its three platforms and wooden footbridge, two signalboxes and characteristic canopy awnings, is the perfect cameo of a rural GWR junction station.

Hampton Loade was the SVR's first destination station when trains began from Bridgnorth in

1970. It is a popular alighting point for anglers and others wishing to cross the river by ferry.

Hub of the SVR

Bridgnorth is the locomotive hub of the SVR. It has a four-road engine shed (previously a part of Portskewett timber seasoning shed), engineering workshops and paintshop and, since 1990, a purpose-built boiler repair works complete with overhead gantry crane.

Apart from two or three working locomotives stabled at Bewdley (for starting each day's services from the Kidderminster end) and a small number of loco restoration projects conducted there by independent locomotive groups, the SVR's working fleet of engines is housed at Bridgnorth.

Appropriately on a former Great Western line, GWR locomotive types predominate. Three of the pre-British Railways companies are represented, as well as BR-built locomotives. Loco overhauls at Bridgnorth are a perpetual process – as soon as one engine has received its mechanical overhaul, another takes its place on the hydraulic lifting jacks. There is no such thing as a slack period in the loco workshop.

◀ GWR 4-6-0 No 6960 *Raveningham Hall*, a Great Western locomotive formerly at the SVR, pulls into Arley station on its way to Kidderminster. A winner of the national Best Restored Station competition, Arley, with its polished oil lamps and flower-trimmed platforms, typifies the small country station of late Victorian times.

Ripe for Beeching

For 70 years, until the nationalization of the railways in 1948, the Severn Valley Railway was a secondary passenger and freight line in the GWR empire, but it always struggled financially. As a result, the line through to Shrewsbury fell to the notorious Beeching axe in 1963, and the track north of Bridgnorth was dismantled.

Passenger trains continued to run on the Kidderminster–Bewdley–Hartlebury triangle at the southern end of the route for another six years. But by 1970, these too had succumbed, along with the coal trains which had operated to and from the colliery beside the line at Alveley, near Highley.

Today's image of the SVR as a neatly restored and efficiently run enterprise, with a permanent staff of 60 and a paid-up membership of almost 14,000, is very different from the image it began with in 1967. Then, amid weed choked and over-grown lines, the first steam locomotive – GWR Collett 2251 Class 0-6-0 No 3205 – arrived with four coaches from BR's Stourbridge loco shed, to make 'exploratory' runs for the benefit of members over three-quarters of a kilometre (half mile) of track, from Bridgnorth to Oldbury Viaduct.

The initial aim of the Severn Valley Railway Society was to buy the closed 8km (five miles) of line south from Bridgnorth to Alveley, for which BR was asking £25,000. After paying the amount, the SVR's first public passenger services, over the 7.25km (4½ mile) section from Bridgnorth to Hampton Loade, were run in May 1970.

◀ The present and the past come together at Hampton Loade. Visiting BR Class 31 diesel-electric No 31413 waits to leave with a train for Bridgnorth. The first coach, its varnished teak bodywork gleaming in the sun, is the leading vehicle of the ex-LNER Gresley set. In April 1988 the locomotive was named *Severn Valley Railway* at Bewdley station – the event reflecting the increased level of co-oper-ation at the time between BR and the private railway.

▶ The River Severn valley forms a tranquil backdrop to a demonstration freight train hauled bunker first by LMS Jinty 0-6-0T No 47383. Gala weekends at the Severn Valley Railway allow the company to show off its collection of mainly ex-GWR goods wagons – one of the most extensive in Britain.

Next target was the acquisition of the 15.25km (9½ miles) through Bewdley to Foley Park – then the limit of SVR expansion, because the final 2.5km (1½ miles) of track into Kidderminster was still being used by BR for freight trains to the British Sugar Corporation's Foley Park factory.

A fund-raising campaign for the £74,000 quoted by BR achieved startling success and services were extended to Bewdley in May 1974. The last piece of the SVR jigsaw was put into place in 1984, when following the cessation of freight trains to the BSC works, the Severn Valley Railway bought the final 2.5km (1½ mile) section of line into Kidderminster – for £80,000.

Visitors to the SVR's Kidderminster Town terminal can be forgiven for thinking that the station is the original one opened by the GWR in the 1870s. In fact, it was opened only in 1984 on the site of the old GWR goods yard and is a faithful re-creation of the former GWR station at Ross-on-Wye, in authentic red and blue engineering brick, complete with working gas lamps. The big signalbox here, completed in 1988, is another GWR replica design.

Kidderminster remains the focal point for the railway's further development. After over 20 years of operating without one, it now has a 21.25m (70ft) locomotive turntable (ex-BR, Fort William) and an extension to the carriage repair facility in the former GWR warehouse. Projects planned for the near future include a new depot to house its diesel fleet.

▲ A line-up of LMS locomotives at Bridgnorth, the northern terminus of the Severn Valley Railway, recalls the kind of bustling activity that seemed to have gone for ever when BR sent its last steam engines for scrap in 1968.

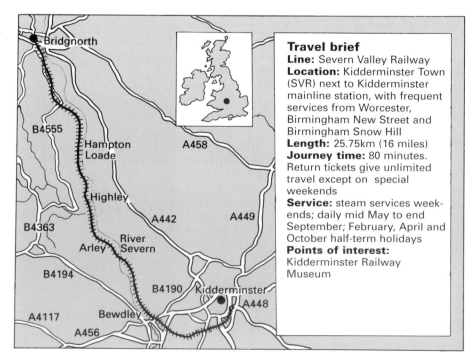

Travel brief
Line: Severn Valley Railway
Location: Kidderminster Town (SVR) next to Kidderminster mainline station, with frequent services from Worcester, Birmingham New Street and Birmingham Snow Hill
Length: 25.75km (16 miles)
Journey time: 80 minutes. Return tickets give unlimited travel except on special weekends
Service: steam services weekends; daily mid May to end September; February, April and October half-term holidays
Points of interest: Kidderminster Railway Museum

The Great Central Railway

**The inspiration of the Victorian visionary
Sir Edward Watkin, the Great Central Railway was intended
as a vital link in his Channel Tunnel scheme. Although the Tunnel
never materialized, the railway was completed,
the last mainline to be built in Britain.**

Nearly a hundred years after the original line was built, the Great Central Railway (GCR) has created a unique opportunity for enthusiasts to experience mainline railway operations as they were during the heyday of steam. From its headquarters at Loughborough, the GCR runs a year-round service on a 12km (7½ mile) stretch of track to Leicester – and it has embarked on an ambitious development programme, laying double track, building loops and sidings, and constructing a prestigious new southern terminus.

Opened for passenger traffic in 1899, the Great Central was the inspiration of Sir Edward Watkin, Chairman of the Manchester, Sheffield & Lincolnshire Railway. Watkin, a visionary, launched the Submarine Continental Railway, with the aim of building a Channel Tunnel which would link the industrial centres of Sheffield and Manchester with markets in Europe.

The scheme failed to come off, but the Great Central – the last mainline to be built in Britain – was constructed to the larger European loading gauge. Designed with gentle gradients and easy curves, it ran from Annesley, a short distance north of Nottingham, to a new terminus at London Marylebone.

'Rapid Travel in Luxury' was the slogan of the GCR – a claim justified by the provision of express services such as the Master Cutler. In the grouping of 1923, the Great Central became part of the London & North Eastern Railway (LNER), but continued to offer travellers a wide range of destinations. Running through the heartland of England, the line was also a natural through route for goods and passenger trains from other railways, and the great variety of locomotives and rolling stock that used the GCR made it a magnet for steam enthusiasts.

Road traffic challenge

The increasing competition from road traffic contributed to the Great Central's decline after nationalization in 1948. Passenger traffic on the rural southern part of the route was light, while services to cities such as Sheffield and Leicester could be provided more economically by other routes. In September 1966, the last through trains to London were withdrawn, leaving a local diesel service between Nottingham and Rugby that existed until May 1969, when the line was closed.

That same year, a group of enthusiasts formed the Main Line Preservation Group (later, the Main Line Steam Trust), with the aim of purchasing a section of the line between Nottingham and Leicester. Shortage of funds frustrated this ambition, but in 1976 the Trust formed the Great Central Railway Company to negotiate the purchase of 8.75km (5½ miles) of single track between Loughborough and Rothley.

Nine years later, the company was granted a lease on a southern extension as far as the former station of Belgrave & Birstall, where a new terminus named Leicester North has been opened with the encouragement and support of Leicester City Council.

From the start, the company's intention has been to recapture the atmosphere of a mainline

▼ A former Great Northern 0-6-2T, London & North Eastern Railway Class N2, No 69523, heads a north-bound train in May 1989. Built more than 70 years ago, No 69523 is the only survivor of the class. Principal duties were on suburban workings out of London's King's Cross – hence the Cuffley (Hertfordshire) destination board.

steam railway, and for visitors this philosophy is apparent from the moment they enter the impressive wood-panelled booking hall of Loughborough Central station – a lovingly restored example of late Victorian railway architecture and the largest station in preservation.

From the booking office, a wooden staircase descends to the two platforms; in the days before BR installed a lift, porters lowered bulky luggage down the wooden slide on the right.

Tradition of excellence

Built on the island pattern, with a handsome glass canopy, the station boasts a small exhibits museum, a gift shop and a handsomely refurbished licensed refreshment room. Reviving a tradition for excellent catering pioneered by the original Great Central, the GCR operates a luxury evening dining train, in addition to buffet cars and Saturday and Sunday lunch services.

The museum, housed in part of the old lift shaft, contains an interesting collection of Victorian photographs documenting stages of the railway's construction. Among the many other items on display are Great Central posters, signs, china and cutlery. Here you can also see a signal-box lever frame and a working model of a 4-4-2, No 361 – an original GCR passenger locomotive.

A footpath leads north to the restored signalbox and to the large locomotive shed. The box controls all train movements at Loughborough Central, but visitors are usually allowed inside to watch the signalman at work.

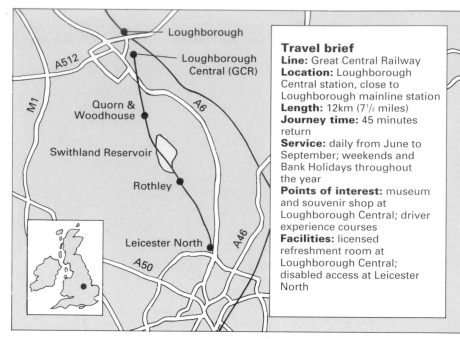

Travel brief
Line: Great Central Railway
Location: Loughborough Central station, close to Loughborough mainline station
Length: 12km (7½ miles)
Journey time: 45 minutes return
Service: daily from June to September; weekends and Bank Holidays throughout the year
Points of interest: museum and souvenir shop at Loughborough Central; driver experience courses
Facilities: licensed refreshment room at Loughborough Central; disabled access at Leicester North

The shed, which was built entirely by volunteers, is 76.25m (250ft) long and 15.25m (50ft) wide, with a 42.75m (140ft) long inspection pit. Here maintenance and restoration work is carried out on the railway's collection of over 20 steam locomotives and diesels. Visitors are allowed access to the shed on guided tours, subject to engineering works in progress.

Only one Great Central passenger locomotive remains in existence – 4-4-0 No 506 *Butler*

Coal train revival

Goods traffic was always an important part of the Great Central Railway's operations. In the 1950s, fast coal trains known as Windcutters set records for productivity and performance on the mainline between Annesley and Woodford Halse, near Banbury.

In 1992, the new Great Central revived this tradition, inaugurating what is planned as a regular service with a run-past at Swithland of 20 Windcutter wagons hauled by a Great Western Railway 2-8-0 tank, No 5224.

◀ One of the Great Central's Bulleid Pacifics, No 35005 *Canadian Pacific*, hauls the 11.45 a.m. service from Loughborough across Swithland Reservoir in July 1990. The reservoir is a haven for bird life.

With such a varied and impressive fleet, a trip on the Great Central is always exciting. Shortly after departure, the train leaves the suburbs of Loughborough behind and steams past fields, spinneys and hedgerows. This is fox-hunting country, home of the Quorn Hunt.

After about 10 minutes, the train pulls into Quorn & Woodhouse station. Marking the original extent of the revived Great Central service, Quorn has the style and atmosphere of a typical GCR country station. A large goods yard adjoins the station, and during the years of World War II this was extended to accommodate traffic for a nearby army camp.

The yard is used for steam rallies and to demonstrate the exchange apparatus for use with the railway's unique LNER travelling post office set. The signalbox is a genuine GCR item which has been transported from Market Rasen in

▼ The GCR is renowned for its demonstration goods workings, exemplified by its re-creation of a Windcutter fast coal train. Here a London & North Eastern Railway Class Y7 0-4-0T, No 68088, painted in the first post-nationalization livery, stands at Rothley station with a short goods train.

▲ The GCR's three-car DMU, made up of Class 120 M59276 and Class 127s M51616 and M51622, passes the Loughborough distant signal at Woodthorpe. It was trains similar to these that worked the final local services between Rugby and Nottingham in the years before the Great Central's demise.

Henderson, which was restored at Loughborough and afterwards displayed at the National Railway Museum at York. Another classic restoration undertaken at Loughborough was that of the unique BR Standard Class 8 Pacific, No 71000 *Duke of Gloucester*. This involved the manufacture of components never before attempted in railway preservation.

Varied steam fleet

The eight steam locomotives in operation include examples from all of the post-grouping Big Four companies. Special mention should be made of the former Southern Railway (SR) West Country class 4-6-2, No 34039 *Boscastle*, bought from Barry scrapyard and recommissioned in 1993 after extensive restoration work had taken place.

Regular runners include GWR No 6990 *Witherslack Hall*, BR 9F No 92212, LNER B1 No 61264 and GNR N2 No 69523. The railway also frequently plays host to locomotives from other lines; one such illustrious visitor was an LNER Pacific, No 4472 *Flying Scotsman*.

Passenger goes wild

One day towards the end of the last century, a goods van containing a live gorilla arrived at Loughborough Central station. The animal was intended for a local gentleman with a taste for exotic pets, but so dismayed were the station staff that they sent it, van and all, to Nottingham. On arrival there, it promptly bit a railway official on the thigh and rushed out into the street, much to the consternation of passengers and passers-by.

'Everybody gave chase with sticks and dogs,' the wounded official later recalled, 'and at length they ran it into a timber yard, where two dogs tackled it. But it knocked them over time after time with its fists. At last two men got a chain and a rope over it, and it was sent back to Loughborough.'

▲ A London Midland & Scottish 5XP Jubilee class 4-6-0, No 5593 *Kolhapur*, passes an unusual signal configuration as it leaves Rothley with a Santa Special. Outshopped in 1934, *Kolhapur* was one of several locomotives previously on loan to the GCR from the Birmingham Railway Museum.

Lincolnshire. There is also a NAAFI style canteen and a picnic area.

Leaving Quorn for Rothley, the train offers fine views of Buddon Wood and Charnwood Forest before it crosses Swithland Reservoir. The reservoir had to be fully drained to allow construction of the two railway viaducts that span the lake via Brazil Island.

At the southern edge of the reservoir, the line crosses the Mountsorrel–Swithland road, close to where the proposed Swithland station was to have been built. The station was demanded by the Earl of Lanesborough, whose land the railway passed through. In the event, it was never completed. The Earl resided at nearby Swithland Hall, which can sometimes be seen through the woods to the west.

Much new construction work is now going on at Swithland, including the installation of loops and sidings, complete with signalling from the original Great Western & Great Central Joint Line. Furthermore, Swithland was the starting point for the railway's double-track laying operations which are now almost complete, leading south to Rothley and north to Loughborough, thus providing the only double track preserved steam railway in the world.

At Rothley, passengers step back into the past. The station, painted in the green and white livery of the GCR, is a faithful representation of the late Victorian era, featuring gas lamps, an original parcels office and old-fashioned advertisements for patent cures.

Located near an Anglo-Saxon burial ground, the station is officially listed as a haunted site. The GCR signalbox, from Blind Lane near Wembley, replaces one which once employed an eccentric signalman who made a habit of bathing nude in the water trough.

A four-track carriage shed has been built for the overhaul and maintenance of the railway's extensive fleet of rolling stock. The standard coaches are BR Mark 1 vehicles, but there are also

a number of vintage carriages, including a Gresley Pidgeon van and LMS sleeping car.

Soon after leaving Rothley, the train crosses Rothley Brook, used in Roman times as a canal. To the west you can see the hilltop Leicestershire landmark of 'Old John'. After passing through a deep cutting, the train reaches the site of Belgrave & Birstall station, which was demolished in 1977. The train terminates 274m (300yds) further south, at a station called Leicester North.

Opened in 1991, the station has a short stub platform and basic facilities. There is, however, easy wheelchair access and ample off-road parking. A restored carriage provides the booking office and refreshments at weekends. The GCR plans to develop Leicester North in a way befitting the terminus of a mainline railway. The proposed complex will feature three platforms, a visitor centre and museum, and a new locomotive shed and turntable. Work is already in progress.

This is not the only initiative being undertaken on the revived Great Central. To the north, another group of enthusiasts has started restoring the track at Ruddington, near Nottingham, with the eventual aim of linking up with the Loughborough–Leicester section, and thereby more than doubling the length of the line.

▼ A tribute to the restoration skills of the modern-day GCR, No 506 *Butler Henderson* has its water tank replenished at Loughborough Central. No 506, on loan from the National Railway Museum, is the only preserved Great Central passenger engine, featured below with its BR number and livery.

The Midland Railway Centre

**Designed as a tribute to a
long-vanished transport system, the Midland
Railway Centre offers many attractions, including a
museum, a country park and three railways – a miniature,
a 2ft (0.6m) narrow gauge and a standard gauge.**

▼ BR 2-6-4T No 80080 leaves Hammersmith for Butterley, passing a fine Midland Railway bracket signal and the unusual, cantilevered signalbox that came from Kilby Bridge, Leicester. The Brighton-built tank was adopted by the television programme *Blue Peter*, which helped to restore the engine to steam in 1987.

Just to the north of the town of Ripley, in Derbyshire, lies the Butterley Iron Works. The works is linked to a railway line which runs west across the Erewash Valley and is now operated by the Midland Railway Trust.

Opened in 1875, the line was a vital artery in an area where collieries, iron foundries and tar works once thrived. The line was closed on 23 December 1968. All the main station buildings were demolished, and the track was removed. The Midland Railway Trust was established the following year.

It established the Midland Railway Centre (MRC) at Butterley in 1973 and ran its first trains (to Ironville) in 1981. Now the line extends for 5.5km (3½ miles) from Hammersmith to Riddings, and there are plans for a further extension, to the mainline at Pye Bridge Junction.

▶ This Kirtley 2-4-0, No 158A, is on display at the MRC's Matthew Kirtley Museum, named after the engine's designer. One of a class of 29 locomotives built for express work, No 158A was outshopped at Derby in 1866 and, with numerous reboilerings, continued in service for an astonishing 81 years.

Two-line choice

Not far from the Richard Levick Workshop at Swanwick Junction, you will find the Butterley Park Miniature Railway. This 3½ and 5in (89 and 127mm) gauge line has a circuit of around a quarter of a kilometre (300yds), and visitors can enjoy a ride behind one of its tiny locomotives. The layout has over and under bridges, and includes signals controlled from a miniature Midland Railway signalbox.

Close to Swanwick Junction is the terminus of the new Golden Valley Light Railway, a 2ft (0.6m) gauge line which crosses the museum site and runs the length of the Country Park to Newlands Inn. A small diesel locomotive hauls passengers in an ex-colliery man-rider along the 1km (1,000yd) route.

A journey on the MRC line starts at Butterley. Although the station buildings have an authentic Midland Railway (MR) air of permanence, nothing was left standing here in the wake of the 1968 closure, and the building you see today was moved stone by stone from Whitwell in north Derbyshire.

At Butterley, there is the immediate atmosphere of a bustling country station, full of interest and activity. You pass through the booking hall, next

to the shop, and out on to the platform. Here the train is waiting. It comprises five former BR Mark 1 coaches in maroon and crimson lake and cream, with an ex-Somerset & Dorset 2-8-0 goods engine, No 53809, at the head.

Before boarding the train, you can visit the 00 gauge model railway layout in a building on the platform and the garden railway display down towards the carriage sheds. Here 16mm scale 0 and 1 gauge trains follow a circuit that is partly outdoors and partly under cover.

Look out also for the first of several distinctive MR signalboxes. The one at Butterley originally stood high up in the Pennines at Ais Gill, the summit of the Settle & Carlisle line.

Echoing exhaust

Now doors slam, whistles blow, and the train eases forward out of the station. The engine can soon be heard working hard on the 1 in 96 climb towards Swanwick Junction, the beat of its exhaust echoing off the sides of a long cutting. As the cutting opens out, you can see the MRC's historic carriage and wagon repair base on the right. On certain days, visitors are allowed inside.

Approaching Swanwick Junction, you can see the old Butterley Iron Works branch leading off to the right. Both the works and the branch are still functioning, and occasional goods trains lumber on to the MRC metals bound for the link with the BR line at Codnor Park Junction.

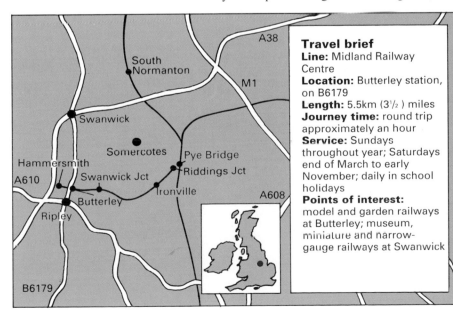

Travel brief
Line: Midland Railway Centre
Location: Butterley station, on B6179
Length: 5.5km (3½) miles
Journey time: round trip approximately an hour
Service: Sundays throughout year; Saturdays end of March to early November; daily in school holidays
Points of interest: model and garden railways at Butterley; museum, miniature and narrow-gauge railways at Swanwick

After steaming under a signal gantry (rescued from Shipley, near Leeds), you pass the massive 41 lever signalbox that once stood at Kettering station. You have now reached Swanwick, where the MRC is developing an impressive museum site. Most visitors prefer to stop off here on the way back.

As the train leaves Swanwick Junction, the 35 acre Butterley Country Park comes into view on the right. This attractive open space includes a pond and a picnic site, as well as two reminders of the industrial past – the remains of Grumblethorpe Colliery and Cromford Canal Tunnel.

The train passes under the rebuilt Golden Valley Bridge and enters the valley itself, with views of cottages by the canal. The Jessop Monument, built to commemorate one of the

▶ Class 55 Deltic No 55-015 *Tulyar*, built by English Electric in 1961, leaves Swanwick for Riddings Junction, passing under the imposing signal gantry rescued from Shipley in Yorkshire. The survival of a good number of Midland Railway (MR) semaphores into the 1970s enables the MRC to control all traffic with authentic MR signals.

founders of the Butterley Iron Works, can be seen in the distance.

You now enter Ironville cutting, site of the MRC's original western terminus, and pass the branch that swings south to Codnor Park Junction. The train halts at Riddings, on a high embankment overlooking Ironville and the Erewash Valley. The locomotive runs round the train and couples up ready for the return to Swanwick.

Here you can get off the train and explore the rapidly expanding museum site. Open to view is the enormous Matthew Kirtley Museum, named after the celebrated Midland Railway locomotive and carriage designer. This houses a magnificent display of locomotives, rolling stock and relics.

Exhibits in the museum include an 1866 built

▼ Stanier's 1936 Pacific, LMS 4-6-2 No 46203 *Princess Margaret Rose*, withdrawn from Carlisle in 1962, was later rescued from Butlin's holiday camp at Pwllheli and repainted as a static exhibit in London Midland & Scottish livery. Now restored to mainline standard, it is finished in BR maroon.

Butterley Iron Works
Just to the north of Ripley lie the extensive premises of Butterley Iron Works, linked by a steeply graded track to the MRC line and the mainline. It still makes cast-iron structures for industry, as it has done for over 150 years, and you will find its name on many old railway and canal bridges all over Britain. Rail transportation of huge girders is an occasional sight on the MRC line.

Probably its most famous creation is the overall roof of the Midland Railway's London headquarters and terminus, St Pancras. This was designed by the company's chief civil engineer, W.H. Barlow, and built between 1867 and 1875.

2-4-0 on loan from the National Railway Museum, a 50 tonne (ton) steam crane, historic passenger coaches including a Midland Railway four-wheeled vehicle from 1865, six wheelers from 1884 and 1896 and a splendid bogie Royal Saloon of 1912. There is also an impressive range of goods vehicles on display in the museum.

The centre houses a vast collection of locomotives including the Princess Class 4-6-2 No 46203 *Princess Margaret Rose*, another 4-6-2 No 46233 *Duchess of Sutherland*, two BR standard 2-6-4 tank locomotives Nos 80080 and 80098, BR standard Class 5MT No 73129, no less than three London Midland and Scottish Railway 3F Fowler tank locomotives and many more.

The centre is also home to the Midland Diesel Group collection of over 25 mainline locomotives including Class 55 Deltic No 55-015 *Tulyar*, Class 40 No 40-012 *Aureol*, Class 44 No D4 *Great Gable* and examples of Class 20, 25, 31, 33, 37, 45, 46 and 47. The centre is even home to a mainline electric locomotive No 27000 *Electra*.

Repair and restoration centre

In a separate building at the rear of the museum is the Richard Levick Workshop. This is where mechanical and restoration work is carried out.

▼ LMS 4F 0-6-0 No 4027 and former Somerset & Dorset Joint Railway 7F 2-8-0 No 53809 double head a train across Butterley Reservoir. The 4F is on loan from the National Railway Museum in York, and the 7F was rescued from Barry scrapyard in South Wales and restored in 1980.

▼ The Midland Railway Centre possesses four examples of Fowler's 3F 0-6-0T shunting locomotive – known as Jinties. No 47357, freshly turned out in maroon livery, hauls the first train of the day towards Ironville on 17 April 1987. The small recess in the side of the tank is for the sandbox, but when asked, locomotive men used to say it was the hole for the key that wound up the engine.

Entry to this and to the nearby Historic Carriage Workshop is restricted, but items can be seen from the paths which run alongside.

At the carriage workshop, several vehicles are being worked on, as time and funds permit, including a six-wheeled ballast brake and a Lancashire & Yorkshire Railway dynamometer car.

Other features to be enjoyed are miniature and narrow-gauge railways (as described on page 81) and a road vehicle and static power display. There is also, of course, the Country Park. Access to the park is through an entrance next to an MR gatehouse brought from St Mary's goods yard in Derby, which has been rebuilt to the original design.

Returning from Swanwick Junction to Butterley – you can walk along a footpath beside the line, if you wish – the train runs through Butterley station non-stop and out over the causeway across Butterley Reservoir, originally built to provide a water supply for the Cromford Canal.

As you approach the MRC's western terminus at Hammersmith, you will see another fine Midland Railway red and cream signalbox, this time from Kilby Bridge, near Leicester.

At Hammersmith, the former junction for Ripley, the train comes to a halt, and you can alight on to the stone platform to watch as the locomotive runs round the train again before hauling it on the short run back to Butterley.

The East Lancashire Railway

Running for more than 13km (eight miles) through the Irwell Valley, the ELR is the ideal way to explore the rugged splendour of the Lancashire hill country. And for those in search of gentler pleasures, it offers riverside picnics and visits to historic market towns.

The original East Lancashire Railway (ELR) opened in 1846 and operated two lines which formed a rough 'T' shape in the county, one feeding freight and passenger traffic southwards to Manchester, the other carrying it westwards to Liverpool and Preston. As the region became more industrialized and the products of its mines and factories were exported throughout the world, so the fortunes of the ELR rose.

Yet it existed as a separate entity for only 11 years. In 1857, it was taken over by the Lancashire & Yorkshire Railway (LYR). The LYR was itself merged with the London & North Western Railway in 1922 before becoming part of the London Midland & Scottish the following year.

In 1948, there was a further change of ownership, with the appearance of British Railways on the scene. Nationalization, however, failed to halt the steady decline in the ELR's business. The passenger service on the Bury–Rawtenstall line was withdrawn in 1972, and the last freight train travelled over it in December 1980.

For the next seven years the ELR was just a memory. Then, in 1987, thanks to a combination

▼ On 27 April 1991, ex-Manchester Ship Canal 0-6-0T No 32 *Gothenburg* and former Meaford power station RSH 0-6-0T No 1 haul a special train over Summerseat Bridge. This was part of the ceremony to mark the reopening of the line's extension from Ramsbottom to Rawtenstall.

85

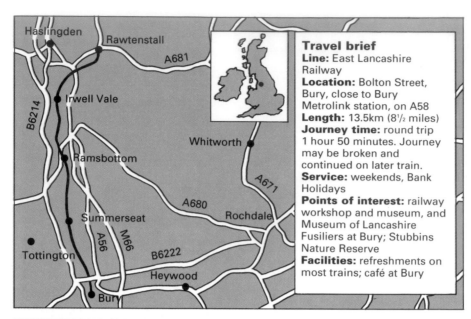

Travel brief
Line: East Lancashire Railway
Location: Bolton Street, Bury, close to Bury Metrolink station, on A58
Length: 13.5km (8½ miles)
Journey time: round trip 1 hour 50 minutes. Journey may be broken and continued on later train.
Service: weekends, Bank Holidays
Points of interest: railway workshop and museum, and Museum of Lancashire Fusiliers at Bury; Stubbins Nature Reserve
Facilities: refreshments on most trains; café at Bury

of voluntary and local authority effort, the line began to carry passengers again. Now the service has been fully restored, running from Bolton Street station, Bury, for 13.5km (8½ miles) to a terminus at Rawtenstall.

Bury is the oldest British Railways station to survive on a preserved line. It is a 1950s structure that could have been designed to serve London Underground or a bus station. There is easy access for the disabled via a side gate from the adjoining car park. The ELR operates a Wheelchair Access coach on one train each weekend.

Tracks still stretch out to the south, seemingly ready to receive the next heavily laden train from Manchester. However, appearances are deceptive, for that section is no longer connected with the railway. Instead, it is part of the Greater Manchester Metrolink.

This important commuter route which, until recently, terminated at Bolton Street station, now

► On a cold February day in 1991, BR Standard 4MT 2-6-0 No 76079 bursts out of Nuttall Tunnel on its way to Ramsbottom. This locomotive was built in 1957 and had only 10 years of service on BR before it was withdrawn. It is now one of the ELR's most stalwart performers.

▼ On 26 January 1992, GWR Manor 4-6-0 No 7828 *Odney Manor*, paired with SR Light Pacific No 34072 *257 Squadron*, haul the 11.00 a.m. Bury–Rawtenstall up the 1 in 132 gradient at Burrs. Both these engines are visitors to the line.

runs to a bus/Metrolink interchange a little way to the south east.

The atmosphere at Bolton Street is that of a busy secondary line station in the 1950s. The enthusiasts who operate the ELR have always been more interested in creating the mood and feeling of a major railway system rather than in slavishly rebuilding a time capsule of the ELR or any of its successors.

The trains are all made up of ex-British Railways coaches, and these are as likely to be hauled by a relatively modern mainline diesel as by a locomotive from one of the companies that owned the line.

Loco roundup

Many of the ELR's own steam stable are being restored. The locomotives currently operating on the line mainly represent those that operated in the area during the days of steam. On a typical working day you may see Black 5, a Horwich Crab or an Ivatt Mogul. Engines from other railways often visit. You may see a West Country Pacific or an LNER locomotive. These powerful engines might share duties with one of the many heavy-duty diesel locomotives which are privately owned but based at Bury.

Almost immediately after leaving Bolton Street station, Bolton Street Tunnel looms up. This runs for about 73m (80yd). As the train emerges from the tunnel, there is a clear view of the Diesel Depot to the left and then two sidings of some of the ELR's impressive diesel locomotive stud.

Within a few minutes the train reaches open country and passes through an area associated with Sir Robert Peel, former British Prime Minister and founder of the modern police force. It was the wealth from Lancashire mills which created the Peel family fortune and enabled Sir Robert to go into politics. Peel Mill can be seen on the left, just after the old California Steel Works.

The Mill marks the site of Tottington Junction, where a 4.75km (three mile) branch line once curved away to the left to Holcombe Brook. Steam railmotors operated the service from 1905 to 1913, when the line was electrified, using the 3600V overhead system.

The experiment was a failure and in 1916 a different supply system was introduced. This worked successfully until 1951, when the equipment wore out. The service was converted to steam operation, only to close to passengers one year later. The last goods train ran in 1963 and much of the trackbed is now covered by houses.

The Irwell follows a winding route from here on and the train is soon clattering over the first of the numerous railway bridges that lie between Bury and Rawtenstall. Touch Hill Cutting leads to Summerseat. This is set in a wooded section of the Irwell Valley and is a popular alighting point for ELR passengers. If you do decide to stop off here, you can always finish your journey on a later train.

On leaving Summerseat station, the train travels over the 183m (200yd) Brooksbottom Viaduct, then plunges almost immediately into Brooksbottom Tunnel. This is 387m (423yds) long

▲ As well as its compliment of ex-BR steam engines, the ELR is also home to a growing collection of diesels. In 1989, two former Western diesel-hydraulics, Class 52 Western No D1041 *Western Prince* and Class 42 Warship *Onslaught*, haul a train through the cutting at Burrs.

and is bored through solid rock. Emerging into daylight, the train passes through a short cutting before entering Nuttall Tunnel.

After crossing the Irwell again, the train enters Ramsbottom station. Here north- and southbound services pass each other. The signalman controls the exchange of tokens, which allow the trains to continue to their next sections. Although the station building dates from only 1989, it has been constructed in the style of the old ELR and it is not too difficult to imagine yourself back in the past. Many 19th century buildings still survive around the station, several of them housing cafés and craft centres.

Ramsbottom itself is an old mill town with many attractions for the visitor, including a Heritage Centre which gives a vivid insight into the town's history. There is also a trail you can follow to Holcombe Hill and its 39m (128ft) monument to Robert Peel.

Beyond Ramsbottom the remains of Stubbins Junction are passed without stopping. The mainline north to Accrington ran on from this point and, when the reopening of the ELR was being considered, one of the proposals was to continue the line along this route.

The plan was abandoned, however, when the impressive Alderbottom Viaduct, three-quarters of a kilometre (half a mile) beyond the junction, was found to be in poor condition. Because of this, the

ELR opted to follow the old route to Rawtenstall. The viaduct can be seen to the left of the line, through the thick tree cover which characterizes this part of the route.

Irwell Vale, only recently built, consists simply of a stone shelter, a car park and some picnic tables, and is intended as a springboard for explorers of the surrounding countryside. Both the Stubbins Nature Reserve and the Helmshore Textile Museum and Mill are within easy walking distance of here.

Triumph at Rawtenstall
The chief architectural triumph of the present-day ELR is its new terminus at Rawtenstall, the station building itself sitting astride the site of the line that once ran on to Bacup and Rochdale. The ELR was able to use the original through platform, but virtually everything else has been constructed from scratch.

Here the locomotive runs round the train and, if it is a steam engine, it tops up at a replica of a Lancashire & Yorkshire water tower some distance beyond the carriages before starting its journey back to Bury.

It is worth spending some time in Rawtenstall. The town, which dates back to the 14th century, has many interesting buildings, as well as numerous shops, pubs and cafés. If you prefer something more strenuous, you can explore the rolling hill

▶ On 7 November 1990, the harsh exhaust beat of BR Standard 4MT 2-6-0 No 76079 sounds out across the Lancashire countryside as it crosses Brooksbottom Viaduct with a train from Bury. With its train of matching BR Mark I maroon coaches, the 1960s scene on BR is superbly recreated.

▶The ELR is careful to maintain the atmosphere of a British Railways station during the 1950s and '60s. Over one million pounds was spent on rebuilding the line. Ramsbottom station was completely re-equipped, with refurbished footbridge, level crossing, water tower, signalling and buildings.

country for which this part of Lancashire is justly famous. Either way, your trip on the East Lancashire Railway will not have been wasted.

The future is very exciting for the East Lancashire Railway. The 6.5km (four mile) extension from Bury Bolton Street eastward to Heywood will be operational by mid 2001. At Bury Bolton Street station, the tracks have been relaid to give two-directional working for three of the four platforms, semaphore signalling is being installed and, with a 65 lever frame, Bury South box is destined to become the largest Heritage Railways signalbox.

Liverpool Road Station Museum

In 1830, the first-ever intercity train steamed into Manchester's Liverpool Road Station. Now part of the Museum of Science and Industry, this historic site still evokes the days when Manchester was the railway capital of the world.

Viewers of Granada Television's famous soap opera, *Coronation Street*, might wonder why they never see a train pass over the brick railway viaduct at the end of the street. Of course, this is only a set and not a real railway viaduct at all. But even so, if you stand outside the Rovers Return, the Coronation Street local, you will more than likely hear a steam locomotive shunting just the other side of those closely packed terraces.

Unknown to most of the viewing millions, Granada's Manchester studios (including the viaduct and the *Coronation Street* set) are back to back with the world's oldest surviving passenger railway station. On most weekends of the year,

▼ **To show visitors how a steam locomotive works, the Museum has sectioned *Pender*, its 2-4-0 tank, by cutting away the right-hand side. An electric motor and chain drive have been concealed under the cab floor so that the driving wheels, piston and motion can be seen in action.**

steam trains are busy at work, shuttling passengers to and fro in a genuine railway environment which pre-dates the neighbouring set by more than a century and a half.

Shrine to the past

Liverpool Road Station, home of Manchester's Museum of Science and Industry, is a shrine to the north-west's industrial past in which railways played such a key part. Built in 1830 as the terminus of the Liverpool & Manchester Railway (L&MR) – the first-ever intercity line – Liverpool Road was the point from which Stephenson's *Planet* used to trundle its train of bone-shaking carriages down the track to Liverpool, at a fearsome 32km/h (20mph).

The station handled passenger trains for 15 years before a much larger station was built, now called Victoria station, but it continued as a goods terminus until the 1970s. Concerned by the absence of

▲ **Class EM2 Co-Co No 1505 *Ariadne* was acquired by the Museum from Dutch State Railways in 1986 and is displayed in its Dutch livery. It was not only built in Manchester at BR's Gorton works, but spent most of its working life from 1954 on the 1500V DC Manchester–Sheffield line via Woodhead.**

on this meagre inheritance, it was rather late in the day – more than a decade had passed since the end of steam on BR – to begin building a collection of historic railway exhibits, especially items from the north-west. As a result, the Museum had to cast its net rather wide.

Its first acquisition, in 1979, was *Pender*, a 2-4-0 tank engine built in Manchester in 1873 by Beyer Peacock and declared redundant by the Isle of Man Railways following the closure of large sections of the Manx railway system.

Exotic arrivals

It was for pioneering the powerful articulated Garratt type engine between 1907 and 1914 that Beyer Peacock was best known, and for this the Museum had to look much further afield. A 1983 request to South African Railways for a Garratt suitable for preservation resulted in the acquisition of a GL Class 4-8-2+2-8-4.

From Pakistan Railways in 1982 the Museum acquired a 5ft 6in (1.75m) gauge SPS Class 4-4-0 steam loco, No 3157, built in 1911 by the Vulcan Foundry works at Newton-le-Willows, Lancashire.

firm plans for the derelict site, the Liverpool Road Station Society began lobbying for its future.

In 1979, with the 150th anniversary of the L&MR imminent, Greater Manchester Council confirmed that the station and its associated goods shed and warehouses – an area totalling nine acres – were to be transformed into the permanent home of the Museum of Science and Industry, replacing a similar but much smaller museum in Grosvenor Street.

The Victorian goods shed was the venue for an impressive collection of locomotives – mostly loaned from other sources – which was assembled for the 150th anniversary exposition in 1980, though the museum itself did not open to the public until 1983.

Twin themes

Liverpool Road's railway exhibition has been designed to tell two stories – the development and operation of the L&MR, and the evolution of locomotive, carriage and wagon building in the north-west. It is the second of these themes that has spawned the Museum's still growing collection of engines and rolling stock, also located in the goods shed, now renamed the Power Hall.

The Grosvenor Street museum had been too cramped to allow the display of complete steam locomotives, and for that reason its railway collection comprised little more than the archives of the famous locomotive builders Beyer Peacock of Gorton, Manchester and some items of track and signalling equipment.

Although Liverpool Road was anxious to expand

Travel brief
Centre: Liverpool Road Station Museum (inside the Museum of Science and Industry)
Location: Liverpool Road, Castlefield, Manchester; nearest station is mainline/metro Deansgate (connections from Manchester Piccadilly)
Opening times: 10 a.m. to 5 p.m. seven days a week
Facilities: car park

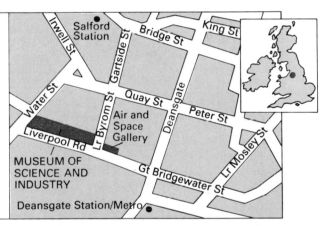

▶ One of the Museum's most impressive exhibits is the 3ft 6in (1m) gauge Beyer Peacock GL Class 4-8-2+2-8-4, No 2352, built in 1929. The 27.5m (90ft) long monster was donated by South African Railways and arrived in Britain in January 1984.

Trial by steam

Look out, too, for *Novelty*, a replica of one of the three participants that took part in the 1829 locomotive trials at Rainhill in Lancashire (the other two were *Rocket* and *Sans Pareil*). It was these trials that persuaded the directors of the L&MR to opt for a steam-hauled railway.

Built in 1929 for the centenary of the trials, the reproduction *Novelty* incorporates one set of wheels and a cylinder from the original. It is too fragile for running on rails.

The fireless 0-6-0 *Lord Ashfield* carries an Andrew Barclay 1930 worksplate. The *Lord Ashfield* has no boiler of its own, but a cylinder for storing steam from an external source. The type was regularly used in industry where the fire risk from a conventional steam locomotive was too great – at paper mills and chemical works, for example. With several working steam engines to draw upon, providing steam for *Lord Ashfield* presents few problems. The Liverpool Road site is virtually alone in the UK in being able to run a fireless engine on a regular basis.

While steam, not surprisingly, is the mainstay of the collection, it is by no means the whole story. Pride of place goes to the Class EM2 Co-Co electric locomotive No 1505 *Ariadne* (ex-BR No 27001), which was originally used on the Manchester–Sheffield Woodhead line. There were two types of locomotive built for the line – six EM2 Co-Cos and 58 EM1 Bo-Bos, all built at Gorton works, Manchester. Although the EM1s have long since been scrapped, the Museum managed to save the cab section of No 26048 *Hector* from the cutter's torch, and this is displayed alongside *Ariadne*.

The heart of the Liverpool Road exhibition is, of course, the station itself. The station building was used as general offices from the cessation of passenger trains in 1845, but has been restored as far as possible to its original state. The single-door entrance gives access to two separate booking halls – first and second class.

▲ The 0-6-0 fireless locomotive *Lord Ashfield* hauls one of the Museum's 1830 replica coaches past the Grade I listed goods warehouse, also dating from 1830. The station building and warehouse are the oldest surviving railway buildings of their kind.

The first-class hall features figures in period dress representing railway employees and passengers of the 1830s. The second-class hall houses an exhibition about the L&MR.

The original 1830 warehouse has now been fully restored and houses various exhibitions including 'Futures' which looks at people's ideas of what the future held in 1830, 1875, 1948 and 1998. Included is a replica of the world's first programmable computer developed in Manchester in 1948.

A Planet in view

Having an 1830 working replica locomotive to go with its carriages has always been the Museum's greatest ambition – and, with financial backing from a number of sources including the British Engine Insurance Group and the English Tourist Board, that ambition is being fulfilled.

Built by a team of experts from the Friends of the Museum, the replica is of one of Stephenson's Planet class locomotives – a type that first appeared at Liverpool Road over 160 years ago.

◄ An early requisition of the Museum was this SPS Class 4-4-0, No 3157, imported from Pakistan Railways. It was built in 1911 by the Lancashire-based Vulcan Foundry works.

The Embsay & Bolton Abbey Steam Railway

With Bolton Abbey, Skipton Castle and the enchanting Yorkshire Dales as nearby attractions, the Embsay Steam Railway is popular with sightseers. But the railway also provides enthusiasts with a good share of steam-age nostalgia.

Just over three kilometres (two miles) from Skipton, the main town in the Craven region of Yorkshire, lies the village of Embsay. Its stone-built main street and attractive setting make it a pleasant if unremarkable place to visit. A short side road leads down to the railway station, where the headquarters and operating centre of the Embsay Steam Railway (ESR) can be found.

Originally, Embsay was a small wayside station on the Midland Railway's line from Skipton to Ilkley. Although a variety of schemes for building a railway on this route had been put forward since 1845, construction did not begin until 1885. Opening took place in two stages in 1888. Trains ran from Ilkley to Bolton Abbey at first, with the full service following a few months later.

The routine existence of the line, with its half a dozen local trains a day, was enlivened by various through workings, particularly on summer Saturdays. There was a considerable amount of excursion traffic to Bolton Abbey, a well-known local beauty spot. And when the Aire Valley mainline was closed for engineering work, trains as prestigious as the Thames–Clyde Express were diverted over the Wharfedale route through Embsay before heading back towards the Settle–Carlisle line.

From early 1959, diesel replaced steam on local

▼ Overlooked by the sweeping expanse of Embsay Moor, the Hunslet 0-6-0 *Beatrice* steams along the track east of Embsay, a rake of three BR Mark 1 coaches in tow. *Beatrice* is currently under restoration.

▲ **Barclay 0-4-0ST No 22 waits beside platform 1 at Embsay, seen here in a previous incarnation. As engines are used by different companies, their name and livery are changed. This engine now sports a black livery with the name of Fishburn Coke Works on its side.**

Haw Bank line

The giant Haw Bank Quarry, which dominates the landscape south of Embsay station, once contained much of railway interest. Between the 1790s and the 1940s, a line connected the quarry with the Leeds–Liverpool Canal near Skipton Castle.

Starting as a wooden wagonway, it was later relaid with narrow-gauge metal rails, equipped with a steam locomotive to replace horse and cable haulage, and finally rebuilt to standard-gauge width to connect with the Midland Railway's siding into the quarry.

passenger services. However, the multiple units, operating a service little changed from steam days, were unable to save the line. After a public inquiry in 1964, closure took place in March 1965. Demolition followed a year later.

It was largely due to chance that part of the route was reopened. The original intention of the preservationists had been to use Embsay as a base for operating the branch north from Embsay Junction to Grassington, which closed to regular passenger traffic as early as 1930.

Trains transporting stone had continued to run, however, and it was a decision to expand Swinden Quarry, just short of Grassington, that saved the branch but thwarted the preservationists. Regular diesel freight trains are still operated to the quarry today.

Undeterred, the Embsay and Grassington Railway Preservation Society moved into Embsay station anyway. It changed its name to the Yorkshire Dales Railway and altered its plans to encompass the revival of the line east to Bolton Abbey. The first official trains of the preservation era ran in 1979 over a short stretch of track from Embsay to Bow Bridge.

Eight years later, trains were running to the newly constructed Holywell Halt, and, by 1991, the new loop at Stoneacre was in use. But Stoneacre was still only halfway to Bolton Abbey, the goal that the railway's preservationists were working towards.

By the end of 1993, the railway was negotiating

to buy the track to Bolton Abbey. The old station was beyond repair, so it was dismantled and an extended replica was all but finished in 1994. It took until 1998 for the track and loop to be laid and the station was opened on 1 May. Sightseers can now visit Bolton Abbey by steam train after a gap of 33 years.

Echoes of the past

Embsay station is little changed from the days when regular services operated on the line. A wooden cab drivers' shelter has been transported from Ilkley and re-erected at the station to serve as a waiting room. Like the rest of the station woodwork, it is smartly painted in green and cream.

The main buildings are on platform 1, where the single-storey stone structure now houses a café and a bookshop specialising in transport. On platform 2, the old shelter contains a display of photographs and railway relics.

Services usually depart from platform 1, though for special events when two trains are operated, you sometimes have to cross the footbridge to platform 2. Most trains consist of four maroon ex-British Rail coaches, including a buffet car.

Departure from Embsay

As the train pulls eastwards out of the station, on the left you can see the locomotive shed where engines under restoration or in store are kept. Almost immediately, the train starts the 1 in 110 climb to Skibeden. To the north rises Embsay

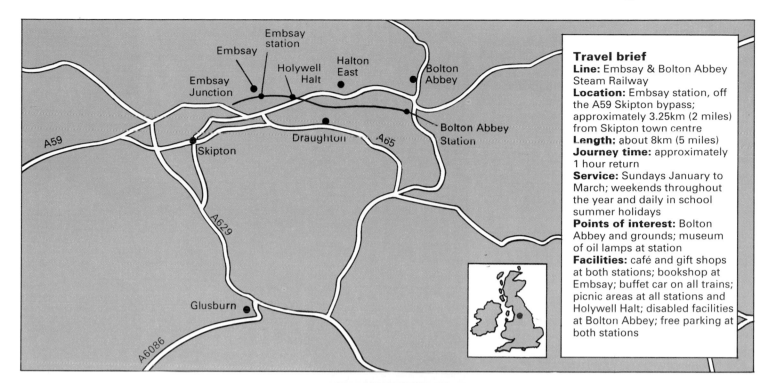

Travel brief
Line: Embsay & Bolton Abbey Steam Railway
Location: Embsay station, off the A59 Skipton bypass; approximately 3.25km (2 miles) from Skipton town centre
Length: about 8km (5 miles)
Journey time: approximately 1 hour return
Service: Sundays January to March; weekends throughout the year and daily in school summer holidays
Points of interest: Bolton Abbey and grounds; museum of oil lamps at station
Facilities: café and gift shops at both stations; bookshop at Embsay; buffet car on all trains; picnic areas at all stations and Holywell Halt; disabled facilities at Bolton Abbey; free parking at both stations

Moor, with limestone outcrops breaking through the grass in places. Prominent in the centre is Embsay Crag.

After reaching the summit, the track drops to 1 in 100 all the way to Bolton Abbey. The line continues to Holywell Halt, where there is a single platform with a wooden shelter that effectively recreates the atmosphere of a rural halt in the days of steam. The train passes into a shallow cutting under the main road and, soon afterwards, enters the loop at Stoneacre. Here, a new brick signal-box, modelled on the Saxby and Farmer type 6 box at Daisyfield station, Blackburn, is used for passing trains at peak times.

Along the line

Leaving Stoneacre, you can see the village of Draughton nestling on the hillside on the right. The train goes under the road leading to the village and then enters a long wooded cutting. As it nears the end of its journey, the remains of quarry workings can be seen.

The train slows down to enter Bolton Abbey station. On the left is a typical Midland Railway wooden signalbox. Near the run-round loop is a water column, and it is here that the locomotive fills up its tanks once it has run round its train. The train comes to a halt with the station in Midland Railway colours, on the left.

With its long platform and extensive run-round loop, the station has won several awards and was highly commended by the Heritage Railway Association. It boasts a very attractive tea room and a shop and there is also a large car park.

▶ One of the ESR's oldest locomotives, Hunslet 0-6-0ST *Airedale*, built in 1923, is seen here awaiting restoration at Embsay. Following the success of Thomas the Tank Engine, many preserved railways have taken to painting faces on the smokeboxes of their engines.

Rural interests

Near Bolton Abbey station there is a newly developed wetland area and next to it are orchid beds that contain some rare species. From here, you can take a pleasant walk along a public footpath to the ruins of the 12th century priory at Bolton Abbey, 2.5 km (1½ miles) away.

Reaching Bolton Abbey is the pinnacle of the railway preservationists' success and a trip to the historic site is certainly recommended. There are walks by the River Wharfe and in Strid Wood, ideal places to stop for picnics. Burden Tower and the retored Cavendish Pavilion, where refreshments are served in the shade of the wood, are worth a visit before returning to Embsay by train.

Special attractions

Thomas the Tank Engine events, when the locomotives sport smiling faces on their smokeboxes, draw big crowds. No 140, a Hudswell Clarke 0-6-0T side tank, is painted as Thomas the Tank Engine and provokes much excitement among the youngest visitors. No 140's popularity means that it is sometimes on loan to other railways.

On selected evenings during the summer, you can take a vintage train and relax in the luxury of

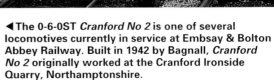

◀ The 0-6-0ST *Cranford No 2* is one of several locomotives currently in service at Embsay & Bolton Abbey Railway. Built in 1942 by Bagnall, *Cranford No 2* originally worked at the Cranford Ironside Quarry, Northamptonshire.

the historic Great Eastern Railway saloons while being served light refreshments. For these trains, booking is essential. There is also an occasional service when the Gresley restaurant car, serving morning coffee and afternoon tea, is attached to the train.

The regular steam service uses only one train to do five return trips, but two trains on special event days. On these days, the signals at Embsay and Stoneacre enable the line to be worked in three sections and this has helped the line to double its capacity. An oddity from the past still survives: a train coming back from Bolton Abbey passes through Embsay without stopping and goes as far as the Bow Bridge loop. Here, the engine runs round its train and then makes its return to Embsay station.

Another highlight on the Embsay Railway is a regular scheduled service using the Class 107 Diesel Multiple Unit. This is a Derby heavyweight two-car unit built in 1961 and withdrawn from Edinburgh Haymarket in 1992. Its restoration was undertaken at Crewe. The diesel service, which was introduced in April 1999, has proved remarkably popular with its users. While the use of diesel is not new to the railway, the emphasis still remains on steam.

◄ Operations at Embsay's crowded goods yard are still controlled by the original Midland Railway signalbox on the right. The unusual triple-armed ground signal in the foreground has now been removed.

▼ Hunslet 0-6-0ST No 69, currently in store, runs round at the western end of its journey, just before Embsay Junction. The preservationists originally intended to run services from here westwards to Grassington, but had to revise their plans when BR announced that it would continue to carry freight traffic over that line.

Enthusiastic volunteers

Without its volunteers, the railway could not run. The Society has about 700 members and 120 of them are active, driving the trains, maintaining the engines and helping in the shops and cafés. About 30 to 40 of these enthusiastic members help out every weekend.

The line has a reputation as Yorkshire's Friendly Line. This is because volunteers take time to welcome day-trippers and answer their questions – if they can!

The fact that the trains are running more often than they ever did, providing a reliable service over weekends and during school holidays, is a marvellous tribute to the dedication of the railway's enthusiasts.

Looking into the future

Even though they have achieved their main goal, the railway preservationists are still planning for the future. At present, the locomotive collection at Embsay is not under suitable cover and the first priority is to restore the locomotive shed. At the same time, the maintenance facilities need to be improved to ensure the safe and efficient operation of the trains.

There is also a more ambitious plan for the railway to run into Skipton and talks have begun with Railtrack and other interested parties. With their determination and the promise of European funds, the Embsay Railway preservationists hope to achieve their aims in the near future.

Isle of Man Railways

Although comprising less than 596 square kilometres (230 square miles), the Isle of Man enjoys a unique railway heritage. As well as three operational lines from Victorian days – two steam and one electric – it also has the only mountain railway in the British Isles worked by electricity.

The Isle of Man offers a variety of railway experiences unrivalled by any comparable area in Britain. Slightly smaller than Cleveland, it has two steam railways, a horse-drawn tramway, a 3ft (914mm) gauge electric railway akin to an American inter-urban, and the 3ft 6in (1m) gauge Snaefell Electric Railway.

Besides being the destination of the car ferry from Heysham and regular summer sailings from Liverpool, Dublin and Belfast, Douglas, the island's capital, is the ideal base from which to explore the railways.

The earliest – and longest – of the five routes is the 3ft (914mm) gauge Isle of Man Railway (IOMR), the first section of which was opened in 1874. Featuring some of the oldest narrow-gauge steam engines in Britain, it runs from Douglas, on the east coast, to Port Erin, on the south-western tip, serving the old capital Castletown and Port St Mary *en route*.

This 25km (15½ mile) line, owned since 1977 by the Isle of Man government, is all that remains of a 74km (46 mile) system that once extended to Peel, Foxdale and Ramsey.

High-season traffic

Until the 1970s, Douglas station boasted two long island platforms with canopies for most of their length, reached through a magnificent red-brick building that served as the IOMR's headquarters. In the high season, before the final closure of the Peel and Ramsey lines in 1968 – the Foxdale branch carried its last traffic in 1943 – four or five engines would be fussing around prior to departure, heading trains that could be anything up to 16 coaches long.

There is now only one island platform, and the canopy has been removed. But the engine shed and workshops, built in the 1880s, can be seen on the right as your train heads out of the station. The train climbs through Nunnery Woods until it reaches the cliffs at Keristal about 61m (200ft) above Port Soderick, affording fine views over the Irish Sea.

The huge station building at Port Soderick seems out of all proportion to the tiny village, but in its heyday Port Soderick had so many visitors that special trains were run there from Douglas.

◀**Its brasswork gleaming in the sun, No 4 *Loch* ascends the IOMR's summit through Oakhill Cutting. One of the oldest working steam engines anywhere in the world, *Loch* was built in 1874 for the opening of the Douglas–Port Erin line.**

Travel brief
Line: Isle of Man Railway
Route: Douglas to Port Erin
Length: 25km (15½ miles)
Journey time: about 1 hour
Service: Easter and summer season
Points of interest: Port Erin Railway Museum
Line: Manx Electric Railway
Route: Derby Castle to Ramsey
Length: 27.25km (17 miles)
Journey time: 75 minutes
Service: end of May to mid-September
Points of interest: Laxey Wheel; Groudle Glen line; Snaefell Mountain Railway; Manx Electric Railway Museum

From Port Soderick a slightly inland course is taken, the engine barking its way up the bank to Santon, the highest point on the line. A meandering route through woods and farmland takes you to Ballasalla, close to the island's airport of Ronaldsway.

Arrival at Port Erin

The next stop is Man's former capital, Castletown. It is worth breaking your journey here to explore the narrow streets that huddle around the glowering medieval fortress of Castle Rushen. From here, the railway turns inland again to Colby, then takes a south-western course to Port St Mary and the terminus at Port Erin.

Beside the station is the Railway Museum, which contains many relics and photographs as well as the youngest locomotive built for the IOMR: No 16 *Mannin* of 1926. All but one of the IOMR's locomotives were 2-4-0 tanks with varying sizes of boiler, and the four currently in service date from 1873 to 1910.

Horse-powered travel

The pace of the IOMR's trains is positively brisk compared with the horse-drawn trams that since 1892 have been plying the three kilometres or so (two miles) between Douglas's Victoria Pier and Derby Castle. In 1902, the tramway was taken over by Douglas Corporation. Now preserved as a tourist attraction, it is the only horse tramway still operating in the British Isles.

About 50 horses pull three types of car, chosen according to the weather: fully open 'toast-rack' with crossbench seats, toast-rack with roof and enclosed. A restored double-deck car is kept as a museum piece for special trips during the high season. The horses are not overtaxed as the line is quite level and all cars are fitted with roller bearings.

▲ Opened in 1892, the Douglas horse tramway provides a 3.25km (two mile) link between Victoria Pier and Derby Castle. The only serious disruption on this normally sedate line occurred when a pet parrot in one of the seafront hotels learned to mimic a tram's starting bell. Tram horses would start immediately they heard the sound – often before the passengers had alighted.

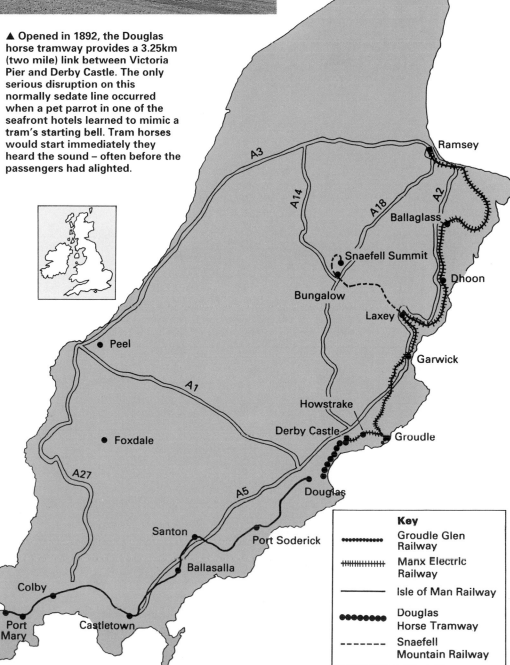

Key
●●●●●●● Groudle Glen Railway
╫╫╫╫╫╫ Manx Electric Railway
——— Isle of Man Railway
●●●●●● Douglas Horse Tramway
------- Snaefell Mountain Railway

▶Dwarfed by the massive headland beyond Groudle Glen, the Bagnall 2-4-0 tank engine *Sea Lion* steams round the clifftop towards its eastern terminus. At one time, the Groudle Glen Railway ran to a seaside zoo where passengers could feed sea lions and polar bears. Although the animals have long since departed, work has been completed on the restoration of this final section of line.

Averting disaster

The most dramatic event on the steam railway occurred on 22 August 1925, when a combined passenger and goods train drew in at Douglas. Due to a flag-signalling misunderstanding during shunting, the heavy train had been running without a guard or brakesman.

Attempts to alert signalmen and station staff ahead had failed, so that it was not until the train approached the station under clear signals that the loco crew realized theirs were the only brakes available – with insufficient power to stop the train in the available distance.

Two members of the station staff attempted to save the day – one jumped into the brake van, the other into the guard's van. They did slow the train, but it still crashed into stanchions, stopping less than four metres (12ft) from the station building. Disaster had been averted, but tragically the fireman was killed.

At Derby Castle you can connect with the Manx Electric Railway (MER) for the journey to Ramsey, on the north-east coast. Owned since 1957 by the Isle of Man government, the MER is a unique mixture of railway and tramway – it runs partly alongside roads on a separate reservation and partly across country on its own right of way.

The first section, as far as Groudle, was opened in 1893 and two of the original cars are still in use. Laxey was reached in 1894 and the final section into Ramsey was opened in 1899.

The MER used to be worked by a mixture of open and enclosed motor cars. But the enclosed cars are now sufficient to maintain the service, including extra trips to Laxey, and the open vehicles are rarely used. One of 24 trailers – three saloon and 21 open – is usually attached to a motor car.

Fine sea views

The 27.5km (17 mile) journey provides wonderful sea views. From Derby Castle the line runs alongside the main road before climbing around Onchan Head and past the site of a pre-World War II holiday camp at Howstrake to the first of many glens along the east coast.

Groudle Glen is the start of the 2ft (600mm) gauge Groudle Glen Railway, which runs, for a limited season only, three-quarters of a kilometre (half a mile) or so out on to the cliffs. Owned and run by volunteers, the line is operated by *Sea Lion*, one of a pair of diminutive 2-4-0 tank engines built by W.G. Bagnall & Co. of Stafford for the opening of the line in 1896. *Sea Lion* and its former twin *Polar Bear* owe their names to a sea lion pool and bear pit that were once situated at the headland terminus.

Reboarding the MER, you travel inland for a few kilometres (two miles) before coming in view of the sea again at Garwick Glen. A section along the coast takes you to Laxey where one of the island's best-known sights is to be found – the

◀ Car No 19, a veteran of the Manx Electric Railway (MER), hauls a trailer and van along the roadside track near Onchan Head. Completed in 1899, the 27.5km (17 mile) MER was one of the world's first electric railways.

▲ The magnificent red-brick Victorian station building at Douglas remains the centre of the IOMR's activities. Seen here pulling away from the platform is a train headed by two of the railway's veterans – No 13 *Kissack* and No 11 *Maitland*, launched in 1905.

Electrifying account
The arrival in the 1890s of an electric railway on the Isle of Man prompted a great deal of enthusiasm. This kind of railway was still a novelty and the writers of local guide books were duly impressed.

One of these described the descent from Howstrake to Groudle: 'Faster and faster we rush down the track, until it seems as if all control over the cars had been lost, and that an accident must inevitably occur. But the fear is entirely unfounded... Within a few yards of the station, and when we are rushing down the road at what seems a terrific speed and with a thunderous roar, (the driver) quietly applies the brake, and the cars, obedient to his hand, stop, without a jar exactly at the stopping place.'

Laxey Wheel, or 'Lady Isabella'. Named after the wife of Man's Lieutenant Governor, this is a huge waterwheel of 22m (72ft) diameter built in 1854 to pump water out of the lead mines under nearby Snaefell.

The summit of Snaefell (Snow Mountain) can be reached from Laxey by the Snaefell Mountain Railway, one of only two mountain railways in the British Isles – the other is Snowdon – and the only one to be powered by electricity.

The Snaefell line, taken over by the Isle of Man government in 1957, has six cars, all enclosed saloons, five of which have been in service since the opening of the railway in 1895.

Approached by gradients as steep as 1 in 12, the 620m (2036ft) summit is the highest point on Man and affords panoramic views of the island; on a clear day, you can see Ireland, Scotland, England and Wales. A stop on the 30 minute trip can be made at Bungalow where there is a Motor Cycle Museum.

Falling embankment
Rejoining the MER for the last leg to Ramsey, you turn 180 degrees and cross the castellated parapets of the Glen Roy viaduct to the opposite side of the valley. Here you begin to climb again, passing the sites of several quarries which provided both mineral traffic for the railway and ballast for its track.

For most of the journey the line is close to the cliffside – almost too close at one point, for in 1967 a section of embankment above Bulgham Bay collapsed, causing a breech that took six months to repair.

Beyond Bulgham, almost 183m (600ft) above sea level, your train cuts across the rolling hills and lush pastures of Maughold Head before descending into the island's second largest settlement, Royal Ramsey, so called since King Edward VII and Queen Alexandra paid a visit in 1902. They also travelled on the electric railway, aboard saloon trailer No 59.

The town, with its excellent shopping centre and picturesque harbour, is well worth exploring. Certainly you should visit the Manx Electric Railway Museum, near the station.

The Ravenglass & Eskdale Railway

A survivor of bankruptcy, closure and neglect, the Ravenglass & Eskdale Railway has been carrying visitors from the Cumbrian coast to the heart of the Lake District for over a century. A quarter of a million passengers now make the 11.25km (seven mile) journey every year.

Ravenglass lies on the unspoilt west Cumbrian coast, where three Lakeland rivers, the Esk, Irt and Mite, form a natural harbour that was used by the Romans. The village is best reached by First North Western mainline train, which follows a picturesque route along the shore from Lancaster or Carlisle. Occasional mainline steam specials also call, providing the perfect way to arrive.

The Ravenglass & Eskdale Railway (RER) station at Ravenglass adjoins the mainline halt. The narrow-gauge line, once very much the junior partner here, has now taken over all the mainline station buildings. The goods shed has become the RER works, the up platform houses the RER Museum and the down-platform building the RER

pub, the Ratty Arms. The museum well repays a visit before or after your journey.

The three-platform RER terminus is smart and well equipped, with good use made of redundant BR materials. The footbridge is from Coniston, while the platform canopies include components from Millom and Whitehaven stations.

Passenger service launched

The original RER was opened in 1875 to serve the iron ore mines in Eskdale. A few months later, the railway operated its first passenger services, using two Manning Wardle 0-6-0T locomotives, *Devon* and *Nabb Gill*. Three coaches were provided, though at busy times travellers were just as likely

▼ The RER is often visited by locomotives from other 15in (375mm) gauge railways. But for Romney, Hythe & Dymchurch Railway 4-6-2 No 1 *Green Goddess*, seen here moving on to the turntable at Ravenglass, the RER is more than just a host line. It was here in 1925 that the engine underwent its steam trials.

to be accommodated rather uncomfortably in iron ore wagons fitted with benches.

The 3ft (914mm) gauge line never prospered. By 1877, two years after opening, the RER had gone bankrupt. With little demand for the poor-quality iron ore and insufficient tourist traffic to compensate, the railway finally closed in 1913.

But that was not the end of the Ratty, as the line was known to the locals. In 1915, the miniature locomotive engineer W.J. Bassett-Lowke and his partner took over the derelict railway. It was rebuilt to 15in (381mm) gauge, by moving the old rails closer together on their sleepers, and reopened in stages, eventually reaching the original terminus at Boot in 1917.

Reversal of fortune

Mineral traffic restarted when Beckfoot granite quarry opened in 1922, but in 1953 quarrying ceased. In 1960, the railway was up for auction and once again its future looked bleak. It was taken over, however, by enthusiasts, supported by the Ravenglass & Eskdale Railway Preservation Society, since when its fortunes have soared.

On bright, clear days the RER operates open coaches, offering magnificent views of the mountain scenery. Waiting at the head of your train by platform 1 may be *River Esk*, a black 2-8-2 built in 1923 for the granite traffic.

Once past the signalbox, the steam shed and diesel depot are on your right. Outside you can see locomotives awaiting their next duty. *Northern Rock* is a light green 2-6-2, constructed at Ravenglass in 1976, while *Bonnie Dundee*, built as

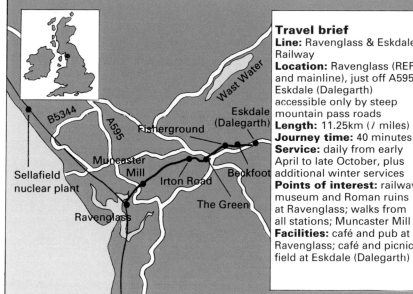

Travel brief
Line: Ravenglass & Eskdale Railway
Location: Ravenglass (RER and mainline), just off A595. Eskdale (Dalegarth) accessible only by steep mountain pass roads
Length: 11.25km (7 miles)
Journey time: 40 minutes
Service: daily from early April to late October, plus additional winter services
Points of interest: railway museum and Roman ruins at Ravenglass; walks from all stations; Muncaster Mill
Facilities: café and pub at Ravenglass; café and picnic field at Eskdale (Dalegarth)

a 2ft (600mm) gauge 0-4-0WT for Dundee Gasworks in 1900, was converted to a 15in (381mm) gauge 0-4-2T at Ravenglass in 1982 and further modified to a tender locomotive in 1996. The railway's diesel locomotives and railcar set are used for off-peak services and the daily winter train.

Forging through floods

The line now curves to the right, falling steeply to run alongside the River Mite across Barrow Marsh. In 1967, trains had to negotiate this section with extreme caution when flood water covered

Export success
Northern Rock, the newest steam locomotive on the RER, was built at Ravenglass to incorporate the best of 15in (381mm) gauge practice. The design proved so successful that the management of the Rainbow Park at Shuzenji, 96.5km (60 miles) from Tokyo, ordered a locomotive to the same pattern from Ravenglass for its own miniature line.

Northern Rock II was delivered in 1990 and performed so well that the Japanese placed an order for a sister engine, *Cumbria*, a year later.

the track. Ahead is England's second highest mountain, Scafell, while to the left the Sellafield nuclear complex can be seen.

A kilometre and a half (a mile) further on, the main road crosses the line, just before Muncaster Mill station. The ancient mill has been fully restored, with both the waterwheel and the mill race clearly visible from the train. The climb through Mill Wood, with gradients sometimes as steep as 1 in 42, can be tough going at times.

Getting off here to push the train uphill used to be a feature of the journey when the combination of wet rail and steep gradient proved too much for the struggling locomotive. However, the track has been realigned to ease the gradient, and this, together with other improvements, means you are unlikely to be asked to help in this way now.

Sailboat shelter

An upturned sailboat by the side of the track provides the shelter at Miteside Halt, shortly before Miteside loop, where your train pauses to allow a train from Eskdale to pass. Its locomotive may be *River Mite*, a 2-8-2 built in 1966 on a chassis that provided extra power under *River Esk*'s tender in the late 1920s. *River Mite*, painted in Furness Railway Indian red, is owned by the

Preservation Society. It was transported across the Pennines by traction engine in 1967.

For just over three kilometres (two miles) the line runs in the shadow of Muncaster Fell. There is a fine walk along its ridge from Ravenglass to Eskdale Green. At Murthwaite you pass the ruins of the crushing plant for granite from Beckfoot Quarry. From 1929 to 1953, standard-gauge tracks reached here from Ravenglass, worked by an early diesel locomotive. The existing 15in (381mm) gauge line was taken up and relaid between the new standard-gauge rails, with interesting point-work at the place where the two gauges diverged. The standard-gauge tracks have been removed.

Climb to the summit

Climbing through woods and open moorland, the train reaches Rock Point, where it runs along a hillside ledge, high above the Mite. Walk Mill

▼ A 1930s Pullman coach outside Ravenglass station contrasts with one of the RER's newer acquisitions, *Lady Wakefield*, a diesel engine dating from 1980. Innovation has always been a feature of the revived RER, which in the 1970s introduced train control by radio. The system, the first of its kind in the United Kingdom, is partly based on the Austrian Zillertalbahn and now operates on some rural lines.

▲ RER 0-8-2 *River Irt*, smoke billowing in its wake, heads a train through the rugged grandeur of Eskdale. Built in 1894 as an 0-8-0 called *Muriel*, and extensively modified over the years, it is now the oldest 15in (381mm) gauge locomotive in active service anywhere.

summit soon follows and then you are hurrying downhill again, with fine views of Scafell looming up ahead. The train curves to the right and stops at Irton Road, just over halfway to Eskdale.

In the 1920s, passengers for this station made their journey in slip coaches which, like those on the mainlines, were uncoupled from non-stop trains at speed. The stone shelter is little changed from when it was first built in the 1870s, and if the bridge seems on the grand scale for miniature trains, remember it was designed originally for the larger 3ft (914mm) gauge stock.

With no train to pass, you are soon off again. Swinging sharply southwards, the train rounds the end of Muncaster Fell, leaving Miterdale and resuming its eastward course along Eskdale. Three-quarters of a kilometre (half a mile) beyond Irton Road, the Green station serves the eastern end of Eskdale Green village.

A local story is still told that, in 3ft (914mm) gauge days, a farmhand sent to collect a henhouse here picked up the station building by mistake and took it away. Erected by volunteers in 1968, the present station is rather more substantial than its early predecessor, which really did resemble a garden shed.

Oldest working locomotive

The line winds round the foot of the hills on the northern flank of Eskdale, with Harter Fell prominent across the valley ahead. At Fisherground loop, you cross another train, hauled by the green 0-8-2 *River Irt*, the oldest working 15in (381mm) gauge locomotive in the world.

It was built in 1894 as an 0-8-0T called *Muriel* by the miniature pioneer Sir Arthur Heywood for his private line at Duffield in Derbyshire. Moving to Ravenglass in 1917, it was comprehensively rebuilt 10 years later, assuming its present form in 1972 with further alterations.

Beyond Fisherground, you continue through Gilbert's Cutting, the railway's major earthwork, dug in 1963 to avoid an awkward reverse curve. Following the valley road on a hillside alignment, the line reaches Beckfoot quarry, now abandoned and almost concealed by undergrowth. This was the major source of granite traffic in the area until the 1950s.

Abandoned line

Beckfoot station, about 9.5km (six miles) from Ravenglass, is the request halt for the former Stanley Ghyll Hotel. A minor level crossing follows before your train enters the woods again, climbing alongside the lane to Dalegarth Cottages. The original line ran behind the cottages to terminate at the top end of Boot village.

Miniature trains ran to Boot for a season, until it was realized that the early locomotives, designed for short pleasure lines, were really not equipped to tackle the final 1 in 38 gradient into the station. The route was then changed to follow the alignment of the abandoned Ghyll Force mineral branch.

It now curves in front of Dalegarth Cottages, crossing Whillan Beck to reach the simple terminus at Eskdale (Dalegarth). As at Ravenglass,

there is a turntable at the end of the line. On arrival, go to the front of the train to watch the engine being turned in a fine mountain setting. The locomotive runs to the other end of the train to take water for the return journey.

It is worth spending some time in Eskdale. Ramblers should acquire the booklet *Walks from Ratty*, written and illustrated for the RER by the well-known Lakeland author Alfred Wainwright. This describes a variety of walks, from the short stroll to Dalegarth Force to more ambitious expeditions up Harter Fell or to the Roman fort on Hardknott Pass.

Mining mementos

Eskdale is full of interest for the railway historian. Behind Boot village you can still make out the inclines and spoil tips of the haematite mines on the hillside. You can also walk the short distance to St Catherine's church on the banks of the Esk.

If you follow the river upstream, you soon reach two rusting girders, disused for almost a century, which cross the Esk. These formed the bridge by which the Ghyll Force branch reached its mines, now long since reclaimed by nature. This wooded glade, with its reminder of the railway's early days, is a fitting place to end your exploration of Eskdale.

▼ The most powerful engine ever built for the 15in (381mm) gauge, 2-6-2 No 10 *Northern Rock*, is coaled up outside Ravenglass engine shed. The locomotive was designed and constructed at Ravenglass and entered service in 1976, the year of the RER's passenger centenary.

The Lakeside & Haverthwaite Railway

Built to transport Victorian tourists who wanted to cruise on Lake Windermere, the Lakeside branch line was closed by BR in 1967. Now, given a new lease of life as the Lakeside & Haverthwaite Railway, the line is a tourist attraction in its own right.

It could be said that the Lakeside & Haverthwaite Railway (LHR) owes its origins to William Wordsworth. The Poet Laureate wrote so passionately about the beauty of the Lake District that many of his readers wanted to see it for themselves. The invention and development of railways made this possible, though Wordsworth himself was horrified, trying to resist the intrusion of the iron road into his beloved and unspoiled private heaven. He failed.

As early as 1846 the Furness Railway began carrying passengers from its station at Dalton, near Barrow, to Newby Bridge. From here they could take a tourist steamer down the River Leven to Lake Windermere.

In 1869, the Furness opened the Lakeside Railway, which carried passengers from Ulverston to Lake Windermere itself. The line, which eventually became part of the London, Midland & Scottish Railway, was very popular for 50 years, but a steady decline followed World War I. World War II did little to improve the line's fortunes, and its last scheduled passenger train ran in 1965. Two years later, the freight service came to an end.

Plans by enthusiasts to reopen the entire 12.75km (eight mile) branch received a fatal blow when Lancashire County Council announced its intention of taking over a large part of Haverthwaite station yard and other stretches of the line for road improvements.

A railway reborn

A more modest revival scheme was agreed, and in 1973 the upper 5.5km (3½ miles) of track from Haverthwaite to Lakeside echoed to the sound of steam trains. Once again, tourists had the option of a combined rail and water trip through some of the most striking scenery in England.

▼ *Cumbria* heads a rake of ex-BR Mark 1 coaches towards Newby Bridge Halt *en route* from Haverthwaite to Lakeside. It was at Newby Bridge that passengers used to transfer to steamers for the voyage down the headwaters of the Leven to Lake Windermere. In 1869, a new line was built leading to the lake itself.

is in daily use as the works and storage base for the whole line.

Whenever you arrive there will be a selection of the railway's 20 steam, diesel and petrol locomotives parked around the edge of the yard in various stages of restoration and completeness. During the working day there will also be a full range of movements by the engines which are in operation. Despite all the activity of a working railway, the Lakeside & Haverthwaite Railway members and supporters work hard to keep the station tidy and attractive.

The tightly packed area of Haverthwaite station and goods yard is full of interest for the railway enthusiast, but this is only one small part of the entire railway/lake experience. The 18 minute trip to the connecting cruisers is through such attractive countryside that, when BR first closed the line, the Lake District Planning Board was keen to convert it into a scenic footpath. It is very easy to see why.

Climbing the gradient

The spectacular scenery of the Lake District is its main attraction, and the Lakeside & Haverthwaite offers dramatic views as it climbs up the Leven Valley. However, the majestic mountains made it difficult to build a level railway line, so trains pull out of Haverthwaite on a 1 in 70 gradient and have to be handled very gently if they are to get enough grip for the climb that constitutes the first part of

▲ No 42085 emerges bunker first from under Newby Bridge. Here the engine is shown decked in its former livery, the distinctive mid-blue of the Caledonian Railway. The locomotive is an LMS Fairburn 2-6-4T, which was built at Brighton in 1951 and spent most of its life on the North Eastern Region of BR.

Close co-operation between railway and cruiser operators means the visitor can combine rail and water travel on a single ticket, but the logical place to start a tour of the railway itself is at Haverthwaite station.

As you enter the old goods yard, you get the impression that this is a working railway, still sending its goods and passengers on to the great industrial towns of Britain, rather than just a severed remnant, isolated from the main network.

At the western platform end two tracks lead into a tunnel. Now it just contains the far end of the run-round loop, but you get the impression that the rails still run on for miles.

Unlike some preserved railway stations, which look as if they are brand new sets for a motion picture, the atmosphere at Haverthwaite is one of gritty realism; hardly surprising as the goods yard

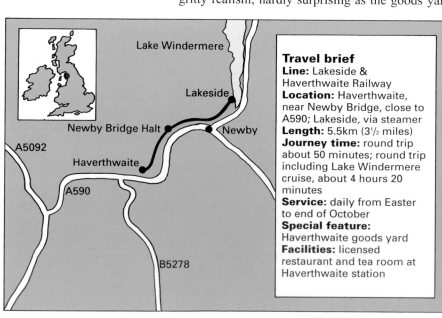

Travel brief
Line: Lakeside & Haverthwaite Railway
Location: Haverthwaite, near Newby Bridge, close to A590; Lakeside, via steamer
Length: 5.5km (3½ miles)
Journey time: round trip about 50 minutes; round trip including Lake Windermere cruise, about 4 hours 20 minutes
Service: daily from Easter to end of October
Special feature: Haverthwaite goods yard
Facilities: licensed restaurant and tea room at Haverthwaite station

the journey. On days when the track is slippery it is a true test of a driver's skills. For this reason the locomotives which operate the line are chosen mainly for their pulling power.

Among the locomotives based at Haverthwaite are two powerful Fairburn 4MT 2-6-4Ts. However, depending on the state of repairs and restoration, many services will be pulled by one of the hard-working 0-4-0Ts, which were manufactured by Peckett, Barclay or Avonside. A lighter GWR Class 56XX 0-6-2T, one of three former industrial 0-6-0Ts, is being restored for use on the line.

Waterfall in view

Whichever locomotive is used, it pulls its train beside steep, wooded rock faces to a short tunnel before passing the entrance to the Backbarrow Iron Works. From here, pig iron was exported down the line until 1967. Then the view opens out and to the right can be seen the Leven Valley, with its waterfall and mature woods. One prominent building is the Whitewater Hotel. This was once an ultramarine works, another important railway customer in the 19th century.

▲ The 0-6-0 Hunslet saddle tank *Cumbria* takes on a fresh supply of coal at Haverthwaite station. Built at Leeds in 1953 for the army, *Cumbria* worked at the Shoeburyness Artillery Range in Essex before arriving on the Lakeside & Haverthwaite in 1973 – the railway's reopening year.

▼ A steamer makes its way towards the pier at Lakeside to disembark passengers for the return train journey to Haverthwaite. Lake Windermere has always been the magnet for travellers on the Lakeside & Haverthwaite.

The only stop before Lakeside is Newby Bridge, closed to regular traffic in 1939, but used when German prisoners of war were being transferred to nearby Grizedale Hall. It was reopened in 1973 by the famous railway photographer, the late Eric Treacy, Bishop of Wakefield.

It was here that the Furness coaches used to meet the Lake Windermere steamers. However, with the building of the branch line from Ulverston, the track was taken on a further three-quarters of a kilometre (half mile) to Lakeside, where a new pier was erected. The extension cut out a difficult piece of navigation down the River Leven for the steamers and enabled larger vessels to be used on the lake.

Arrival at Lake Windermere

Newby Bridge is a convenient alighting point for passengers wishing to explore the beautiful countryside. For those remaining on the train, there is another kilometre or so (mile) of ever-changing scenery to pass through, including the first dramatic views of Lake Windermere. At some

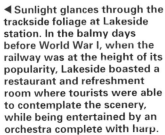

◄ Sunlight glances through the trackside foliage at Lakeside station. In the balmy days before World War I, when the railway was at the height of its popularity, Lakeside boasted a restaurant and refreshment room where tourists were able to contemplate the scenery, while being entertained by an orchestra complete with harp.

▲ **Getting up steam at Lakeside station, the 1950 Hunslet 0-6-0 tank engine *Repulse* prepares to haul a train to Haverthwaite. The oblong chimney is part of a Giesl ejector system, added after the locomotive was built.**

Combined tours

Close co-operation between the Lakeside & Haverthwaite Railway and Windermere Lake Cruises has produced a range of combined tours to various local attractions including the Steamboat Museum and the Beatrix Potter Story in Bowness, and Brockhole National Park Centre. Trains are steam hauled throughout the spring and summer, but the final train of the day in high season may be pulled by one of the LHR's five diesel locomotives.

places, the train runs next to the lake, at others it passes through cuttings or steams past gently rising hills and open fields.

The train pulls round a sharp turn to the left and, suddenly, there is Lakeside itself. Sadly, much of the once-grand rail terminus and dockside canopy was demolished between 1965 and 1973 when the railway reopened, although passengers with combined tickets will hardly notice this as they simply cross the platform to the quayside and continue their excursion on one of the Windermere Lake Cruises' four boats.

Travelling in style

But, no matter how enjoyable the journey, it is unlikely to be as luxurious as that of a certain Mr H.W. Schneider, an ironmaster, in the 1860s. This most stylish of early Victorian commuters would leave his house in Bowness (now the Belsfield Hotel), on the lake shore, accompanied by his butler, who carried a heated silver salver containing Mr Schneider's breakfast.

The ironmaster's private steam yacht, *Esperance*, would cruise the nine kilometres (six miles) to Lakeside while Mr Schneider ate his

meal before he transferred to a reserved first-class railway compartment for the remaining stretch of his journey to Barrow. *Esperance* was such a familiar sight that Arthur Ransome used it as the model for the houseboat in his classic children's story of adventure afloat, *Swallows and Amazons*. It is now preserved at the Steam Boat Museum in Windermere.

Rail passengers can choose to include the museum in their trip; or they can settle back for a round trip cruise of Lake Windermere.

Shares in the steamers

The popularity of the Lake Windermere passenger steamers was so important to the profitability of the line to Lakeside that the Act of Parliament which authorized its construction also entitled the Furness Railway to buy £10,000 worth of shares in the Windermere United Steam Yacht Company, which then operated the boats. In 1872, the Furness Railway bought the remainder of the shares outright. With the closure of the railway, the ships continued to run as part of BR's operations under its Sealink wing until privatization.

Passengers on the Windermere cruisers can choose to travel between Ambleside and Bowness or cruise the longer distance to Lakeside. Boats depart at regular intervals throughout the day with the last boat running during the late afternoon. You can disembark at any of these stops and continue the cruise on a later boat.

The Tanfield Railway

**Opened in 1725, the Tanfield Railway is the
oldest surviving railway in the world. Its first rails were
made of wood and horses supplied the motive power for the small
coal wagons that moved along it. The line was faced with
extinction in 1970, but is now flourishing again.**

The Tanfield Railway (TR) has two major claims to fame: it is the oldest working railway in the world and it offers visitors the magnificent sight of the world's oldest surviving railway bridge. Moreover, few other railways can operate locomotives and carriages of such antiquity in normal service, as opposed to special events.

It is not surprising that the TR should have such a long history, for its location in the heart of the County Durham coalfield places it amongst the earliest concentration of mining activity, which began centuries before the Industrial Revolution. Crude wagonways are believed to have been in existence on the banks of the River Tyne as early as 1530, but wooden rails and sleepers were not recorded with certainty until 1671.

These early wagonways were developed into a network of lines that carried coal from the Durham and Northumberland coalfields to the wharves beside the Tyne and Wear. It was a development of one of these lines, the Ravensworth, that became the Tanfield Wagonway. The route ran from Dunston Staithes on the Tyne to Tanfield Moor, and is thought to have been opened in stages between 1712 and 1725. It is the southern part of this wagonway that forms today's Tanfield Railway, which runs over the 4.75km (three miles) from Sunniside to East Tanfield.

For over a century, horse-drawn wagons made almost entirely of wood trundled along the wooden rails to waiting colliers. For much of the 18th century, the line carried more coal than any other wagonway in Britain, with a vehicle passing every three-quarters of a minute.

By the time the nearby Stockton & Darlington Railway was opened in 1825, the Tanfield's

▼ **Robert Stephenson & Hawthorns' 0-4-0ST No 7409 *Sir Cecil A. Cochrane*, built for Redheugh Gasworks, Gateshead, passes the site of sidings at Marley Hill with a train from Sunniside. Immediately behind is North Eastern Railway full brake van No 92189 of 1899 – one of the most modern items of passenger coaching stock on the TR.**

equipment was outdated and work began in 1839 to rebuild the wagonway as an iron railway. This conversion was carried out by the Brandling Junction Railway, named, unusually, after its founders, John and Robert Brandling.

Horses were retained on the flat sections, but steam winding engines or self-acting inclines were used where the gradient was too steep. Even more unusual for such a railway was the start of a short-lived passenger service, in 1842, between Tanfield Lea Colliery and Gateshead.

Steam locomotives appear

By 1854, the Tanfield branch had become a part of the huge North Eastern Railway (NER), which introduced steam locomotives to the flatter sections in 1881. After the end of World War II, colliery closures gradually reduced the length of the Tanfield branch, the last section of the future Tanfield Railway closing in 1962.

The reason for the Tanfield line becoming the focus of a preservation project, however, had as much to do with the Bowes Railway, which crossed the Tanfield branch on the level at Marley Hill, as the Tanfield itself. For it was the survival of the 1854 built engine shed there, serving collieries which outlasted those linked to the Tanfield branch, that attracted the attention of preservationists in search of a suitable base.

The repair of National Coal Board steam locomotives continued at Marley Hill shed until November 1970, and the following year a group of local enthusiasts took over with the intention of relaying track along the Tanfield branch. Another objective was to save locomotives that were either built or worked in the north east.

Within two years, steam open days were being held. Trains began running northwards to Bowes

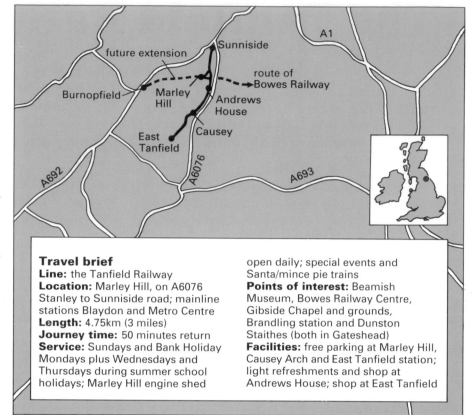

▼ 0-4-0ST *Sir Cecil A. Cochrane* and 0-6-0ST works No 7298 *Progress* haul a rake of wagons round the sharp, check-railed curve between Marley Hill and the main running line of the TR. Like *Sir Cecil A. Cochrane*, *Progress* was built by Robert Stephenson & Hawthorns. Outshopped in 1946, it worked at a colliery in Derbyshire.

Bridge in 1977 and to Sunniside in 1981; Causey on the southern section from Marley Hill was reached in 1991 and the final stretch to East Tanfield was reopened in 1992.

Most visitors to the Tanfield Railway start at Marley Hill, where they can admire the collection of industrial locomotives and varied rolling stock that has been built up. The scene beside the huge area of waste ground on which once stood the colliery, coke works and village of Marley Hill still evokes the atmosphere of the colliery railway from days gone by.

Tidiness was never a priority on most industrial lines since there was no public to impress or to complain, and the site does not compromise authenticity for the sake of visitors worried about getting their shoes dusty.

Protection for veterans

An effort is being made to provide more covered accommodation: an engine shed covering five roads has been built and extended, and a steaming shed is to be built round the rare 5.5m (18ft) turntable that was made by Cowans Sheldon in 1894 for Nostell Colliery near Pontefract. The veterans are protected from the elements.

The 29 steam locomotives of various gauges date from 1873 to 1958, the oldest being 0-4-0ST *Wellington*, built by Black Hawthorn in nearby Gateshead. Besides the dozens of very different four- and six-coupled industrial tank engines are two oddities – a 2ft (600mm) gauge 0-4-0ST built by Black Hawthorn in 1883, which was rescued from a Spanish industrial railway; and a 1951 Robert Stephenson & Hawthorn Pacific built in Darlington for the 3ft 6in (1m) gauge Tasmanian Government Railways. This had stood for years in

▲ The TR's oldest locomotive, No 266 *Wellington* of 1873, passes the bracket signal for the loop at Andrews House after drifting over the crossing at Marley Hill. The line to the right of the rebuilt signalbox ends after a few yards, but used to continue to the River Tyne as the Bowes Railway.

a park in the north coast port of Stanley before it was repatriated.

Equally remarkable is Tanfield's collection of carriages. The majority of them are former main-line railway carriages that were bought by colliery railways to transport miners from the pit village to the mine shaft. Consequently, they are mostly four- or six-wheeled third-class coaches, but there are a few magnificent NER family or inspection saloons.

It is not often that the workshops of preserved railways are of intrinsic historical value, but the machine shop beside Marley Hill engine shed has been used as the set for filming a Catherine Cookson novel, so authentic is its atmosphere. Powered by various steam, gas or diesel engines, the machines were made by a host of British and American machine-tool manufacturers.

Trains leave from Andrews House station, close to Marley Hill shed, and first head north. There was never a station here, but a siding for farmers, known as the manure siding, meant that the cutting was wide enough for two platforms. Before departure, your engine, possibly the 1873 veteran *Wellington*, will have to replenish its water tanks from the rivetted torpedo-shaped tanks on the stone base at the end of the northbound platform, and its tiny coal bunker will be refilled.

The locomotive eases the three-coach train out of the loop and under Gibraltar Bridge; the 1765 structure had to be rebuilt by the TR following its inexplicable demolition by British Rail 11 years after leaving the site. Almost immediately, the train crosses what was formerly the Bowes Railway, protected by a tiny signalbox that was rebuilt on the site of, and in the same style as, the original.

The Causey Arch

Built in 1725–27 by Ralph Wood, a stone mason from the area, the Causey Arch was erected for Colonel Liddell, a member of the local coal- and land-owning consortium, the Grand Allies, and carried the Tanfield Wagonway 24.5m (80ft) above the Causey Burn.

Thoughtfully provided with a sundial on one of its piers, the bridge had two tracks of wooden rails. Colliery closures from 1733 began to reduce the traffic using it, until by the 1770s it was virtually redundant. Two centuries of neglect were remedied by a county council restoration that was completed in 1981.

The line to the east ends at an embankment. As *Wellington* tackles the climb up to Bowes Bridge, the connecting curve from the engine shed joins the line from the west. It is hard to believe that the uneven waste ground to the left, largely colonized by saplings, marks the site of a colliery, coke works and several rows of miners' houses with their allotment gardens.

Change of gradient

Observant passengers can still detect the site of the NER engine shed at Bowes Bridge on the right, marked by the small turntable pit and the remnants of the coal stage. The two-road shed is thought to have been adapted from the winding house for northbound wagons, which then dropped down to the present terminus at Sunniside. The gentler exhaust from *Wellington*'s chimney indicates the change of gradient, as the train ambles past fields of wheat on the right and pasture to the left, with the village of Marley Hill on the horizon.

At the simple loop and single platform of Sunniside, the locomotive is uncoupled to run round the train and return to Andrews House. The train pauses for passengers at the southbound platform at Andrews House before the regulator is cracked open to get the train moving downhill, under a timber footbridge and out of the cutting. Wide views open up over the pastoral valley on the right as the line briefly borders the main road before moving on to an historic piece of civil engineering – the vast embankment that was built about 1725 to carry the wagonway over Causey Burn.

It was to see this and the nearby Causey Arch that people came from far and wide, wishing to find out if comparisons with the Via Appia, the

▼ The Causey Arch, depicted in many paintings and engravings following its completion in 1727, was the largest single-span bridge in Britain for 30 years. A footpath now crosses the bridge, enabling visitors to walk along the bed of the branch that once carried 930 wagons a day in each direction.

The Grand Allies

The Tanfield Wagonway was built for Sir John Clavering and Thomas Brunell, local colliery owners, but control passed in 1726 to a consortium that went under the name of the Grand Allies. Formed by the Bowes, Liddell, Ord and Wortley families, the partnership was to dominate the coal trade in County Durham and Northumberland for over a century.

It was the Grand Allies who built the Pontop & Jarrow Railway (PJR), renamed the Bowes Railway in 1932. An impressive, and still functioning, legacy of the PJR is the Marley Hill engine shed, built in 1854.

greatest Roman road in Italy, were justified. The eulogies of contemporaries suggest that most thought they were, and it is not difficult even for today's sophisticated visitors to see why.

The burn was first covered by a stone culvert 91.5m (300ft) long, and a 30.5m (100ft) high embankment was then heaped on top. Nothing on this scale had been built for centuries. The thickening of trees as your train drops down the hill towards Causey station makes it difficult to appreciate the size of the construction; a walk beside it on your return will help.

A minor road off the A6076 opposite the Causey Arch Inn leads to a car park from which easy footpaths lead through the gorge beside the railway. A circular walk takes in the embankment, with a short deviation to the culvert under it, the Causey Arch, a replica wooden wagon and the delightful section of railway through the woods. Oak trees predominate with a scattering of beech, ash and silver birch. Along the east side of the Causey Burn, the path is just inside the perimeter of the wood, affording views over the surrounding farms towards Beamish.

▼ The atmospheric interior of Marley Hill shed, built in 1854 and thought to be the oldest working locomotive depot in the world. On the left is Hawthorn Leslie 0-4-0ST No 2 of 1911. On the right is *Wellington*, and behind it Hudswell Clarke 0-4-0ST *Irwell*, dating from 1937.

If you do not intend to walk through the woods, it is advisable to alight at Causey station to admire the Causey Arch and catch the next train on to East Tanfield, especially during the summer. The density of the surrounding woodland makes it difficult to catch more than a glimpse of the bridge from the train, since it is situated on a branch that ran off the main route of the Tanfield Wagonway. It is a sight not to be missed, the graceful masonry arch of 32m (105ft) standing 24.5m (80ft) above the stream in a sylvan setting worthy of an idealized landscape painting.

From Causey station, the line twists downhill, flanked by foxgloves and the deepening gorge, full of trees. At times, the trees arch right over the railway, forming a dense tunnel of branches and leaves. Suddenly, *Wellington* emerges from the woods and rolls into East Tanfield where a new station with a run-round loop and a bay platform have been built together with a large free car park and shop. The line used to continue on to Tanfield Moor, but any thoughts of extension are blocked by the Ever Ready factory that is built over the route.

The return to Andrews House is no anti-climax, for it is uphill nearly all the way, culminating in a stretch of 1 in 39 that *Wellington*, in spite of its years and size, tackles with vigour. No other preserved railway evokes so well the experience once common to generations of miners of riding to work in spartan wooden carriages.

The Bowes Railway

**Built to carry coal from the Durham
pits to the River Tyne, the Bowes Railway offers visitors
two working preserved rope inclines – the only examples in
Britain. Their summit is reached by steam-hauled train
from the historic complex of Springwell Yard.**

Of the various districts of Britain that can make some claim to be the cradle of the Industrial Revolution, the north east probably has a better case than most. To understand why, and to witness one of the most extraordinary railway operations ever devised, a visit to the Bowes Railway can hardly be bettered. Its origins go back to the early years of the 18th century, when an alliance was formed between four of the principal landowning families of Northumberland and County Durham to develop the coal trade.

The families of Bowes, Liddell, Ord and Wortley became known locally as the Grand Allies, and it is with the sinking of a shaft on a farm they owned at Springwell, in 1821, that the history of the Bowes Railway begins. The opening up of the new mine coincided with a developing crisis in the north east coalfields.

In contrast to other areas of early industrial activity, the north east did not lend itself to the construction of canals, due to the region's moors and steep-sided valleys. So wagonways were built to take coal to staithes on the Tyne and Wear rivers where it was tipped into waiting vessels.

However, the staithes upriver could be reached only by small sailing vessels called keels, which had to transfer their loads into waiting colliers downstream. It was to overcome this double handling, increase capacity and serve the new pit at Springwell that the Bowes Railway came into being. George Stephenson was chosen as engineer for the line. This appointment was predictable, since Stephenson had previously been in the employ of the Allies, at Killingworth colliery in Northumberland, where he rose to become colliery enginewright.

Following construction of his first locomotive, *Blucher*, with the Allies' support, Stephenson was appointed engineer of the nearby Hetton Colliery Railway (HCR) and the Stockton & Darlington

▼ A century and a half of colliery locomotives are spanned by the replica of George Stephenson's *Locomotion No 1*, on a visit to the Bowes Railway, and the Barclay 0-4-0ST, No 22 (Works No 2274). No 22 came to Bowes on permanent loan from St Anthony's tar works at Walker in Newcastle. On the right are the wagon shops which formerly stored coal during the winter months.

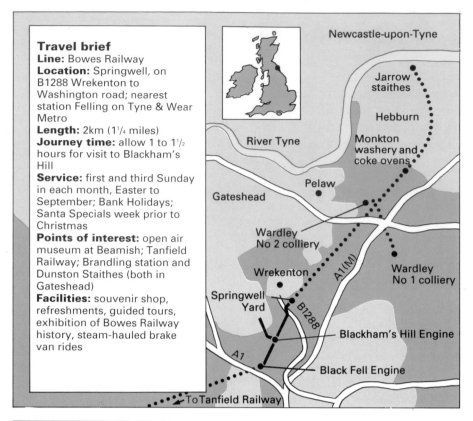

Travel brief
Line: Bowes Railway
Location: Springwell, on
B1288 Wrekenton to
Washington road; nearest
station Felling on Tyne & Wear
Metro
Length: 2km (1¼ miles)
Journey time: allow 1 to 1½
hours for visit to Blackham's
Hill
Service: first and third Sunday
in each month, Easter to
September; Bank Holidays;
Santa Specials week prior to
Christmas
Points of interest: open air
museum at Beamish; Tanfield
Railway; Brandling station and
Dunston Staithes (both in
Gateshead)
Facilities: souvenir shop,
refreshments, guided tours,
exhibition of Bowes Railway
history, steam-hauled brake
van rides

▶ Blackham's Hill engine house with a rake of
wagons waiting to descend to Black Fell. Invisible
beneath the wagons and track is a horizontally
positioned colliery winding wheel which is used to
bring the rope round to its required direction and
alignment.

Springwell Bank Head
A sharp left turn on the way
into Springwell Yard brings
visitors to the top of the
gravity-worked Springwell
Bank incline. With an
average gradient of 1 in 24,
it stretches for 2km (1¼
miles) down to the start of
the long flat section of the
Bowes Railway that led to
the staithes at Jarrow.

The weight of the full
descending wagons brought
up the same number of
empties from Springwell
Bank Foot. The cable was
controlled from the tall
brake cabin that still stands
at the top of the incline,
close to the pit that once
contained the large return
wheel for the 2.5km (1½
mile) long rope. Speed was
held at about 40km/h
(25mph). Much of the route
of the Bowes Railway is
now a public footpath.

▶ A rake of wagons begins to
descend the 686m (750yd)
incline from Blackham's Hill to
Black Fell. Wagon No 289 is an
example of the 800 or so
standard Bowes Railway 10
tonne (ton) hopper wagons
which were built at Springwell
from about 1900. Apart from
springs, drawbar gear and
wheels, which were bought
in, all parts were produced at
the works.

wagons over the new line, and opened it on 17
January 1826, although the two locomotives
ordered from Robert Stephenson & Co. had yet to
be delivered; horses were used until their arrival in
April. One of the pair is thought to be the engine
named *Billy*, now preserved at the Stephenson
Railway Museum in North Shields.

The line was gradually extended to the west to
link up with other collieries, and by 1854 it had
reached the Tanfield Railway, which it crossed on
the level near Marley Hill and Andrews House
collieries. To reflect its increased importance, the
line was named the Pontop & Jarrow Railway
from the previous year. By 1860, the 24km (15
mile) line was serving nine pits, and had seven
rope-worked inclines and three sections worked by
locomotives. Renamed the Bowes Railway in
1932, the line carried coal until colliery closures
brought its work to an end in 1974.

Exceptional status

That would have been the end of the railway had it
not been for the foresight of Tyne & Wear County
Council. They realized its historic value and
bought 2km (1¼ miles) between Black Fell, at the
foot of the western incline from Blackham's Hill,
and Springwell. The engine houses and 40 wagons
were included in the purchase, and the engineering
and wagon repair shops were added in 1977. As
the only preserved working inclines in Britain, the
whole site, including parts of the trackbed where
track has been lifted, buildings and even trees, has
been given Scheduled Ancient Monument status
by English Heritage.

It is at Springwell that visitors begin their tour
of the Bowes Railway; there is no road access to
Blackham's Hill. Although substantial buildings
remain on the site, they are mostly related to railway activity and it is hard to imagine that the

Railway (SDR). Preoccupation with the latter
probably prevented Stephenson playing more than
a supervisory role in the construction of what
became the Bowes Railway; it is thought that the
resident engineer was one of George's three
brothers, Robert. The wagonway was to follow the
practice of the HCR and SDR in being a combination of rope-operated inclines and leveler sections
worked by steam locomotives.

A winding engine found on Blackham's Hill,
just over a kilometre (nearly a mile) east of
Springwell, was built to haul coal wagons up from
another of the Allies' pits at Mount Moor and
lower them down to Springwell. From there they
would descend a gravity incline to Springwell
Bank Foot, where locomotives would take over for
the next 7.75km (4¾ miles) to the staithes at
Jarrow. The Allies were impatient to move their

Steam trio
Besides *W.S.T.*, the Bowes Railway has two other steam locomotives – 0-4-0ST No 22, outshopped by Andrew Barclay in 1949, and 0-6-0ST *Norwood*, built by Robert Stephenson & Hawthorn in 1948. No 22 is the only surviving steam locomotive delivered new to the Bowes Railway. After working at East Tanfield and Tanfield Lea collieries, it was based at Marley Hill shed from 1959 to the shed's closure in 1970, when it was transferred to a tar works in Newcastle-upon-Tyne. *Norwood*, which is currently under restoration, worked at Norwood coke works at Dunston near Gateshead until closure in 1983.

colliery, which ceased operations in 1932, employed several thousand men. On the left as you enter Springwell Yard is the massively buttressed stone building that once served as a coal bunker. When the colliery closed, it was converted into a wagon repair shop, a function it still retains.

At the rear of the building is an obelisk marking the site of the colliery engine house and headgear. The relatively small coal tubs used down the pits were repaired in a separate shop on the other side of the running lines which was fitted with a steel floor to make it easier to move them around by hand.

Opposite the wagon shop, beyond the six parallel lines where wagons awaited dispatch, are the engineering shops, tub shop and locomotive shed. They form a three-sided courtyard, once a common layout for such buildings in the north east, but now believed to be the only surviving example. Part of the tub shop is given over to a small museum containing three underground locomotives as part of a mining display.

Relaunching the *Rocket*
Crossing the courtyard to the far side of the engineering shops, you come to the joiners' and blacksmiths' shop. Upstairs is an exhibition of photographs, memorabilia and scale models of the site. Next to this building is a well-equipped machine shop, where the replica of Stephenson's *Rocket* was built for the 150th anniversary of the Liverpool & Manchester Railway in 1980.

Outside the shops, alongside the nearest of the six shunting lines, is a simple wooden platform from which a train of three converted brake vans leaves for the winding house at Blackham's Hill. They are hauled by a 1954 built Andrew Barclay 0-4-0ST *W.S.T.*, named in honour of William Stuart Trimble, one of the directors of British

Gypsum, which ordered the locomotive for its Long Meg mine at Lazonby near Carlisle.

Passing the former colliery manager's house on the left as the train curves to the right to cross the B1288 Wrekenton to Washington road, the locomotive tackles the 1070m (1170yd) climb up the east incline on a gradient which averages 1 in 70. A steel stockyard on the left and a stonemason's yard on the right give way to fields.

As the train nears the summit of the climb, *W.S.T.* veers to the right and draws to a halt at a platform from which the engine house at the top of Blackham's Hill is only a few minutes' walk. Although the two inclines worked from the engine house date from the railway's opening in 1826, the present building was erected in 1915. A new stationary steam engine commissioned from Andrew Barclay was installed at the same time.

▲ Two men are required for the skilful task of dragging the rope out of the way as wagons breast the summit of Blackham's Hill from the west. A special slip coupling releases the rope. On the left is a roller capstan for the rope that lowers the wagons down towards Black Fell.

Replica *Rocket*

The well-equipped workshop at Springwell was chosen by Mike Satow and Locomotion Enterprises as the ideal place to build the replica of *Rocket* that the Science Museum in London commissioned from them for the 150th anniversary celebrations of the Liverpool & Manchester Railway in 1980. Although the external appearance of the replica adheres closely to the original (now in the Science Museum), safety regulations dictated the use of welding rather than riveting for the construction of the boiler. The well-travelled replica has its present home at the National Railway Museum, York.

▼ Barclay 0-4-0ST *W.S.T.* (Works No 2361) passes the wagon repair shop at Springwell Yard. Built in 1954, *W.S.T.* is on permanent loan from British Gypsum, which last employed the locomotive at its Cocklakes works south of Carlisle. Between 1969 and 1981, when it arrived at Springwell, *W.S.T.* was left marooned in a disconnected engine shed.

This was replaced in 1950 by the present engine, a 300hp electric hauler made by Metropolitan Vickers Ltd of Manchester.

Visitors can enter the engine house to watch the procedure of moving wagons up and down the inclines. The ropes are wound round two drums – one of 8ft (2.5m) diameter for the rope on the east side and one of 6ft (1.75m) diameter for the rope on the west side – and each is provided with indicators to show the position of the set on the incline and dials to monitor the speed of the rope in feet per second.

Climbs and descents are directed from a cabin built on stilts, which gives the driver a clear view of both inclines. In National Coal Board days, they were worked simultaneously, but for the present they are operated one at a time. Two vertical handwheels control the clutch for each drum, and two horizontal handwheels control the brakes, supplemented by foot pedals. Downward runs are controlled by the brake alone.

The ropes for both inclines can be seen emerging from the west side of the engine house, that for the eastern incline being redirected by a colliery winding wheel, 4.25m (14ft) in diameter, positioned beneath the track. The procedures for hauling sets of six wagons on the west incline and 12 on the east are quite different.

Considerable skill and judgement are required to process wagons at the summit, and these operations have changed little since the inclines were built. Empty wagons cresting the east incline pass over an artificial hump, or kip; this releases tension on the special slip coupling between the rope and the leading wagon, and the coupling drops down between the tracks. The wagons are then braked manually and brought to rest at chocks to await their descent to Black Fell.

Dramatic ascent

On the west incline, which is about 686m (750yds) long on a gradient varying between 1 in 18 and 1 in 37, the top of the hill is used as the kip. The operation for ascending wagons from the west is much more dramatic than the one for those climbing from the east. This is because the west rope, instead of simply dropping between the tracks, has to be dragged out of the way of the wagon wheels as soon as the coupling has been slipped. This is done by two men running alongside the leading wagon as the rake breasts the summit.

Using special hooks, they drag the heavy coupling device and attached rope out of the path of the rotating wheels. Any error of judgement could have serious consequences, so new operatives have to undergo careful training, though many of those giving demonstrations to visitors once earned their living from the skill.

That is part of the fascination of the Bowes Railway, for many of those who give their time to it were once involved with mining or colliery railways in the north east. Conversations with them can give a more vivid idea of how vital mining was to the region, and how far back its history goes, than any number of exhibition panels in a museum.

The horizontal winding wheel at the top of Springwell Bank, which dates from 1826.

The North Yorkshire Moors Railway

Set in the heart of the North York Moors National Park, the 29km (18 mile) line from the market town of Pickering to the village of Grosmont offers an irresistible combination of scenic splendour and steam power.

Described by Charles Dickens as 'a quaint old railway', the line owes its origins to George Stephenson, who designed and built a horse-drawn tramway from Whitby to Pickering, opened in 1836. The line left the valley of the River Esk at Grosmont, and followed its tributaries, the Murk Esk and Eller Beck, to beyond Goathland, but needed to rise 152.5m (500ft) in a distance of less than 6.5km (four miles). So, from the intermediate village of Beck Hole, a 457m (1500ft) rope-worked incline was used to get trains to and from Goathland.

Beyond Goathland Summit, at 162m (532ft) the highest point on the line, Stephenson utilized the natural gorge of Newton Dale – a glacial overflow channel from the Ice Age – to descend to Levisham and Pickering. From Pickering the line eventually continued, via Rillington Junction, to Malton and York.

As traffic increased and speed became more critical, the Beck Hole incline grew into an operational albatross and was replaced in 1865 by a new line or deviation, mainly at a gradient of 1 in 49, between Grosmont and Goathland. With the incline abandoned, part of the old route remained open as a goods-only branch line from Deviation Junction at Grosmont until closure in 1951.

The Whitby & Pickering Railway became part of the North Eastern Railway (NER) in 1854, which itself was absorbed into the London & North Eastern Railway (LNER) in 1923. In the 1948 nationalization, it became part of British Railways.

Never a heavily used line, except during the summer months, there was no real surprise when the Beeching axe fell on it in 1965. While the 9.5km (six mile) section between Grosmont and Whitby survived as part of the Esk Valley line linking Whitby with Middlesbrough, the route southwards to Rillington Junction was closed.

However, in 1967, the North Yorkshire Moors

▼ K1 2-6-0 No 62005 waits for passengers amid the wooded setting of Goathland station. It is one of 70 mixed-traffic locomotives designed by A.H. Peppercorn for the LNER and built in Glasgow in 1949–50. In 1984 it was given a temporary number – 62052 – prior to its withdrawal from service for a major overhaul.

North east veterans

With 22 steam and 15 diesel locomotives, the NYMR mounts one of the best rosters in the country. Not surprisingly, the original emphasis was on engines from the north east, which range from two eight-coupled NER locomotives, to an LNER Class J72 0-6-0T, No 69023, built under BR auspices in 1951.

There are two 10 coupled War Department locomotives – Nos 3672 and 90775, both of which were transported for use in Egypt. Other engines include No 60532, an LNER Class A2 Pacific *Blue Peter*, No 34101 *Hartland*, a Southern Railway West Country Class 4-6-2 and three Black Fives.

▲ Completed in 1918, the still impressively powerful eight-coupled NER T2 No 2238 hauls a train down grade through the lush valley of Newton Dale. The engine was withdrawn as BR No 63395 in 1967, but was saved from the scrapyard through a last-minute deal between BR and north-eastern steam enthusiasts.

Railway Preservation Society was formed and, with help from the North Riding County Council, it was able to purchase the 29km (18 miles) of track from Grosmont to Pickering. Trains began running on the line again in 1973, since when the railway has built up one of the best collections of steam locomotives in the country.

Along the line

There can be no better setting for the southern terminus of the North Yorkshire Moors Railway (NYMR) than its station at Pickering. Steam locomotives can regularly be seen within a few feet of the High Street, giving visitors an early glimpse of the pleasures to come.

Pickering is the administrative HQ of the line

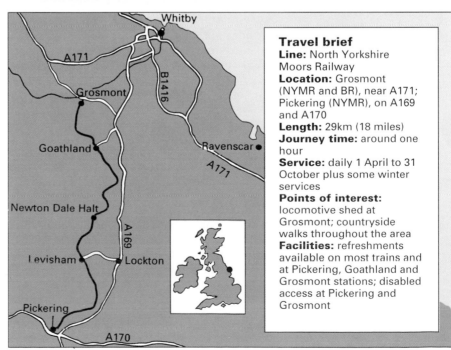

Travel brief
Line: North Yorkshire Moors Railway
Location: Grosmont (NYMR and BR), near A171; Pickering (NYMR), on A169 and A170
Length: 29km (18 miles)
Journey time: around one hour
Service: daily 1 April to 31 October plus some winter services
Points of interest: locomotive shed at Grosmont; countryside walks throughout the area
Facilities: refreshments available on most trains and at Pickering, Goathland and Grosmont stations; disabled access at Pickering and Grosmont

and the starting point for over half the journeys made. Visitors parking in the NYMR's own car park, reached via High Mill level crossing, pass the railway's carriage and wagon workshop on the left as they make their way to the station.

The main platform can take rakes of up to eight coaches and passengers can see the engine on their train prior to departure. When Pickering's starting signal shows green, the train edges forward, passing High Mill and the famous trout farm on the east side of the line; the fish are clearly visible.

The train slows for New Bridge crossing, where the signalbox on the left controls the Pickering colour light signalling. Here, the fireman collects the single-line token for Levisham and the locomotive begins to work harder. On the left, after the crossing, lies the railway's permanent way yard.

Travelling brooms

The train now enters Newton Dale, which extends for almost 19.25km (12 miles), as far as the summit of the line at Fen Bog. The driver slows for the sharp Kingthorpe curves and shortly after whistles for Farwath cottages. The train used to stop here to pick up a cargo of traditional besom brooms made by local residents to transport to Pickering market.

From Farwath, an almost three kilometre (two mile) straight leads to the first intermediate station and passing place at Levisham. Here the fully semaphore signalled station lies no less than

Crowning achievement

In 1965, Mr and Mrs F.F. Clough travelled on the last train from Grosmont to Pickering. The Beeching axe had just fallen and it seemed that the line had closed down for good. Eight years later, however, on Easter Sunday 1973, the Cloughs returned from North Wales to ride on the first public train over the newly restored tracks.

On 1 May that year, the railway was officially opened by the Duchess of Kent. After unveiling plaques at Whitby and Grosmont, she journeyed to Pickering on the train.

▲ Three locomotives owned by the North Eastern Locomotive Preservation Group prepare for the day's work at Grosmont depot. LNER K1 2-6-0 No 2005 takes water, while NER P3 0-6-0 No 2392 and T2 0-8-0 No 2238 raise steam.

▼ K1 No 62005 passes the magnificent slotted-arm bracket signal at Goathland station. The slotted arm, a distinctive feature of NER signalling, can also be seen at Levisham. These lower quadrant signals were generally superseded by upper quadrants.

2.4km (1½ miles) distant and 91.5m (300ft) lower than the village it purports to serve.

Apart from the station house, some cottages and one nearby house, there is no other sign of human habitation. Levisham is the starting point for some attractive forest walks and therefore a popular alighting point.

Rural tranquillity

If you decide to take one of the walks, it is worth waiting a while until the train has departed; as the exhausts fade on the wind and the ringing of bells in the signalbox ceases, the rural tranquillity resumes at this charming wayside station, only to be broken by another flurry of activity the next time a train approaches.

Beyond Levisham, the train soon gets well into its stride, attacking the ever-steepening gradients past Raindale on the left and the ruined Skelton Tower high up on the right. This might look like an ancient castle keep but is in fact a folly built by the vicar of Levisham in Victorian times.

The noise from the engine is very noticeable as it climbs the 1 in 49 gradient to the site of the former Newton Dale signalbox. The change in gradient here is very pronounced and the engine eases off past the isolated house at Kidstye before calling at Newton Dale Halt, 14.5km (nine miles) from Pickering.

With no public road access, the halt was opened in 1981 to allow passengers to make the most of the footpaths in and around the forests; for example, you can alight here and walk back along clearly waymarked trails to Levisham to catch a later train.

Even the forest tracks peter out as the train climbs further up Newton Dale, home to a rich variety of wildlife, including deer and hawks. Beyond Carter's House, a ruin on the left where the forestry plantations end, the valley begins to open out and the continuous climb from Pickering nears its end at Fen Bog.

Sheep's fleeces

Despite recent drainage works, the waterlogged ground is still very evident and Stephenson had a tough job to build across the bog a century and a half ago. He reputedly used timber, heather, brushwood and even sheep's fleeces to make a firm bed for his railway. After passing the summit, away to the right can be seen the Fylingdales nuclear early warning station pyramidal structure which replaced the three giant 'golf balls'.

With a warning blast on the whistle, the engine shuts off steam for the descent to Grosmont and the fireman takes a well-earned rest. The train crosses Lyke Wake Walk, the 67.5km (42 mile) trail across the moors between Osmotherley and Ravenscar.

The line now falls nearly 152.5m (500ft) in approximately 8.75km (5½ miles) to Grosmont. The scenery changes from open, windswept moorland to green meadows at Moorgates, where keen-eyed passengers may spot a stone arched bridge and embankments on the left. These are the earthworks of the original 1836 line from Grosmont via the Beck Hole incline, now a public footpath known as the Historical Railway Trail.

Before reaching Goathland the line crosses the Eller Beck three times. Goathland station, 22.5km (14 miles) from Pickering, is a cameo North Eastern Railway (NER) branch line station. It is the newest station on the line and features a small signalbox complete with fireplace, slotted-post signals, watercranes and attractive platform gardens. On the line's 150th anniversary in 1986, an authentic NER footbridge from Howdon, on the Tyne & Wear Metro, was installed.

Unlike Levisham, the station is immediately adjacent to the village it serves – home of the Goathland Hunt and the Plough Stotts folk dance group. Not far away is the impressive Mallyan Spout waterfall.

Once the up train has arrived, the Grosmont – or down – train can depart. When the driver has the single-line token, the signal is lowered to the clear position, the guard waves his green flag and the train embarks on the last leg of its journey.

▼ BR 4MT No 80135 has its smokebox cleared of ash beneath the Grosmont coaling plant, the first such facility to be constructed by a preserved railway. Built at Brighton in 1956, No 80135 worked commuter trains over the London, Tilbury & Southend lines and traffic over the Cambrian coast routes before being withdrawn in 1965. It was rescued from the scrapyard in 1972 and went into service on the NYMR in 1980.

▲ Surrounded by autumn colours at the approach to Newton Dale, LMS Class 5MT 4-6-0 No 44767 *George Stephenson* heads a train to Pickering. No 44767, built at Crewe in 1947, was unique among the 842 Stanier Class 5s in having Stephenson link motion valve gear, which many drivers found to be freer running than conventional gears.

Volcanic displays

This is perhaps the most spectacular section of the route. Immediately the train pulls away from the platform, the line starts to fall for 5km (three miles) at an unbroken gradient of 1 in 49 – one of the steepest in the country. While northbound trains coast down the hill, southbound trains have to work very hard and can give truly volcanic exhaust displays in the process.

The line crosses the Eller Beck three times in quick succession, then runs on a ledge at the side of the valley which widens to reveal, down to the left, the trackbed of the Beck Hole branch and, further on, Esk Valley cottages, without road access until 1951.

By now the train is slowing for Grosmont and whistling a warning of its approach. On the right can be seen the locomotive sheds, home of a fine collection of steam locomotives, with examples from all the Big Four companies, as well as BR standard and industrial engines.

The first building is the refurbished Deviation shed, built on the site of Deviation signalbox, which controlled the junction with the Beck Hole branch. This is the home to the locomotives of the North Eastern Locomotive Preservation Group. Next to this is the imposing mechanical coaling plant, the first purpose built one of its kind since BR steam days.

Beyond lies a recently excavated area that will

ultimately house the John Bellwood Centre, a museum and workshop complex. The Centre will complement the NYMR's repair and running sheds, which can be seen on the right just before the train plunges into the dark depths of the 109.75m (120yd) Grosmont tunnel. This parallels the smaller bore tunnel used by Stephenson's horse-drawn railway, now the footpath access to the railway's sheds.

As it emerges, the train crosses the Murk Esk for the second time, negotiates the level crossing and enters Grosmont, 29km (18 miles) from Pickering. In earlier days, the station had only three platforms but now there are four making it much more efficient and less crowded. There is also a magnificent signalbox with an impressive collection of instruments including a 52-lever frame from Horden, near Hartlepool.

Like Pickering and Goathland, Grosmont has a station shop and buffet, with a car park in the station yard. There is also a railway shop in the shed complex, which is reached from the station via a footpath that crosses a suspension bridge and passes through Stephenson's tunnel.

With the journey completed, the train engine will be uncoupled and may be taken to the shed for coal and water. A different engine will probably couple on to the front of the train for the journey back to Pickering – and that fearsome 1 in 49 climb out of Grosmont.

The Keighley & Worth Valley Railway

Climbing steeply from the industrial town of Keighley to the Pennine village of Oxenhope, the KWVR gives visitors a memorable impression of what country rail travel was like in the days of steam.

Short it may be, but the Keighley & Worth Valley Railway (KWVR) is one of Britain's most successful private railways, with over 5,000 people belonging to the preservation society and many of them actively involved in operating the line. Indeed, the KWVR is operated entirely by volunteers and is proud to have relied almost exclusively on this source of labour since the line reopened as a preservation society in 1968.

This pride is also evident in the beautifully tended stations and gardens, the spick-and-span carriages and shining locomotives – all in sharp contrast to the atmosphere of neglect which pervaded the line when it was finally discarded by British Railways in 1962.

Taking its name from the company which promoted the railway in the 1860s, the present-day KWVR has a well-developed sense of identity. It aims to give visitors a memorable impression of what country rail travel was like in the 1950s, while at the same time recapturing some of the flavour of the old Midland Railway (MR), which operated the line from its beginning.

For ease of access, visitors are advised to join the train at Keighley, which is also served by the mainline between Leeds and Settle. Keighley offers an excellent buffet housed in the type of kiosk which adorned station platforms in the steam age. Adding to the period feel is the wooden ramp which leads down to the imposing canopied platform.

Legendary turntable

Just beyond the end of the platform is a working turntable, used occasionally to turn the railway's smaller locomotives. This is from the windswept Hawes Junction (now named Garsdale), high up on the nearby Settle–Carlisle line. Legend has it that in 1900 a violent storm caused it to rotate out of control for many hours, before railway workers

◀ The 0-6-0WT *Bellerophon*, owned by the Vintage Carriages Trust, heads towards the southern terminal of Oxenhope with a train formed of stock from the Metropolitan and South Eastern & Chatham railways. The locomotive was built in 1874 by Haydock Foundry.

re-erected at Ingrow, where it blends in perfectly with its new surroundings.

Ingrow has acquired an atmosphere all of its own, doubtless enhanced by the oil lamps – other Worth Valley stations are lit by gas – which cast an eerie glow on gloomy winter afternoons. Ingrow is also home to the Vintage Carriages Trust Museum of rail travel. This houses an interesting collection of rolling stock, as well as several small steam engines. There is a display of small exhibits, a shop and a video viewing room.

New home for Bahamas

Emphasizing the renaissance of Ingrow is the new workshop and museum of the Bahamas Locomotive Society (BLS), currently nearing completion. This long-established society, formed originally to preserve LMS Jubilee class 4-6-0 No 45596 *Bahamas*, was forced to vacate its premises at Dinting, near Glossop, Derbyshire in 1989.

The following year, it approached the KWVR with a view to relocating at Ingrow. When it is finished, the BLS premises will form a welcome addition to a complementary range of attractions to be known collectively as Ingrow Railway Centre.

Rejoining the train, you pass through Ingrow Tunnel and encounter a particularly steep stretch of line before halting – if the request has been made to the guard – at the tiny station of Damems. With its crossing keeper's house, small signalbox and tiny station building, Damems forms a delightfully tranquil backwater, a place to savour the atmosphere of the country branch line.

Just south of Damems there is a loop that was installed by the KWVR in 1971 to help it cope with a sudden growth in traffic. The main reason for this increase was the success of the film *The*

arrived at the solution of shovelling ash into the turntable pit to bring the spinning locomotive to a halt.

The climb out of Keighley is steep and sharply curved, and taxes the locomotive, especially in wet weather, when skilful use of the sanders is required. Indeed, the inaugural train in 1867 slipped to a standstill on the 1 in 58 gradient here. Once into its stride, however, the train climbs steadily away from Keighley, giving a clear view over the town, with the hills enclosing the Worth Valley in the distance.

Replacement station

In a short time, the site of Keighley Great Northern Junction is passed. The dense undergrowth now makes it hard to believe that the Great Northern Railway line to Queensbury – closed in 1955 – once branched off here. Services to Oxenhope and Queensbury shared the same line up to this point, but now only the Worth Valley survives and the train forges on to its first stop, Ingrow West.

Formerly an unkempt halt, Ingrow West has undergone a remarkable transformation. The original station was heavily vandalized after the closure of the line and was demolished by the Society in the mid 1960s. However, such has been the success of the KWVR that, from the mid 1980s, Ingrow started to be developed as a park-and-ride centre aimed at reducing congestion elsewhere on the line. A replacement MR station was purchased from Foulridge in Lancashire and

◄ A Riddles class 4MT No 75078, formerly in service at KWVR, contrasts with the Edwardian trimmings of Oakworth station. A winner of the Best Preserved Station award, and the centrepiece of the film *The Railway Children*, Oakworth was once a busy centre for goods traffic, with general produce and animal feed coming in, and cattle and the products of the local woollen mills going out.

▼ KWVR's Stanier 8F 2-8-0 BR No 48431 simmers at Oakworth station during an annual Christmas service excursion. The engine first entered passenger service on the KWVR at the end of 1975 and will have its next major overhaul during 2001.

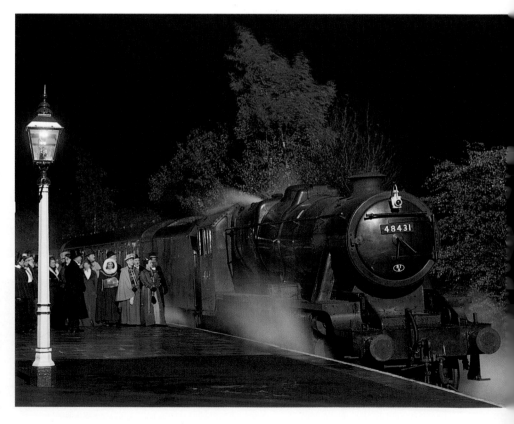

Railway Children, much of which was made on location in the Worth Valley. It certainly immortalized the next station on the line, Oakworth. Here, visitors can inspect the haunts of Mr Perks – the porter in the film – and, if lucky, catch a glimpse of the flag-waving guard, Mr Mitchell, the former chairman of the preservation society, who played the part of the guard.

Edwardian splendour

A conscious effort has been made to restore Oakworth to its Edwardian splendour. Both the station building and platform are lit by gas, and lanterns adorn the prize-winning goods shed. Next to the shed, the weighbridge, hut, hand-operated crane and goods yard are still in existence. Competing for attention is an impressive array of enamel signs on the platform fencing, as well as an unusual piece of platform furniture in the shape of a coffin trolley.

Shortly after leaving Oakworth, the train passes over the three-arch Mytholmes Viaduct before plunging into a short tunnel. This considerable structure forms part of a new alignment of the branch, dating from 1892, replacing a wooden trestle bridge and sharply curved section of track.

The railway's headquarters at Haworth are now quickly reached. The station here is the busiest on the line, as tourists flock all year round to this famous moorland village which was once home to the Brontë sisters. Haworth is the ideal place to buy a souvenir of a visit to the Worth Valley. The station shop here is the largest on the line.

The former goods warehouse at Haworth is used for maintenance of the railway's locomotives. A large locomotive shed is also being built in the adjoining yard as funds permit. The best times to visit Haworth yard are early morning and early evening, when locomotives are being prepared for service or disposed after a hard day's work. Time-honoured tasks such as oiling round

▲ A former visitor King Arthur, No 777 *Sir Lamiel*, runs into the passing loop at Damems. The controlling signalbox comes from Frizinghall near Bradford and was transported whole to its present location. When the box is open, tokens are exchanged between the train crew and the signalman.

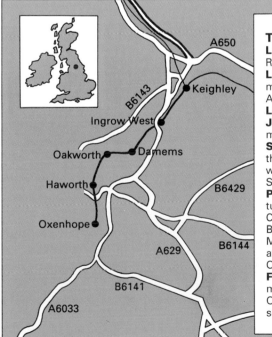

Travel brief
Line: Keighley & Worth Valley Railway
Location: Keighley (KWVR, mainline and MetroTrain), on A650; Oxenhope, near A6033
Length: 7.75km (4¾ miles)
Journey time: round trip 50 minutes
Service: weekends throughout the year and daily from third week in June to first week in September
Points of interest: historic turntable at Keighley; Vintage Carriages Trust Museum and Bahamas Locomotive Society Museum (under construction) at Ingrow; Railway Museum at Oxenhope
Facilities: refreshments on most trains and at Keighley and Oxenhope; some dining car services; shop at Haworth

or raking out ashpans can be observed, all accompanied by that special aroma peculiar to steam locomotives. There is a particularly rich variety of motive power on the KWVR, ranging from humble tank engines to heavy freight and express passenger locomotives.

Varied steam stable

Currently, there are some 30 steam engines based on the line and, of these, up to 10 are maintained in working order at any one time. Given the line's early history, it is appropriate that locomotives with Midland Railway associations should have played an important role in its revival. A 4F 0-6-0, No 43924, the first engine to be purchased from the celebrated Barry scrapyard in South Wales and restored to traffic, was a stalwart performer in the 1970s and 1980s. It is currently being overhauled at the Haworth workshop.

Also showing clear MR influence is No 47279, an LMS Jinty 0-6-0T dating from 1924. This engine, currently being restored, will be used regularly on the lighter trains. It will share these duties with No 85, a 0-6-2T tank locomotive built for the Taff Vale Railway in 1899. Still in the realm of tank engines, the Worth Valley boasts some vintage gems in the shape of *Sir Berkely* and *Bellerophon*, dating from 1891 and 1874 respectively. These industrial engines may be seen operating on special occasions.

The heavyweight

On gala weekends, and in the summer, train sizes increase accordingly and more powerful locomotives are used. At present, such services are hauled by the heavy freight engine No 48431, a 2-8-0 built at Swindon in 1944. This locomotive is a representative of the celebrated 8F class designed for the LMS by Sir William Stanier. This engine was active until the end of steam on BR in 1968.

In the final stages of a long restoration period is another 2-8-0, No 1931, an ex War Department locomotive built in England in 1945 and repatriated from Sweden in 1973. This unique survivor of almost a thousand locomotives of its class will

▲ Smoke billows across the snow-covered landscape as 0-6-0 Pannier tank No 5775 heads out of Haworth with a Santa Special bound for Oxenhope. Built for the GWR in 1929, No 5775 took on a new role almost half a century later, featuring in the film *The Railway Children*.

◀ No 80002 BR Standard Class 4 first hauled passenger traffic in the early 1970s, performing regularly between 1971 and 1973. It has since been extensively restored and is a regular sight on the Keighley and Worth Valley Railway.

soon be available for passenger service. The historical significance of this Austerity type locomotive, as a precursor of the later locomotives built by BR, can be especially appreciated in comparison with the attractive collection of BR Standard engines at Haworth. This includes 4-6-0 No 75078, 2-6-0 No 78022 and 2-6-4T No 80002, all of which were built in the 1950s.

On to Oxenhope

From Haworth the train steams on to Oxenhope, amid increasingly picturesque moorland scenery and with the waters of Bridgehouse Beck as a frequent companion. This is excellent walking country, with numerous footpaths offering clear views of the trains and plenty of scope for picnics. Overlooking the line just before Oxenhope is Three Chimneys, the house used for outdoor scenes in *The Railway Children*.

Strenuous efforts have been made in recent years to improve Oxenhope station and its environment, and it now bears comparison with the finest on the line. Certainly, its gardens are outstanding and a visit to the landscaped picnic area while the locomotive is taking water or running round its train is recommended, as is a visit to the museum. This houses numerous locomotives not currently in use, as well as the railway's elegant diner train, the White Rose Pullman, which runs on a number of occasions throughout the year.

Included in this rake is No 84 *Mary*, dating from 1930, perhaps the best surviving example in

▶ A Standard class 4MT, No 75078, simmers gently on the track at Keighley station, while members of the cast of the film *Yanks*, a wartime drama set in the North of England, play out a civic welcoming ceremony on the wrought-iron footbridge between platforms 3 and 4.

◀ Two stars of the big screen – No 5775 appeared in *The Railway Children* and No 5820 in *Yanks* – double-head a train up the sharp gradient out of Keighley. Built in 1945 for the US Army, No 5820 – nicknamed Big Jim – worked on Polish State Railways before arriving on the KWVR in 1977.

Britain of a third-class Pullman car. These, and the railway's other carriages, are cared for by the carriage and wagon department, also based at Oxenhope.

The Lancashire & Yorkshire Preservation Society own the diminutive Pug shunting engine No 51218 which is usually found in Haworth yard.

All these contribute to a remarkable collection of larger locomotives and coaches which present a fascinating recreation of Edwardian railway travel on the Worth Valley line.

The National Railway Museum

The National Railway Museum, on a 16 acre site near York station, is the largest museum of its kind in the world. Its exhibits span almost two centuries and range from a full-sized working replica of Stephenson's *Rocket* to a section of the Channel Tunnel.

'It is nothing short of a national disgrace,' an indignant reader wrote to the *Railway Magazine* in 1917, 'that no All-British Railway Museum exists for preserving in chronological sequence the inception and progress of our national railway. It is high time that this was remedied and the Government should provide the necessary funds.'

The Government, however, had other priorities at that time – it was still desperately searching for a way to beat the Kaiser – and almost 60 years were to elapse before the opening of the National Railway Museum (NRM) in York in 1975. In that year, two separate collections – one from the Museum of British Transport in Clapham,

London, and the other from the London & North Eastern Railway (LNER) Museum in York – were combined under one roof.

The new museum was housed in the 19th century York engine shed, later to become the Great Hall. However, despite extensive rebuilding work, in 1988 it was discovered that the roof was structurally unsound. A £6 million renovation scheme incorporated the repair work, and the new-look National Railway Museum was completed in April 1992.

It is now the largest railway museum in the world. In July 1999, a new £4 million wing, The Works, opened offering visitors more of Britain's railway heritage than ever before.

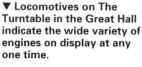

▼ Locomotives on The Turntable in the Great Hall indicate the wide variety of engines on display at any one time.

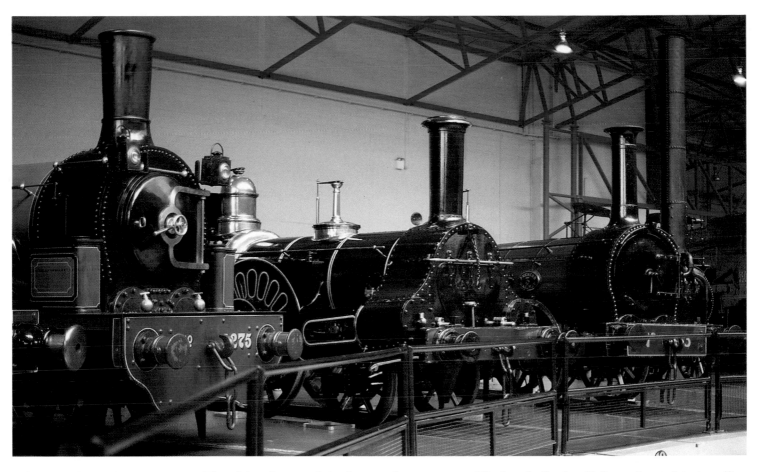

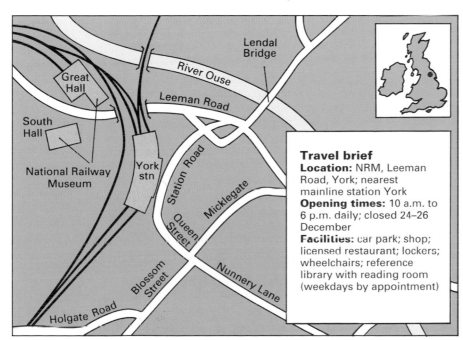

▲ **Standing side by side are North Eastern Railway 0-6-0 No 1275 of 1874; London & North Western Railway 2-2-2 No 1868 *Columbine* of 1845; and Furness Railway 0-4-0 No 3 of 1846, nicknamed *Coppernob*. *Columbine* is now to be seen at the Science Museum in London.**

The visitors' car park is close to the entrance, which leads directly into the Great Hall. If you want to come by train, York station is 540 metres (600yds) from the main entrance. The entrance is a steel and glass building that gives access both to Station Hall and, via a subway under the busy Leeman Road, to the Great Hall.

Station Hall, once the North Eastern Railway's goods depot in the city, was originally used by the NRM for storage purposes. However, during the redevelopment of the Great Hall, it served as an exhibition centre, and this function continues.

Displays in Station Hall are devoted to travelling by train, a theme that applies to passengers and freight. There is a rich variety of rolling stock – freight, express, suburban and royal – and some of them are displayed with appropriate locomotives.

Freight lines during the steam age provided extensive cartage services, so alongside the trains, horse-drawn and motor vehicles are displayed. These are a reminder that door-to-door transit involved railway-operated road services.

Passenger trains

Passenger travel did not bring in as much money as freight. However, rail companies competed for it by making their services more attractive.

Towards the end of the 19th century, the Midland Railway company abolished second class, upgrading its third-class facilities and providing them on all trains. The reforms meant a drastic break with tradition, but they soon achieved their aim of attracting more passengers, many of whom travelled in the new and better carriages exemplified by No 901, an 1885 MR six-wheeled compartment carriage.

Soft upholstery was provided in both first- and third-class compartments, the only real difference between them being the latter's lack of arm rests and slightly smaller dimensions.

The Midland's 1914 third-class dining car, superbly restored and complete with kitchen facilities, is a good example of the quality they offered. It has wide, comfortable seats, tables with a mahogany wood veneer and silver-plated holders for the wine bottles. But for sheer luxury, wealthy passengers chose to travel by Pullman.

Travel brief
Location: NRM, Leeman Road, York; nearest mainline station York
Opening times: 10 a.m. to 6 p.m. daily; closed 24–26 December
Facilities: car park; shop; licensed restaurant; lockers; wheelchairs; reference library with reading room (weekdays by appointment)

▲ On display in the Great Hall is the London & North Eastern Railway 4-6-2 No 4468 *Mallard*. This was just one of the Class A4 Pacifics designed by Sir Nigel Gresley, but it achieved lasting fame on 3 July 1938 by breaking the world rail speed record, touching 202km/h (126mph), which no steam locomotive is likely to beat.

◄ Located in the South Hall, the Treasure Trove features items from the NRM's vast collection of railway memorabilia. Items include luggage labels, presentation watches, china and models.

Travelling in style

Pullmans were introduced into Britain from America in the 1870s. The 1913 first-class Pullman, *Topaz*, that originally ran on the South Eastern & Chatham Railway, epitomizes the grand epoch of railway travel. The car has individual velvet armchairs in which to relax, polished brass tablelamps and inlaid marquetry panels. There are also bells to summon the waiter.

One way of travelling to Paris in style was on the Orient Express. The carriages were supplied by Compagnie Internationale des Wagons-Lits, the company that also produced carriages for the night ferry service to France, started in 1936. Wagons-Lits No 3792, a sleeping car from this service, is in the Museum in the famous blue and gold livery. The builders made it entirely of metal, rather than the traditional wood veneer of other Wagon-Lits cars, to comply with shipboard fire regulations.

A few of the very wealthy could afford their own train, for example the Duke of Sutherland. He had his own private station near his home in Scotland. The Duke's carriage is on display at the Museum.

Palaces on wheels

One of the NRM's most popular attractions is its collection of royal rolling stock, which ranges from Queen Adelaide's coach of 1840 to a 1941

LMS saloon built for HM Queen Elizabeth, the Queen Mother, and later used by HM Queen Elizabeth II until her Silver Jubilee year in 1977.

Queen Victoria's favourite carriage comprised a silk-clad drawing room and a damask-lined bedroom, with retiring rooms for ladies-in-waiting. Her son Edward VII called it a 'stuffy old tub' and was delighted when the London & North Western presented him with a Royal Train made up of two saloons and a dining car. White enamel decorated the walls and the cars boasted all electric mod cons. Later George V had silver-plated baths installed. The dining car continued to be used on royal journeys until 1956.

The new coaches built for George VI in 1941 were comfortable but far less grand. Because it was during the war, the train had to be fitted with protective armour-plating. The most recent royal coaches in the Museum were last used by Queen Elizabeth II.

Railway giants

The theme of the Great Hall is the technology of railways, and the displays reflect not only the past, but also the present and the future. Locomotive enthusiasts will be impressed by a line-up spanning a period of 150 years, with steam, diesel and electric traction all represented.

If you are interested in the internal workings of a steam engine, look out for a replica of *Rocket*. The original was built in 1829 and this replica built in 1935, has been sectioned to show how the

original was constructed. Also sectioned is No 35029 *Ellerman Lines*, a Southern Railway 4-6-2 of 1949 vintage. An electrically powered drive rig enables its motion and driving wheels to be turned.

Of special interest to steam enthusiasts is the London & North Eastern Railway 4-6-2 *Mallard*. It is paired with the dynamometer car in memory of the famous run of 1938, when the blue-painted Pacific became the world's fastest steam locomotive at 202km/h (126mph).

For sheer size, the prize must go to the 192 tonne (ton) 4-8-4 built by the Vulcan Foundry in Newton-le-Willows in Lancashire in 1935. It was one of 24 locomotives supplied to the Chinese National Railways.

From 1959, steam trains started to be replaced by the light but powerful Deltic two-stroke diesel engine. Two of these now pull the Orient Express. The engine responsible for their demise was the High Speed Train (HST), the prototype of which, introduced in 1972, can be seen in The Warehouse.

The Royal Mail

Mail was transported by train from 1830, and by 1838, it was actually being sorted on board in trains known as travelling post offices. But harsh conditions meant that workers on the TPOs often fell ill. On show is the 1883 West Coast Joint Stock TPO, one of the coaches built to improve working conditions by reducing vibration, and introducing seats for sorters and better ventilation.

▶ This superbly restored Midland Railway third-class dining car, with kitchen facilities and passenger accommodation, dates from 1914. A few years earlier, the Midland had shocked the other railway companies by abolishing second class on its trains and upgrading the third-class facilities.

Today the Royal Mail has its own electric trains to transport mail round the country – one of their cabs is on display at the Museum. Over 20 TPOs still operate to facilitate the first-class postal service that we have come to expect.

The Works

In July 1999, the NRM opened a new wing called The Works. This consists of three galleries with unique displays and tributes to those who made the railway a reality.

From the balcony of The Workshop gallery, you can watch engineers repairing and restoring the Museum's rolling stock collections. Members of staff are on hand in the gallery to answer any specific questions about the work in progress. You can also see a film of a locomotive being built in the 1930s.

The next gallery, The Working Railway, shows many aspects of railway control, from a policeman using hand signals to alert a driver to modern sophisticated computer communications. There is a live link to the computerized signalbox that controls all trains through York. Visitors can step outside on to the trackside balcony to watch the East Coast Mainline trains pass by.

The third gallery, called The Warehouse, has a collection of over 6,000 items of railway memorabilia, including gold and silver travel passes, nameplates and gallantry medals awarded to railway employees. It houses the world's largest collection of headboards and some wonderfully quirky railway signs. Also on display is a marvellous collection of model trains, all handcrafted by one man, James Peel Richards, who made it his life's work to build every type of stock from the London & North Western Railway 1921 range.

The future looks interesting for the NRM with plans to expand the whole site so that the latest developments in railways can be shown as they take place.

▼ The Working Railway gallery, part of the NRM's new wing, is devoted to the control and safe operation of the railway. There are many interactive displays but visitors can also step out on to a balcony to watch the East Coast Mainline trains go by.

SCOTLAND

The Strathspey Railway

Situated in the heart of the Scottish Highlands, the Strathspey Railway once specialized in timber, livestock and whisky. Then came the Victorian tourist boom, only to be followed by years of steady decline. Now the line is flourishing once again.

The Strathspey Railway (SR) runs for 8.75km (5½ miles) from Aviemore to Boat of Garten in the Scottish Highlands. It passes through a region of outstanding natural beauty which has become one of Scotland's major tourist centres, attracting nearly two million visitors a year.

Aviemore itself is dominated by the slopes of Craigellachie. The lofty Monadhliath mountains lie to the west and the majestic Cairngorms to the east, beyond the River Spey. The view across the swift-flowing river and wide, sweeping valley is imposing. In summer and early autumn, the area is vivid with purple heather and golden bracken. At the foot of the Cairngorms can be seen stands of pine, a remnant of the ancient Caledonian Forest that once covered much of the Central Highlands.

It is a landscape that has changed very little in the 130 years since the railways first arrived here.

The Aviemore–Boat of Garten–Forres line was opened in 1863 as part of the Inverness & Perth Junction Railway, later to become part of the Highland Railway (HR).

At first, the line carried mainly livestock and timber, with a healthy whisky traffic off the Speyside branch of the Great North of Scotland Railway (GNSR), which joined the SR at Boat of Garten. Then the Victorians realized the tourist potential of the area and trains crammed with sightseers began to come to the area.

▼ Birmingham Railway Carriage & Wagon Co. Class 27 Bo-Bo D5394 pulls out of Boat of Garten with the luxury Royal Scotsman train, which had been stabled overnight at the station. Restoration work on the diesel was carried out in Glasgow following its withdrawal from BR service in 1987.

◄Former Caledonian Railway 0-6-0 828, built at St Rollox works, Glasgow in 1899, hauls the 12.40 train from Boat of Garten to Aviemore.

is No 828, a Caledonian Railway 0-6-0 tender engine built in 1898 at St Rollox works in Glasgow. Ex BR engine No 46512 will soon be appearing on the line after undergoing a long restoration. Awaiting an expensive overhaul is a Black Five – the London Midland & Scottish Railway (LMS) Class 5 4-6-0 No 5025. Built in 1934, this locomotive worked on the Highland mainlines.

On occasion, No 5025 has been sent back to its old stamping ground, travelling to both Perth and Inverness.

Tank engine line-up

There are a number of tank engines at the SR, including No 60, an Austerity 0-6-0 built in 1948, and No 2 *Balmenach*, a little 0-4-0 built by Barclays of Kilmarnock in 1936 and which, appropriately, used to shunt distillery traffic on the Speyside branch.

The SR has several diesels used for shunting and works trains, the largest of which is No D5394, a BR Class 27 dating from 1962.

Rolling stock consists primarily of British Railways Mark 1 standard coaches of the 1950s and early '60s. These form the backbone of passenger services and include a restaurant car once used on the famous *Flying Scotsman*. During the 1990s a number of Mark 2 coaches from the 1960s and '70s were also purchased.

Currently, the journey is confined to the Aviemore–Boat of Garten stretch but this is set to change very soon. Track has been relaid between Boat of Garten and Broomhill adding a further 6.5km (four miles) to the journey, making the entire trip a total of 15.25km (9½ miles).

However, in later years, the increasing threat from the motor vehicle, changing holiday habits and declining freight traffic all contributed to the demise of the SR. Passenger services were withdrawn in 1965 and the line running north of Boat of Garten to Forres via Grantown-on-Spey closed down completely.

The Speyside line had a brief reprieve, but that, too, closed to freight traffic in November 1968. All of the track north of Boat of Garten was lifted in 1969.

By then, however, the Highlands and Islands Development Board and the Scottish Railway Preservation Society (SRPS) were already embarked on a scheme to preserve the line from Aviemore to Boat of Garten. Although the SRPS later withdrew from the scheme, some of its members decided to press ahead on their own, with the result that the Strathspey Railway Company was born.

Steam service resumed

Work on the line began in spring 1972 and, because the basic railway infrastructure was in good condition, it was possible to run the first steam train of the preservation era two years later. Regular passenger services resumed in 1978.

Since then, the SR has made impressive progress, expanding its locomotive fleet and rolling stock, refurbishing buildings and repairing or replacing equipment.

Motive power is varied. The oldest locomotive

▼ Hunslet 0-6-0ST No 48, was built in 1943, and came from Backworth Colliery, close to George Stephenson's home at Killingworth in present day Tyne & Wear. Although not in use, the engine is still on show.

Station changes

At one time, the SR shared Aviemore station with British Rail, whose mainline from London to Inverness ran through it. With the enlargement of the Aviemore Centre complex of restaurants, hotels and sporting facilities, and the subsequent increase in tourist traffic on the BR line, facilities at Aviemore became overcrowded. The SR had to build its own station, Speyside, which fortunately for its passengers was only 457m (500yds) away. Rolling stock was transferred between stations through the sidings. The preservation of the unique character of the line was essential, thus the buildings and equipment used were, where possible, HR and GNSR originated.

Nowadays the station at Speyside is closed and serves as a storage depot. In 1998, a multi-million pound restoration of Aviemore station enabled the SR to run its trains once again from this point.

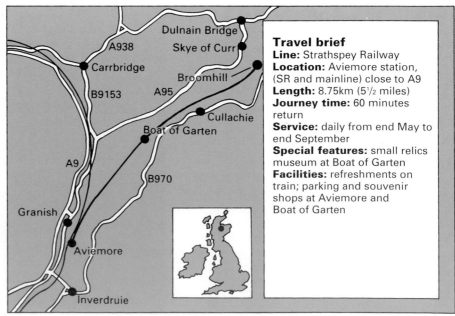

Travel brief
Line: Strathspey Railway
Location: Aviemore station, (SR and mainline) close to A9
Length: 8.75km (5½ miles)
Journey time: 60 minutes return
Service: daily from end May to end September
Special features: small relics museum at Boat of Garten
Facilities: refreshments on train; parking and souvenir shops at Aviemore and Boat of Garten

New lease of life

As the train passes by the old Speyside station, on the right is the four-road locomotive shed. This stone structure was completed in 1898. It survived closure in 1965 by being leased to local firms and at present, it is being used once again as it was originally intended.

You will also see the main track to Inverness on your left. Between the two railways stands Spey Lodge, a former railwaymen's holiday home which is now used to provide accommodation for volunteers working on the Strathspey.

After a short distance, the train slows as it approaches a modern automatic crossing installed in 1980 to accommodate the road to Dalfaber. This was once an isolated farm, but now it is a holiday village following the burgeoning of the Aviemore tourist industry.

Out in the country, keen-eyed passengers may catch glimpses of the local wildlife, including deer, rabbits, red squirrels and tortoiseshell butterflies.

The halfway point of the journey is marked by the summit of the line. The next feature is the

◄The SR's connection with the mainline at Aviemore means that visiting locomotives and trains can operate on its tracks. In 1986, the Scottish Railway Preservation Society's North British Railway 0-6-0 No 673 *Maude* ran over the BR line. *Maude* is based at the Bo'ness & Kinneil Railway.

▼ No 5025, dating from 1934, was one of the first batch of the famous Black Fives, and operated out of Perth on the Highland mainline. On withdrawal from service with BR in August 1968, it was purchased privately for use in Scotland. Currently, No 5205 is awaiting overhauled.

Kinchurdy bridge, which crosses over the road to the farm of the same name. The line, which had risen gently, begins to fall equally gently on the route to Boat of Garten. In fact, the SR is 243.75m (800ft) above sea level and four of the five highest mountains in Britain are within 16km (10 miles).

From Kinchurdy the train swings west through an area of woodland. Silver birches abound, but do not preclude superb views of the Cairngorms away to the right. Soon the train pulls into Boat of Garten. The spaciousness of the station is a reflection of its days as a junction for the Speyside branch of the GNSR.

▲ During 1985, former distillery shunter No 1 *Dailuane* stands painted in fresh undercoat in the shed yard at Aviemore, Speyside, while Hunslet 0-6-0ST No 60 moves off to join its train standing on the island platform. *Dailuane* is now at Aberfeldy distillery.

▲ No 60 stands beside the south cabin at Boat of Garten. Built in 1922, the cabin is of the type used by the Highland Railway during its final years.

Highland Railway heritage

At Boat of Garten, all the original main station buildings and the stationmaster's house, erected in the 1860s, were destroyed in a fire, and the present structures date from 1904. However, the two signalboxes have survived and one of them is of typical HR all-wood design. The original footbridge was removed in the 1960s, but has been replaced by a splendid HR lattice footbridge from Dalnaspidal.

Unfortunately, the GNSR carriage shed and locomotive depot have long since vanished. So, too, has the goods yard, though the SR has relaid some track for storing rolling stock.

Boat of Garten takes its name from the chain-operated ferry across the Spey, which was replaced by a bridge in 1899, but it owes its existence to the coming of the railway. Without that it would probably consist of no more than a few scattered dwellings. Nowadays, it is a village which is growing in size.

No one visiting Boat of Garten should miss the opportunity of a trip to Loch Garten, the home of the osprey. After an absence from Scotland of half a century, a pair of these fish-eating birds of prey

nested close to the Loch in the 1950s and ospreys have returned regularly from their winter quarters in Africa since then. The Royal Society for the Protection of Birds has set up a public observation hide at Loch Garten. This is about five kilometres (three miles) away from Boat of Garten.

Next stop for the SR

As for the Strathspey Railway, the near future promises some exciting developments. The Highland Regional Council has reinstated the bridge over the road at the north end of Boat of Garten station, which was removed in 1974 for road widening. This facilitated the relaying of the 7.25km (4½ miles) of track to Broomhill which will serve as the new terminus. This stretch of line is due to open as soon as the work is completed to bring it up to passenger-carrying standard.

Grantown-on-Spey is the next stop for the SR and it is hoped that in the future the railway line will extend as far as this destination.

The Bo'ness & Kinneil Railway

Steaming along the southern shore of the Firth of Forth from the Victorian station of Bo'ness to Birkhill, visitors could be forgiven for thinking that nothing has changed here over the years. In fact, it is not so long ago that the area was a wasteland.

Standing on the footbridge at the western end of Bo'ness station, it is difficult to believe that everything around you has been created since members of the Scottish Railway Preservation Society (SRPS) began work here in May 1979. They had not so much as the remains of a platform, the foundations of a signalbox or even trackbed on which to base the new station of Bo'ness.

The original terminus, which lost its passenger service in 1956, was three-quarters of a kilometre (half mile) to the west, and the nearly 18 kilometres (11 miles) of sidings that once served the harbour along the foreshore of the upper Firth of Forth had long since been lifted. Today, there is little to indicate that Bo'ness station is not a well-restored station like those on any other preserved railway, a measure of the SRPS's achievement.

The remarkable transformation came about through the determination of the local government bodies to find a new use for the land around what was once Scotland's second largest port. Industrial and residential developments were ruled out by earlier mining activity, so a recreational use looked the most promising alternative.

The SRPS had been searching for a suitable railway line on which to demonstrate the huge collection of locomotives and rolling stock that it had been amassing at a depot in nearby Falkirk since 1964. The two objectives came together and the Bo'ness & Kinneil Railway (BKR) was born.

▼ The oldest operational engine on the BKR, North British Railway 0-6-0 No 673 *Maude* (BR No 65243), emerges from one of the tunnels outside Edinburgh Waverley with a Santa Special on a tour of the suburban circle in 1986. The excursions operated by the Scottish Railway Preservation Society over this route proved extremely popular, and raised vital funds for the BKR.

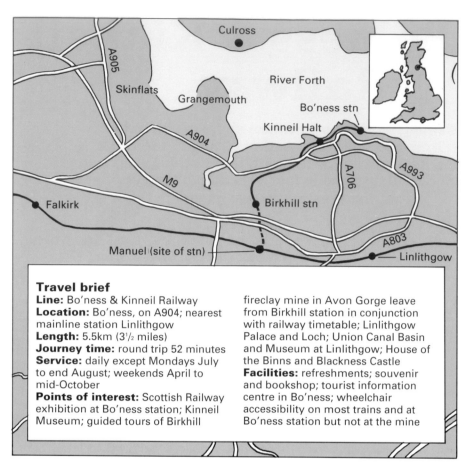

Culross
River Forth
Bo'ness stn
Kinneil Halt
Skinflats
Grangemouth
A905
A904
M9
A706
A993
Falkirk
Birkhill stn
Manuel (site of stn)
A803
Linlithgow

Travel brief
Line: Bo'ness & Kinneil Railway
Location: Bo'ness, on A904; nearest mainline station Linlithgow
Length: 5.5km (3½ miles)
Journey time: round trip 52 minutes
Service: daily except Mondays July to end August; weekends April to mid-October
Points of interest: Scottish Railway exhibition at Bo'ness station; Kinneil Museum; guided tours of Birkhill

fireclay mine in Avon Gorge leave from Birkhill station in conjunction with railway timetable; Linlithgow Palace and Loch; Union Canal Basin and Museum at Linlithgow; House of the Binns and Blackness Castle
Facilities: refreshments; souvenir and bookshop; tourist information centre in Bo'ness; wheelchair accessibility on most trains and at Bo'ness station but not at the mine

Museum venture
In 1996, a three-road building was opened on the north side of the site as the Scottish Railway exhibition. This displays a wide variety of vehicles under cover and is open when the railway is operating. The railway became a registered museum in 1999.

It must have seemed a daunting task when the first volunteers moved on site; the only hint of the former railway was a grassy embankment that led to where one of the coal hoists used to tip wagons over the holds of colliers berthed in the harbour. Everything had to be brought in, including the ballast. Gradually, track was laid and suitable buildings were found that could be dismantled and re-erected on the railway.

The intention has been to recreate an authentic

atmosphere, where possible in the style of the North British Railway (NBR), since it was that pre-grouping company which owned the 7.25km (4½ mile branch from the junction with the Edinburgh–Glasgow line at Manuel.

The building that dominates Bo'ness station is the cast- and wrought-iron train shed built for Haymarket station in 1842, then the terminus in the Scottish capital of the Edinburgh & Glasgow Railway before it reached Waverley station. The ornate columns and spans are the oldest surviving examples of early train-shed design.

Tickets for the 5.5km (3½ mile) journey to the present terminus at Birkhill are bought in the 1880s station building that once served Wormit at the south end of the Tay Bridge. Before you board the train standing under the train shed, it is worth spending an hour looking around the station and the exhibition building.

Over the footbridge

The visitor trail takes you over the former Highland Railway lattice footbridge to a path that leads to the main exhibition hall, opened in 1996. The SRPS has a magnificent collection of locomotives and rolling stock, some of which can be seen here. Most of the locomotives and rolling stock worked on Scottish railways, and all five of the great pre-grouping Scottish railway companies are represented.

Probably the most illustrious carriage in the collection is the elegant Great North of Scotland Railway bogie saloon No 1, built in 1897 at the company's works at Kittybrewster in Aberdeen. With two saloons, kitchen, lavatory and servants' compartment, it was sufficiently luxurious to be part of King Edward VII's royal train.

However, most of the coaches to be seen here are of humbler origin, illustrating the spartan accommodation that was on offer to third-class passengers. The exhibition is the first phase of an

▶ No 673 *Maude* leaves Bo'ness station with a demonstration goods train. The Airdrie headboard on the smokebox recalls the days when North British Railway locomotives regularly carried such boards to inform passengers of the train's destination.

Mainline excursions

The SRPS is unique in maintaining a rake of carriages passed for use on Railtrack metals. Thirteen Mark Is are in mainline order, although only 11 are registered in any year, made up of three first-class coaches, one restaurant car, one buffet, two brakes and four standard class TSOs.

Since the 1960s, a programme of excursions has been operated over scenic lines in Scotland, and to such centres as York and Chester. Diesel traction is normally used, but steam locomotives are allowed over certain routes. This operation has proved an invaluable source of income to fund restoration work on the BKR.

▼ In this view of Bo'ness station from the footbridge, a North Eastern Railway J72 0-6-0T, No 69023, at the time on loan from the North Yorkshire Moors Railway, is seen leaving with a train for Birkhill.

ambitious scheme to create a Scottish National Railway Museum.

The bothy just beyond the signalbox, typical of the small buildings found at the entrance to goods yards, came from Dunfermline, but the huge goods shed was built from scratch, though in keeping with NBR style.

Some of the SRPS's collection of industrial shunting locomotives may be seen, reminding visitors of the time when the railway formed the lifeblood of industry. Among them can be found a rare example of a tank engine equipped with the obligatory skirts for running along a public road, providing road users with some protection from the wheels and motion: *City of Aberdeen* once shuttled wagons between the mainline and sidings at the city's gasworks.

In recent years, the SRPS and associated groups have added a number of former mainline diesel electric locomotives of classes 08, 14, 20, 25, 26, 27 and 47. Most are in running order and the last train of each operating day is usually hauled by one of the diesel fleet. Work is also taking place, assisted by grant funding from the Heritage Lottery Fund, to restore a Swindon DMU set. Standard 2-6-4T No 80105 was rescued from Barry scrapyard and returned to steam in 1999; London Midland & Scottish Class 5 4-6-0 No 44871 was one of the two engines to haul the last steam train on British Railways, in 1968; and London & North Eastern Railway D49 4-4-0 No 246 *Morayshire* is the sole survivor of a class of 76 locomotives, many of which spent all their working lives on passenger traffic in Scotland.

But pride of place must go to the two mainline veterans – Caledonian Railway 0-4-4T No 419,

built at St Rollox works in Glasgow in 1907, and the SRPS's oldest mainline engine, NBR No 673 *Maude*, one of hundreds of humble 0-6-0s that formed the backbone of the Scottish goods fleet.

Rather improbably named after a World War I general, *Maude* was built in 1891, but is still a regular performer on the BKR and could be the motive power for your train.

Also beside the footbridge is the former Caledonian Railway signalbox from Garnqueen South Junction, near Coatbridge. The box has been restored to full operation and controls a fine array of former North British Railway lower quadrant signals. All the hard work of the volunteers of the S & T Department was rewarded when in 1998 they received the prestigious Westinghouse Signalling Award for the best restoration project that year in the UK. The plaque is proudly displayed in the entrance to the station buffet.

Source of prosperity

Shortly after the train leaves the station, you come to the dock upon which Bo'ness depended for its prosperity. Coal was sent out – 756,000 tonnes (tons) of it in 1900 – and iron ore and timber brought in. On the left, by the approach road to the station, are former offices of the Bo'ness Iron Company.

For the first five minutes the train runs between the shore and the tiered rows of solid stone buildings that line the hillside on which much of Bo'ness stands. As the town is left behind and the belts of young trees thicken, the train slows for Kinneil Halt, which was the terminus of the line between 1986 and 1989. It is now sometimes used by birdwatchers visiting a nearby sanctuary.

For the footplate crew, this is where the hard work begins. Leaving the halt, locomotives have a straight run to the point at which the line joins the route of the original branch to Bo'ness. This is near the bridge that carries the A904 over the railway. The noise from the engine's exhaust testifies to the steepening climb as the line turns inland and runs on to an embankment at a gradient of 1 in 95. Grades as steep as 1 in 60 continue for most of the journey to Birkhill and tax the skill of the driver when the rails are greasy, which is often the case in mist or light rain.

Site of experiments

The line crosses a small stone bridge over the old road and enters a woodland of ivy-covered trees. The exhaust echoes off the cutting walls, in places buttressed by massive blocks of masonry, as the line skirts the perimeter of Kinneil House estate. It was in an outbuilding here that James Watt carried out some of his experiments on the cylinders for his steam engine.

Glimpses of the fields that run down to the Firth can be had before the train twists through another cutting and provides a panoramic view of the immense Grangemouth oil refinery. It is not an object of beauty, but it soon disappears from sight as the line turns to the south and leaves the estuary behind.

A high bridge over a deep cutting is close to the place where the Roman Antonine Wall once stood to deter the Caledonians from southerly excursions. Running through a pastoral landscape of fields and mature broadleaved trees, the train passes the site of an earlier passing loop.

Steam to the locomotive's cylinders is shut off and the train coasts under an attractive stone arch

▲ **Caledonian Railway 0-4-4T No 419 passes gorse in full flower as it pulls out of Bo'ness station with a rake of Swedish State Railway carriages. Built in 1907, and one of a class of 92 similar locomotives, No 419 was shedded at Lockerbie, Beattock and Carstairs before being withdrawn as No 55189 in 1962. Note the Highland Railway lattice footbridge recovered from Murthly station.**

▼ **Visitors to the mines at Birkhill descend these steps to reach the entrance beside the River Avon. The wagons, known as hutches, carried the extracted fireclay along the cable tramway to the incline, where they were lifted to the top by the weight of 12 descending wagons.**

Back to Manuel
The SRPS intends to reopen the 1.5km (one mile) stretch of track from Birkhill to the junction with Railtrack's Edinburgh–Glasgow mainline at Manuel as soon as possible. The track is in place and used by the empty SRPS mainline coach set, but it is not yet up to a satisfactory standard for passenger use.

Work is in progress to rectify this with the aim of opening this extension in the year 2000.

Double tragedy

To Victorian railwaymen, Manuel was a place with a bad reputation. In October 1862, 15 people died when two trains met in head-on collision in a deep cutting between Manuel and Winchburgh. In January 1874, there was a second collision, this time between an express travelling from Edinburgh to Perth and a goods train which had come on to the line at Manuel from Bo'ness. The station staff may have mistaken the Perth for the Glasgow express, which had passed a few minutes earlier.

In any event, so great was the impact that the driver of the express, which was running tender first, was crushed against the backplate of the firebox. The leading Caledonian third-class coach was smashed to pieces and 16 of its occupants were killed. In the following coaches, 28 more were injured. The irony is that the absolute block system, which would have prevented the tragedy, was already being installed at the time and was brought into operation only 10 days after the accident.

bridge into Birkhill station. Like Bo'ness, this is a station created by SRPS volunteers, for there was never one on this site. The cutting had to be widened to accommodate a platform and the station building, which came from Monifieth in Angus.

The platform had to be shortened to fit into its new location. The building's most prominent feature is the row of ornate cast-iron brackets supporting the canopy. More have been used than is strictly necessary, with the result that the interior of the building had to be cross-braced to prevent it toppling over with the weight of the brackets.

Passengers who accompany the return working miss one of the highlights of a visit to the BKR. A path from Birkhill station leads to a group of mill buildings almost hidden from view by trees. These were opened during World War I to process the fireclay extracted from mines in the Avon Gorge.

An inclined plane, originally operated by a stationary steam engine, enabled the small mine wagons, called hutches, to be hauled up the hill from the mine entrances to the mill buildings above. Hoppers of the processed fireclay were emptied into railway wagons on sidings from the Bo'ness branch that once ran behind the station.

Nothing seen on the journey to Birkhill prepares you for the sight beyond the mill buildings. The precipitous sides of the wooded Avon Gorge belong more to the Peak District than the pleasant but unexceptional scenery on the way from Bo'ness. A long flight of steps (regrettably it has not proved possible to provide access for wheelchairs) takes you down alongside the

inclined plane to the tumbling River Avon, which is crossed on a bridge that leads to the mine entrance. Guides take hard-hatted parties through some of the 9.5km (six miles) of tunnels that were worked as recently as 1980, when the last load of fireclay was extracted and sent on its way to Sweden.

Underground excursion

A tour of the mine is not to be missed. Hundreds of feet beneath the surface you can see the clear fossilized remains of tree trunks 1.25m (4ft) across that were alive 170 million years before the first dinosaurs. Around you are 11 million tonnes (tons) of unworked fireclay. What was removed was converted into the firebricks that were vital to many industries; this particular type was used in the fireboxes of every steam locomotive on Irish railways. After listening to the mine guide, you will look at the bricks in the locomotive's firebox in a different light before returning to Bo'ness.

▶ Caledonian Railway No 419 passes under a high bridge close to where the Roman Antonine Wall once stood. Remains of the wall may be seen within the grounds of Kinneil House. The locomotive is approaching the site of a crossing loop to the north of Birkhill, which was doubtless of use when the fireclay mine at Birkhill was served by a rail connection.

WALES

The Snowdon Mountain Railway

The Snowdon Mountain Railway is Britain's only public rack and pinion line. Clinging to the north-western slopes of the famous peak – the highest in England and Wales – it offers an exciting journey and spectacular views.

Professional carrier
Unlike the other steam railways of Wales, the SMR is in no sense a preserved line. There is not even a society to provide volunteer help in running it. The line was built to earn money from carrying visitors to the summit of Snowdon and has continued to do exactly that in a highly professional manner ever since.

Fares may at first sight seem expensive, but they reflect the high cost of maintaining a railway of this nature in a hostile mountain environment. Fuel costs are approximately £50 per round trip for steam and two men are required on the footplate. The introduction of diesel has helped control costs.

When Sir Richard Moon, chairman of the London & North Western Railway, opened the Caernarfon–Llanberis line in 1869, he remarked that the next extension should be to the summit of Snowdon itself. He may not have been entirely serious, but by the late 19th century Snowdonia was popular with visitors, many climbing Snowdon with the help of local guides.

Also in 1869, the world's first mountain rack railway carried passengers to the summit of Mount Washington in the United States. Two years later, Niklaus Riggenbach opened his Vitznau–Rigi line, near Luzern in Switzerland. Both lines used a ladder-like rack, laid horizontally between the running rails. When engaged by a pinion or cogwheel on the locomotive, gradients steeper than 1 in 5 could be surmounted.

The opening of these lines increased interest in the construction of a railway to the 1085m (3560ft) summit of Snowdon. Schemes were put forward for various routes from Llanberis and from Rhyd-Ddu, west of the mountain, but all were opposed by local landowner George Assheton-Smith, whose Vaynol Estate encompassed most of Snowdon as well as the Dinorwic slate quarries.

However, towards the end of the century Llanberis was in decline. Demand for Dinorwic

▼ Clinging to the rockface like a tenacious beetle, an SMR locomotive pushes its coach up the final section of line to Summit station. To find a similar scene, you would need to visit some of the mountain railways of Austria and Switzerland.

slate was low and walkers were favouring the shorter path up Snowdon from Rhyd-Ddu. To revive the town's economy, Assheton-Smith supported the formation of a company in 1894 to build the Snowdon railway.

Parliamentary approval was unnecessary for a route entirely on private land; construction of the 7.75km (4¾ mile) line began at once. There were no precedents for a British rack railway so Swiss practice was adopted. The Snowdon Mountain Railway (SMR) remains unique in Britain today.

Designing the line

The rack system adopted for the 2ft 7½in (800mm) gauge line was devised by Roman Abt, Riggenbach's chief engineer. Two parallel vertical steel bars, with teeth cut into the upper edge, are laid between the running rails. Each locomotive has four pinions – two on each driving axle – and the rack bars are staggered so that one is always engaged. The locomotive drives its rack pinions, not its running wheels, which are there solely to support it on the rails.

By early 1896, SLM of Winterthur, Switzerland, had delivered three rack locomotives, five coaches had arrived from Lancaster, and the opening was arranged for Easter Monday, 6 April. The day was a nightmare for the railway. Shortly after the first downhill train had left the summit, its locomotive, No 1 *LADAS* – the name was derived from Mrs Assheton-Smith's initials – disengaged from the rack in a cutting above Clogwyn.

Out of control, it left the rails to plunge down the mountain face above the Llanberis Pass. The engine crew jumped clear and were unhurt. As for the passengers, they were in no real danger. On rack railways the locomotive is marshalled at the downhill end of a train, but not coupled to it. Coaches, with their own independent braking systems, are pushed uphill but return by gravity, resting against the locomotive.

Sadly, before *LADAS*'s coaches had stopped, two passengers, seeing the engine crew jump, leapt out too. One was caught between the train and cutting wall, dying of his injuries the next day.

New safety measure

Investigations found nothing inherently wrong with the Abt rack system. The tragedy was probably caused by a slight subsidence on one side of the track after ice under the sleepers had thawed. To prevent a recurrence, a further safety measure was installed before trains ran again.

Inverted L-shaped guard rails, known as gripper-girders, are laid on either side of the rack bars. Angled grippers, fitted to engines and coaches, engage the girders and prevent locomotives from being lifted off the rails. The SMR reopened on Easter Monday 1897 and has operated safely ever since.

The station lies at the east end of Llanberis, near the ruins of the 13th century Dolbadarn Castle. In summer, the SMR is very busy and although a reservation token system operates when queues build up, passengers are regularly turned away. You should arrive early and bring warm

▲ The long operating schedule of the SMR, from mid-March to the end of October, means that trains often climb through snow at each end of the season. Even in summer, weather conditions can change rapidly on Snowdon and visitors are always advised to bring warm clothing.

clothes – weather conditions can change quickly on Snowdon and the summit often attracts cloud.

You buy your ticket from the original wooden station building before boarding a red and cream carriage. Simmering behind may be locomotive No 2 *Enid*, the oldest survivor of the three SMR engines built in 1895. Like other locomotives on the line, its boiler slopes distinctively forward, becoming level only on the steeper gradients.

Although the engines were designed to be able to push two coaches, single-coach operation is now standard. All the original coaches have been rebuilt over the years, but are still divided into compartments by crosswise wooden benches. The guard's compartment at the front contains the

Challenge to steam

Steam's 90 year monopoly on Snowdon ended in 1986 when Hunslet supplied two rack diesels with a third and fourth following in 1991 and 1992. The diesels may lack the charm of the Swiss steam engines, but they permit much more operational flexibility when bad weather suddenly improves. They also mean the season can be extended and, perhaps most importantly, they keep costs down.

The diesel influence on the line was further extended in 1995 with the delivery of a three-unit diesel-electric railcar set, built in South Wales by H.P.E. Tredegar Ltd.

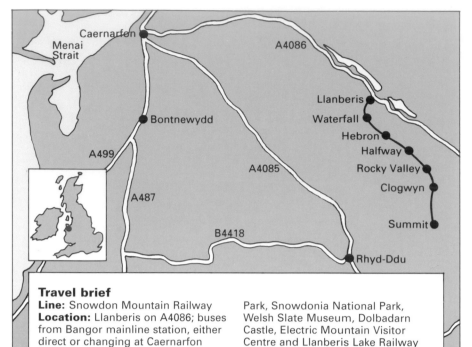

▶ No 3 *Wyddfa* (now with red livery) climbs steadily through spectacular scenery towards Rocky Valley Halt. *Wyddfa* is the Welsh name for Snowdon's highest peak and refers to the burial place of a mythological giant, said to be interred on the summit, just above the SMR terminus.

Travel brief

Line: Snowdon Mountain Railway
Location: Llanberis on A4086; buses from Bangor mainline station, either direct or changing at Caernarfon
Length: 8km (4³/4 miles)
Journey time: round trip 2¹/2 hours
Service: daily mid-March to end October
Points of interest: nearby attractions include Padarn Country Park, Snowdonia National Park, Welsh Slate Museum, Dolbadarn Castle, Electric Mountain Visitor Centre and Llanberis Lake Railway
Facilities: snacks, souvenir shop, restaurant at Llanberis station; bar, café, gift shop and special railway postal service at the summit

Rack specialist

The Swiss company SLM has justly built up a reputation as the world's leading producer of quality rack locomotives. Much of its expertise is in constructing power cars for the electrified lines that proliferate in Switzerland, though motive power of all types has been exported worldwide.

In 1992, SLM returned to its roots and produced three brand new rack steam locomotives. These oil-fired but otherwise traditional engines were for two private Swiss 800m (2ft 7¹/2in) gauge lines and the 1m (3ft 3¹/2in) gauge mountain routes of Austrian Federal Railways. More are to follow – but they are out of the SMR's price range.

handbrake and provides an unrivalled view of the track ahead.

Leaving the station, the wooden locomotive shed, containing the SMR's only level track, is on the right, with its imposing water tank alongside. To the left are the carriage sidings. The line crosses the River Hwch and straightaway starts to climb, winding past the last houses in Llanberis before reaching the impressive 14 arch Afon Hwch Viaduct.

The shorter upper viaduct soon follows, with views of the Ceunant Mawr waterfall. The train follows the river before curving left and passing the closed Waterfall station. The Hwch is crossed again by a bridge at Bishop's Falls.

After a stone bridge over a minor road, a short climb above the reedy valley of the River Arddu brings the train to Hebron station, named after a disused chapel nearby. At 283.5m (930ft) this is the first of three intermediate passing places, each with basic and functional station buildings.

In the loop you may see the works train, consisting of a brake van and open wagon, which takes supplies to the summit every morning. Heading it downhill is No 10 *Yeti*, one of two diesels supplied by Hunslet in 1986.

Railway vantage point

As *Enid* propels your train out of Hebron, curving on to a long stretch of straight track, the ruins of abandoned farms can be seen in the valley below. Climbing across the open hillside, a reverse curve leads on to a bridge across the bridle path to the summit. For climbers, this path, broadly following the railway, is the easiest route up Snowdon. It is also a good vantage point from which to observe the SMR in action, with trains always in sight.

Views of the sweeping range of hills across the Arddu disappear as the train approaches Halfway station through a deep cutting. Here, at 492m (1614ft), *Enid* takes water from the large concrete tank set into the hillside. In the loop, the downhill passenger train may be worked by No 4 *Snowdon*,

▶ Immediately after leaving Llanberis, No 3 *Wyddfa* (now with red livery), built in Switzerland in 1895, propels its single coach over the SMR's gentlest gradient of 1 in 50. The line winds away towards the Hwch Viaduct, the major man-made landmark on the railway.

▲ No 8 *Eryri*, the SMR's 1923 steam locomotive no longer operational, receives attention in Halfway station, over 488m (1600ft) above sea level. *Eryri* is the Welsh name for the chain of peaks that makes up the Snowdon massif and means Place of Eagles.

The end of LADAS

It is said that when No 1 *LADAS* plunged from Clogwyn ridge into Cwm Glas above the Llanberis Pass, at the opening of the SMR in 1896, a climber was making his first-ever ascent there. So alarmed was he to see a steam locomotive hurtling past him through the mist that he never set foot on a mountain again.

As for *LADAS*, the boiler separated from the rest of the engine and survived remarkably intact. It was recovered and sold to the nearby Dinorwic Quarry for use as a stationary boiler. The rest of the locomotive fared less well and was strewn over a wide area of mountain. *LADAS* was not replaced and the SMR has never had a No 1 since then.

▶ No 5 *Moel Siabod*, on its way up from Llanberis, approaches the passing loop at Clogwyn as No 10 *Yeti* waits to descend from the summit. One of a pair of SMR diesel locomotives delivered in 1986, *Yeti* is dedicated to 'all creatures of the mountains – living and legendary'.

one of two locomotives built by SLM in 1896 to the same design as the 1895 trio.

Climbing above the now derelict Halfway House refreshment hut towards the top of the Llechog ridge, the views become more extensive. The mountains beyond Beddgelert can be seen to the right, while to the left are the Glyders and the dark terraces of the Dinorwic slate quarries.

Around the line, glacial boulders lie randomly scattered and a simple platform below a craggy outcrop marks Rocky Valley Halt. Trains terminate here when high winds make the exposed Clogwyn ridge unsafe

At Clogwyn station, 774.5m (2541ft) above sea level, the descending train may be headed by No 6 *Padarn*, the only one of three steam locomotives built by SLM in 1922 and 1923 still operational.

These three superheated engines, distinguished by their much shorter side tanks, were more powerful than their predecessors but they proved to be more difficult to maintain. Consequently, with the advent of the diesels, Nos 7 and 8 were withdrawn. Each of the SMR's steam locomotives has three independent braking systems.

Clogwyn is the terminus when the line beyond is blocked by snow. Crags fall steeply away from both sides of the ridge, with superb views all around. Behind, Llyn Padarn and the coastal plain are visible, while to the left is the sheer drop to the Llanberis Pass, where *LADAS* plunged in 1896. Ahead, looms Snowdon itself, the railway clinging to the mountainside.

Another bridge over the Llanberis Path is incorporated into the stone embankment taking the railway across Clogwyn ridge. Curving to the right, the train climbs across the hillside, approaching Summit station along a rocky edge. This dramatic ascent from Clogwyn includes the railway's steepest gradient of 1 in 5.5.

Cresting the summit

At 1065m (3494ft), Summit station is the highest in Britain, and an hour's journey from Llanberis, 957m (3140ft) below. There are two tracks here and the complexities of the rack pointwork repay examination. At the other platform stands diesel No 9 *Ninian* and a new metal-bodied coach with picture windows. The Summit Hotel nestles against the mountain beyond the platform end.

You are guaranteed a return seat only on the train by which you arrived. It waits 30 minutes at the summit, ample time to climb the last 18.25m (60ft) to the cairn, the highest point in England and Wales. On a clear day, the panoramic views are breathtaking, which makes a fitting climax to what may be Britain's slowest rail journey, but is unquestionably the most spectacular.

The Llanberis Lake Railway

**The Llanberis Lake Railway in North
Wales combines historical appeal with scenic splendour.
Running along the shores of Lake Padarn, under the shadow of
Mount Snowdon, it follows the trackbed of a line that once
served one of the world's largest slate quarries.**

Near the Snowdon Mountain Railway (SMR) station in Llanberis, a minor road leads past Dolbadarn Castle, across the isthmus between Lakes Padarn and Peris and into the Padarn Country Park. The Llanberis Lake Railway's Gilfach Ddu terminus is next to the car park but, before boarding a train, it is worth pausing to explore the area a little.

Slate quarrying in North Wales dates back to Roman times at least, but it was only from the late 18th century that the Dinorwic quarries at Llanberis were fully developed by their owners, the Assheton-Smiths. During the 19th century the quarries assumed their now familiar appearance – a series of grey terraces, spoil tips and jagged rock faces rising 609.5m (2000ft) up the side of the Elidir mountains.

The Dinorwic quarries operated two separate rail systems. The galleries where the slate was extracted were served by a network of 1ft 10¾in (578mm) gauge railways, with well over 80.5km (50 miles) of track. It was on these lines that the locomotives which work the Llanberis Lake Railway (LLR) today, now slightly regauged, spent the first part of their existence.

A series of rope-worked inclines connected the different levels. Rail was also used to transport slate away from Llanberis. In 1824, a 2ft (600mm)

▼ Named after the mountain in the background, No 1 *Elidir* pounds along the track towards Penllyn. The locomotive, a Hunslet 0-4-0ST, was in pieces when bought by the LLR and its reconstruction involved fitting the cab from sister engine *Irish Mail*. Now the oldest working locomotive on the line, *Elidir* celebrated 100 years of service in 1989.

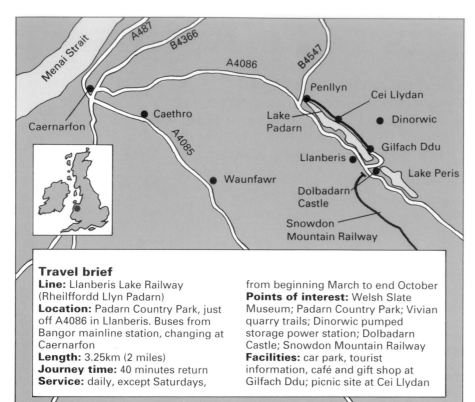

locomotive operation in 1849 when two 0-4-0 tender locomotives, built by L.A. Horlock & Company of Northfleet in Kent, entered service.

They were replaced, in turn, by three Hunslet 0-6-0T locomotives, *Dinorwic*, *Pandora* (later *Amalthaea*) and *Velinheli*, built between 1882 and 1895. The Padarn Railway owned more than 80 transporter wagons, each carrying four narrow-gauge slate wagons piggy-back fashion, two abreast. Passenger services ran for the quarrymen.

The Dinorwic quarries suffered a long, slow decline in the 20th century. The Padarn Railway closed in 1961 and *Holy War*, the last working quarry steam locomotive, was retired in 1967. Two years later, the 300 quarrymen, a tenth of the number once employed, became redundant when production ceased.

Workshop museum
The story of the quarries is told in the Welsh Slate Museum, alongside the Gilfach Ddu car park. The imposing slate building housing it was originally the quarry workshops, where locomotives and machinery were overhauled. Among the rail exhibits is the 0-4-0ST *Una*, which is periodically steamed and occasionally works on the LLR. A typical Hunslet quarry tank, it was built in 1905 for the Pen-yr-Orsedd quarry at Nantlle and never worked at Dinorwic.

Part of the old workshops is still used by the LLR as its own shed and works. Nearby is the restored cable incline which brought wagons down from the quarry to Gilfach Ddu, ready for loading on to the 4ft (1.25m) gauge trains. Several slate wagons are preserved on the tracks round the wagon turntable here.

A rough arch in the adjacent slate embankment leads to the spectacular Vivian quarry, where sheer walls of slate, rising dramatically from the flooded

Historic survivor
The Padarn Railway's first 4ft (1.25m) gauge engines were highly unusual 0-4-0 tender locomotives, built by Horlock of Northfleet in Kent in 1848. Their steeply inclined cylinders, fastened half-way along the boiler, recalled Stephenson's *Rocket*, while their amazingly long wheelbase – each wheel was mounted towards the end of the frame – gave them a curiously ungainly appearance. The general impression of antiquity was heightened by the tall chimney and complete lack of protection for the crew. They were the only engines built by Horlock.

Although one of them, *Jenny Lind*, was scrapped in the 1880s, the other, *Fire Queen*, survived for many years, preserved in a shed at Gilfach Ddu. It can now be seen at the National Trust's Penrhyn Castle Industrial Railway Museum near Bangor, along with several other narrow gauge engines, mainly associated with the local quarries. Sadly, all three of the Padarn Railway's later 4ft (1.25m) gauge Hunslet 0-6-0Ts were cut up in 1963.

gauge horse-worked tramway was opened, starting high up in the quarries and winding its way down to Felinheli or Port Dinorwic on the Menai Strait, where the slate was loaded on to ships.

This tramway soon proved inadequate and by 1843 a new railway, built to the unusual gauge of 4ft (1.25m), had replaced it. Starting by the lake at Gilfach Ddu it ran to Penscoins, just above Port Dinorwic, with a quarry gauge incline down to the quayside. This line, known as the Padarn Railway, was also worked initially by horses, changing to

▲ *Dolbadarn* drifts into Cei Llydan loop with a train for Penllyn. Built in 1922, the locomotive originally saw service shunting wagons on the quayside at Port Dinorwic. Here *Dolbadarn* was known simply as No 2, acquiring its name only after it had moved to the quarry itself.

◄ Visiting from the West Lancashire Light Railway, *Irish Mail* stands outside the entrance to the old quarry workshops at Gilfach Ddu. Now converted to the Welsh Slate Museum, this splendid building houses many fascinating exhibits, including one of Britain's largest waterwheels. It takes two men 10 minutes a week to wind the fine slate clock above the arch.

pit in the centre, provide training grounds for rock climbers and divers alike. A narrow-gauge wagon, suspended from the 'Blondin', or cable winch, spanning the quarry, demonstrates how slate was once raised from the bottom of the 15.25m (50ft) deep pit.

Two marked trails lead round the quarry, one leading past the industrial archaeology of the site and the other climbing steeply alongside the table inclines right to the top of the excavation. The panoramic views of Snowdon and the lake well repay the effort involved in tackling it.

Summoned for the off

A loudspeaker announcement from Gilfach Ddu recalls you to the Lake Railway. The first train on the new pleasure line ran in 1971, when 1ft 11⅝in (600mm) gauge track was laid as far as Cei Llydan along the abandoned Padarn Railway. Extension to the present Penllyn terminus, giving a 3.25km (two mile) run, followed in 1972.

Three Hunslet 0-4-0ST locomotives from the Dinorwic quarries work the trains. No 1 *Elidir*, previously named *Enid* and *Red Damsel*, was built in 1889 and is turned out in maroon livery, while No 2 *Thomas Bach*, previously *Wild Aster*, dates from 1904 and is painted light blue. No 3 *Dolbadarn*, in distinctive yellow ochre livery, was delivered in 1922 and is working today's train. The railway also owns several small diesel locomotives.

Dolbadarn is standing alongside Gilfach Ddu's broad gravel platform at the head of a train of six green bogie coaches. These wooden-seated carriages were all constructed in the railway's own workshops. Extensive use of glass is made above waist level, and this provides excellent all-round visibility. A post-box, with Welsh Dragon logo, is situated on the side of the guard's compartment for the railway letter service.

Leaving the station, there are stock sidings on both sides of the line, which is hemmed in by slate tips. At the end of the yard, a slate arch, dated 1900, spans the track. This carried a siding for tipping waste from the Vivian quarry on to the lake foreshore. Once through the arch, the railway immediately adopts the course it follows for the whole of the journey, with Lake Padarn on the left and slate cuttings or dense woods on the right. Often the train runs above the water's edge on a low slate embankment, providing wonderful views.

At first, the grey and white houses of Llanberis are prominent across the lake, with the church tower at the east end of the village. The SMR station can be distinguished by the pall of smoke hanging over it and it is possible to see SMR trains making their steady progress across the lowest slopes. Looking back, there are fine views towards the Llanberis Pass, the defile between Elidir and the Snowdon massif, the entrance guarded by Dolbadarn Castle on its wooded mound.

Back to nature

As the level route curves gently along the lakeside, Snowdon slowly recedes into the distance. A few

▶ No 2 *Thomas Bach* – the name means Little Thomas – receives a final polish outside the shed at Gilfach Ddu, which is part of the former workshop building. Because all the LLR's locomotives look very similar, painting each one in a distinctive livery helps visitors to distinguish them.

Quarry racehorses

Over the years, more than 20 1ft 10 ³/₄in (578mm) gauge 0-4-0ST locomotives were built by Hunslet for the Dinorwic quarries. There were some differences between them, depending on whether they were intended to work in the quarry, on the mill tramway or down at the port, but the basic concept remained the same.

At first, steam locomotives were either simply numbered or named after local places or members of the Assheton-Smith family, the quarries' owners. Later, however, much renaming took place as Charles Assheton-Smith, a keen racing man, decided to commemorate his most successful horses. Thus *Alice* became *King of the Scarlets* and *Enid* became *Red Damsel*, while *Vaenol* and *Port Dinorwic* were changed to *Jerry M* and *Cackler*. Rather inappropriately, several of the little shunters were eventually named after Grand National winners.

canoes and windsurfers glide across the lake as, to the right, the landscape opens up a little. Scrubby woodland grows around a valley formed by a small stream, which flows into the lake across a tiny promontory, briefly removing the railway from the water's edge.

Across the lake, the prominent spoil tips of the Glynrhonwy quarries are gradually returning to nature. These quarries had their own narrow-gauge railway system, connecting with the London & North Western Railway's Llanberis branch, which ran along the opposite bank of the lake from the Padarn Railway. All the Glynrhonwy locomotives were scrapped on closure in the 1930s.

Trains from Llanberis run non-stop through the halfway station, Cei Llydan. Just beyond it there is an interesting cutting dug through solidified lava from an extinct volcano rather than slate, followed by a siding into the National Grid's Lakeside Cooling Station.

This slate-built pumping house draws water from the lake to cool cables associated with the Dinorwic pumped storage scheme. The power station itself is sited in a huge cavern within the Dinorwic quarries and is well worth visiting. The LLR occasionally carries goods traffic for it.

The train continues along the shore, with little promontories intervening between railway and lake. The wooded ridge across the water, studded with rocky outcrops, becomes gradually lower. Ducks ride the waves near the shore, while boat-houses can be seen on the opposite bank. On the

other side of the train rivulets of water run down the slate cuttings.

Finally, the train stops in Penllyn loop, at the head of the lake. There is no platform here and notices advise passengers to remain seated in the train while *Dolbadarn* runs round and the guard checks tickets. With both operations quickly completed, the train returns to Cei Llydan, this time stopping in the shady station. The beach here is equipped with picnic benches and a panorama board, identifying the mountains around Llanberis.

Return service

Most passengers return to Gilfach Ddu on the same train, which continues its journey after about five minutes. But if you wait at Cei Llydan for a later service back, you can visit the Cwm Derwen Woodland & Wildlife Centre. When the peak timetable is in operation, a second locomotive, such as *Irish Mail,* works the next train for Penllyn. Although *Irish Mail* is a standard Dinorwic Hunslet 0-4-0ST, built in 1903, it is only a visitor to Llanberis from its home on the West Lancashire Light Railway.

The two-train service involves passing at Cei Llydan, adding extra interest to a stop at the remote lakeside halt. In the intervals between LLR trains, you can sit by the tranquil shore, watching out for steam from the Snowdon Mountain locomotives, improbably high on the mountain that dominates the scene.

◀ The appeal of the LLR is summed up by this picture of one of its little trains running along a narrow slate embankment with the tranquil lake on one side and the wooded mountainside on the other. The area abounds with wildlife, including snakes, squirrels and many species of bird.

The Ffestiniog Railway

**Deep within Snowdonia National Park lies the
Ffestiniog Railway. Opened more than 150 years ago to
carry slate from mountain quarries to the ships at Portmadoc,
it is a fine example of a working narrow-gauge railway.**

The Festiniog Railway (FR) was opened in 1836 to transport roofing slates from the quarries of Blaenau Ffestiniog, some 213.25m (700ft) above sea level, to Portmadoc (now known as Porthmadog), 21.75km (13½ miles) away on the coast. For more than a quarter of a century the line was worked by gravity, the wagons rumbling down laden from the quarries and being hauled back empty by horses.

However, with the introduction of steam in 1863, the Ffestiniog Railway – it now uses the Welsh form of two Fs in its title – began to carry passengers. After years of decline, it has become a mecca for tourists attracted by the prospect of an exciting journey through the mountains and forests of Snowdonia. Excursions usually begin at Porthmadog, and to get there you pass through some of the best scenery in Wales.

In high summer, the crowds throng the booking hall, shop and platform of Porthmadog Harbour station, while alongside stands a rake of red and cream coaches, some newly built in the FR's own workshops, others restored originals dating back to 1873, when the Ffestiniog became the first British railway to use bogie coaches.

You can travel first or third class. Although first class is obviously more expensive, it entitles you to travel either in the observation car or near the engine in one of the old non-corridor coaches – a treat in itself, though the disadvantage is that you get no on-train refreshment services.

True to the original

At the head end stands a unique and remarkable locomotive, the brass plate on its tank sides proclaiming it to be *Merddin Emrys*, a double-ended 0-4-4-0 built by the Ffestiniog Railway in 1879 to the patent of Robert Fairlie. It is painted a glorious deep red and, though rebuilt, captures the spirit of the original.

An articulated machine, with twin boilers and a central cab, its double bogie is a forerunner of the

▼ Dwarfed by the slopes and slate tips of the Moelwyn Mountains, the Fairlie double engine 0-4-4-0 *Merddin Emrys* hauls a down train from the terminus of Blaenau Ffestiniog past the waters of Llyn Ystradau. The engine, built by the Ffestiniog Railway in 1879 and restored to its Victorian splendour, was one of the pioneering double bogie units. During the 1870s, such locomotives went into operation on a number of other railways.

arrangement now standard for diesel and electric locomotives.

Just before the start of the hour-long journey, a deep whistle echoes along the platform and *Merddin Emrys* moves its train off on to the Cob, the great 19th century sea wall which lies round the curve from the station exit. On the left are magnificent views of Snowdonia, with a toll road immediately below and the open sea to the right.

At the end of the Cob are the Boston Lodge Works, which not only overhaul but also build engines for the Ffestiniog Railway. And what a fascinating variety there is.

The roster includes two modern double Fairlies, *Earl of Merioneth*, completed at Boston Lodge in 1979, and *David Lloyd George*, built in 1992; two 2-4-0 saddle tanks, *Linda* and *Blanche*, which both

started life on the old Penrhyn Quarry Railway and have been modified to cope with the arduous hauls on the FR; an American Locomotive Company 2-6-2 tank, *Mountaineer*, built for use on military supply lines in France during World War I; and the 0-4-0 saddle tank, *Prince*, one of the pioneer engines used by the FR when it converted to steam in 1863, and the oldest steam locomotive in the world still running on its original line.

Converting to oil
Today all the FR's steam locomotives are fired by oil instead of coal – a change forced through because the sparks of the coal burners were a threat to lineside forestry. Waste oil is no longer used due to emission regulations, and the FR's fuel bill is huge. It has reduced costs by using its

▶ The FR's latter-day version of a Fairlie double engine, *Earl of Merioneth*, steams across the Cob, the great 19th century sea wall linking Porthmadog and the railway workshops at Boston Lodge. Completed at the workshops in 1979, the *Earl* was the first Fairlie to be built for 68 years.

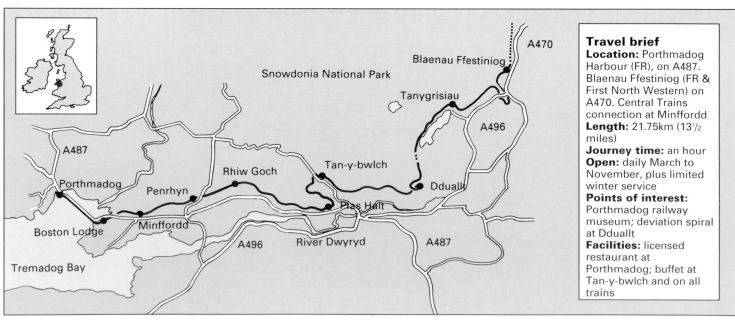

▶ One of the first four steam engines brought into service on the FR in 1863, 0-4-0 *Prince*, makes its way through the lush woodland between Penrhyn and Tan-y-bwlch. Such tracts were often set on fire by flying sparks from coal burners, so in the 1970s the company decided to convert its fleet from coal to oil firing.

▼ A lone motorist gives way to a summer season train hauled by *Earl of Merioneth*. The *Earl* and its vintage stable companion, *Merddin Emrys*, completed 100 years earlier, take on the bulk of the FR traffic at busy times since each one is in essence two engines back to back and so has the power to handle the heaviest trains.

more economical diesel locomotives for off-peak working.

The first stop on the way from Porthmadog is Minffordd, which is an interchange station with Central Trains Cambrian Coast line. A mile or so away is the famous Italianate village of Portmeirion, and well worth a visit in itself. It was created by Sir Clough Williams-Ellis, and was used as a setting for the 1960s television series, *The Prisoner*.

Climbing the foothills beyond Penrhyn, *Merddin Emrys* rattles and hisses into the platform at Tan-y-bwlch, the halfway point of the journey, and draws up alongside the water tower. In the 1930s and 1950s, passengers would be greeted by the station mistress, the late Bessie Jones, dressed in Welsh national costume and handing out tea from the station house.

Although there is no longer free refreshment, Tan-y-bwlch remains a popular tourist attraction. A nature trail starts from the station car park and runs by Llyn Mair, a picturesque lake with picnic areas from which you can watch the many types of water fowl.

To the east, the Moelwyn Mountains look down on the Vale of Ffestiniog and far to the south the skyline is marked by the silvery shape of the nuclear power station at Trawsfynydd – an incongruous symbol of the present in a world that has remained largely unchanged since the whistle of the steam engine first shrilled through the woods across Llyn Mair.

After the deluge

From Tan-y-bwlch the train crawls up towards Dduallt. Before World War I, the stationmaster here was a Welsh bard whose writing lamented the effects of working in such isolation. The line used to pass through a long tunnel beyond the station, but this was blocked up in the 1950s, when the Llyn Ystradau reservoir was built for a hydro-electric power station at Tanygrisiau, and the far entrance now lies below the normal water level.

The revised route makes a 220 degree turn around a huge deviation spiral – the only one of its kind in Britain – crosses over the original track by a new bridge and enters the 274.32m (300yd) long Moelwyn tunnel, which was carved out by volunteer miners working for the FR in 1975-76.

Beyond the tunnel, the line runs by the side of Llyn Ystradau, its waters almost lapping the low carriage steps as *Merddin Emrys* steams past to regain the old track formation at Tanygrisiau.

Passengers alighting here can go on a guided tour of the nearby power station; or they can take the path that leads to a secluded lake and the ruins of a once thriving slate mining community.

Within a couple of minutes, the train pulls into Blaenau Ffestiniog. This final section of the old line was reopened in 1982; and the new terminus, incorporating a souvenir shop and travel and tourist centres, was built jointly by the FR and British Rail. The terminus connects with First North Western's Conwy Valley branch, enabling tourists to continue on to the north Wales coast.

But there is plenty to see around Blaenau Ffestiniog itself, including the old slate mine at Llechwedd, which is now open to visitors. A special battery electric train will take you into the heart of Llechwedd.

Attempt at revival

The attempt to revive the Ffestiniog Railway began in 1951, with the formation of the Ffestiniog Railway Society. The line had lain derelict since 1946 – a state of affairs which the Ffestiniog Railway Company, heavily in debt and with neither income nor prospects, could do little to change.

But in 1954 the company was taken over by a wealthy benefactor of the society – his shares were subsequently transferred to a charitable trust – and from then on the two organizations worked hand in hand to relaunch the railway. After eight years of total neglect, the line was so overgrown with

▲ A crowded passenger train pulled by *Earl of Merioneth* brushes past the front gardens of cottages at Tanygrisiau. The remains of the temporary terminus can be seen to the left of the train. The run-round loop and sidings were lifted after the line was finally reopened to Blaenau Ffestiniog, but have subsequently been restored to increase line capacity.

In the wake of 'Little Wonder'

The first Fairlie locomotive, named *Little Wonder*, appeared on the Ffestiniog Railway in 1870. It was designed by Robert Fairlie and consisted of two boilers back to back, a firebox and a central cab. This arrangement enabled it to have more than double the power of its predecessors.

Furthermore, by mounting each boiler on a power bogie, Fairlie ensured that his engine could negotiate sharp curves and steep gradients.

Other Fairlie locomotives soon followed, including *Merddin Emrys* (shown below), which is still in use after more than a century. Moreover, a number of foreign railways decided to take up the engine and the Russians even used some broad-gauge versions, but its main effect was to increase the efficiency of narrow-gauge lines.

---

brambles, bushes and even small trees that for much of its length it was impossible even to walk along it.

Thanks to the efforts of volunteers from the society, the line was gradually cleared, and in 1955 the 0-4-0 *Prince*, fitted with a new boiler, travelled the first section to be reopened – the 1.5km (mile) from Porthmadog to Boston Lodge.

By 1968, the line had been made operational as far as Dduallt. But beyond there, the volunteers faced the toughest obstacle of all – the Llyn Ystradau reservoir. The electricity authorities had obtained permission to go ahead with this scheme before the FR's revival and it was only after a prolonged legal battle that they were forced to pay compensation to the FR.

This helped to fund the deviation spiral, but again much of the work was carried out by volunteers. In 1978, their efforts were rewarded with the reopening of the 4.5km (2³/₄ mile) section from Dduallt to Tanygrisiau. Four years later, with the line clear once again all the way to Blaenau, the rebirth of the FR was complete.

The Bala Lake Railway

**Once part of the Great Western Railway,
the Bala Lake line runs past the largest body of natural
water in Wales. The views on the 7.25km (4¹/₂ mile) journey are
spectacular, and passengers can stop off for a swim,
a picnic or a mountain hike.**

The first railway to reach Bala was the Ruabon –Barmouth cross-country route, opened in stages between 1861 and 1869 by several small independent companies. The Great Western Railway (GWR) provided backing and subsequently acquired the whole line.

From Ruabon the railway followed the valley of the River Dee, or Dyfrdwy, through Llangollen and Corwen to Bala. It ran along the southern shore of Lake Bala, and crossed the Dee watershed to join the narrow, wooded valley of the Wnion down to Dolgellau. The final stretch was along the Mawddach Estuary, in the shadow of Cader Idris, to Barmouth Junction.

Bala station, opened in 1868, was a little way from the town, on the site of the present-day Bala Lake Railway (BLR) terminus. A more convenient town station opened in 1882 with the construction of the Bala Junction–Blaenau Festiniog line, promoted by the GWR to tap into the lucrative slate traffic from Blaenau Festiniog. (Ffestiniog is now

spelled with two Fs.) Only the most incurable optimist, however, would have expected any return from providing a passenger service along this remote railway through the wild Arenig mountains.

By January 1961, all traffic had ceased on the Bala–Blaenau Festiniog line, except for the section from Blaenau Festiniog to the Trawsfynydd nuclear power station (now closed although the track remains). Shortly after that, Dr Beeching selected the old Cambrian mainline via Welshpool as the favoured route to the mid-Wales coast and passenger services were withdrawn between Ruabon and Barmouth Junction in January 1965.

Because the line ran through some outstanding scenery, it attracted considerable interest from preservationists. In 1970, Merioneth County Council, having bought the trackbed, put forward a plan for a narrow-gauge line all the way from Bala to Barmouth Junction. This ambitious proposal came to nothing, but it was decided, instead,

▼ **With Llangower Point in the background, Hunslet 0-4-0ST** *Holy War*, **shown in a former livery, skirts Lake Bala with a well-filled train. The scenic attractions of the route were exploited by BR during the 1950s by running circular 'Land Cruise' trains from North Wales resorts, taking the Rhyl–Corwen line to Bala, and returning via Barmouth and Caernarfon.**

to create a railway from Bala to Llanuwchllyn – 'the village above the lake' – one of the most attractive sections of the route.

The new line was to be of 1ft 11⅝in (600mm) gauge, and in 1971 the Bala Lake Railway company was formed to build it. The Council leased the trackbed and buildings to the company for 99 years and, with financial support from the Welsh Tourist Board, construction began during Whitsun 1972. Work started from Llanuwchllyn, where the station buildings provided a ready-made headquarters, and the first 2km (1¼ miles) of track opened in August 1972.

The initial motive power was a four-wheeled Ruston diesel from a Blaenau Ffestiniog slate quarry. Two bogie coaches were supplied by Severn Lamb of Stratford upon Avon, which also built the Bo-Bo diesel *Meirionnydd*, and they were delivered in 1973.

By the end of the 1972 season, trains were running the 3.5km (2¼ miles) to Llangower. The line eventually reached Bala for the start of the 1976 season, providing a single journey of 7.25km (4½ miles).

Steam double act

By now, steam had already returned to the shores of Lake Bala. *Maid Marian*, a Hunslet 0-4-0ST, built in 1903 for the Dinorwic quarries at Llanberis, was transferred from the Llanberis Lake Railway to the BLR in 1975. It proved ideal for the line and was joined a few months later by *Holy War*, a sister locomotive built in 1902 for the Dinorwic quarries. These two engines now work almost all the scheduled trains.

The BLR has limited facilities and no parking at Bala, so most passengers join the train at Llanuwchllyn where the station complex has been fully developed as the line's headquarters. The restored station offers a buffet and a souvenir

shop. Extensions have incorporated components from closed stations as far afield as Liverpool Exchange, while the platform canopy previously served at both Pwllheli and Aberdovey.

Holy War, resplendent in navy blue livery, can be seen taking water from the tank by the headshunt bufferstop. Its footplate crew, who bring it through the station loop to couple on to the five-coach train, are probably volunteers. Most BLR trains have been volunteer-operated since the mid 1980s, when declining traffic led to a reduction in the paid staff.

Hardy survivors
The BLR's two principal work-horses, *Holy War* and *Maid Marian*, both belong to the Alice class, 15 of which were built by Hunslet of Leeds for the Dinorwic quarries between 1886 and 1904. These robust little locomotives were used to shunt slate wagons along the quarry terraces, connected by inclines, overlooking Llanberis. Most were not fitted with cabs because of restricted clearances and their drivers must have been a hardy breed to survive the days 609.5m (2000ft) above sea level.

Larger Hunslets were used at ground level by both the Dinorwic quarries and the nearby Penrhyn quarries. Many of the engines have survived and can be seen working on pleasure lines throughout England and Wales.

◀ **The difficulty of shovelling coal into the firebox of some narrow-gauge locomotives is illustrated by the contortions of the fireman on *Holy War* as it heads west from Bala. Built in 1902, *Holy War* (now with blue livery) had the distinction of being the last steam locomotive to work in a slate quarry – the Dinorwic at Llanberis – from which it retired in 1967.**

◄The 1896 signalbox which dominates the station at Llanuwchllyn still controls the signals and points. In BR days, heavy westbound goods trains were banked from Llanuwchllyn to the line's summit at Garneddwen.

Unmistakably Welsh

Bala lies at the heart of a Welsh-speaking area and the Bala Lake Railway is more properly known as the Rheilffordd Llyn Tegid. Indeed, the BLR, which was set up with money raised from shares sold locally, was the first company ever to be registered wholly in the Welsh language. The supporters' association is known as Cymdeithas Rheilffordd Llyn Tegid. However, in spite of its Welshness, the railway is always happy to welcome volunteers – even those from across the border.

▼ Hunslet 0-4-0ST *Maid Marian*, here in previous livery, runs round its train at Llanuwchllyn after taking water in the headshunt. The characteristic Great Western Railway brick building on the left is the waiting room on the platform at which standard-gauge trains bound for Dolgellau and Barmouth called.

The narrow-gauge coaches, all of which were purpose built for the line, are dwarfed by the impressive 1896 signalbox on the station platform. The box still controls semaphore signals, but now of Lancashire & Yorkshire Railway origin. In good weather, much better views can be obtained from the semi-open toast-rack coaches than from the rather spartan closed carriages.

Leaving Llanuwchllyn, the BLR sheds and works are passed immediately on the left. Locomotives not in use, including some industrial diesels, are stabled here. It is possible to look around the sheds, where visiting steam locomotives can be found from time to time.

A long straight leads down through a cutting towards the end of the lake. The gradient downhill sharpens to 1 in 70 – the BLR's steepest – and from the open meadow of the Dee's flood plain there are good views along the whole length of the lake. Llyn Tegid, as Bala Lake is known in Welsh, is the largest natural body of water in Wales. Its excellent fish stocks, including a unique species, the gwyniad, attract many anglers.

Raising the flag

Pentrepiod Crossing, the first request stop, was the BLR's first terminus. From there, a long right-hand bend takes the train to Glanllyn Halt, with its old wooden building protected by a row of tall pine trees.

This was a station in standard-gauge days, but a private one, serving Glanllyn Hall, the large house visible across the lake. Now an outdoor activities centre, it was then the home of Sir Watkin Williams Wynne, a major shareholder in the company that built the line and later a director of the GWR. When he arrived at Glanllyn, a flag would be raised to call his boat from the opposite shore,

giving rise to the halt's alternative name of Flag station. This was the only GWR halt to be referred to in the timetable by a nickname.

Running alongside the lake, though sometimes hidden from it by the dense summer foliage, the train soon reaches Llangower station, almost halfway along the line. The BLR station is not on the site of its standard-gauge predecessor, which was on the opposite bank of the River Glyn.

Llangower is a pleasant place to break your journey. There are short lakeside walks on the wooded Llangower point, with its attractive bay

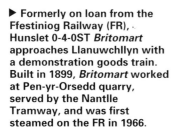

▲ *Maid Marian* was built in 1903 for the Dinorwic quarries. Following its withdrawal in 1964, it worked at Bressingham Gardens in Norfolk until 1971, when it was moved to the Llanberis Lake Railway, finally transferring to Bala Lake in 1975. *Maid Marian* is now to be seen in a new black livery and without the 'dumb' buffers.

► Formerly on loan from the Ffestiniog Railway (FR), Hunslet 0-4-0ST *Britomart* approaches Llanuwchllyn with a demonstration goods train. Built in 1899, *Britomart* worked at Pen-yr-Orsedd quarry, served by the Nantlle Tramway, and was first steamed on the FR in 1966.

and pebble beaches. More energetic hikers can head away from the lake up the valley of the Glyn, where there is access to the forests and open slopes of the Berwyns.

Departing from the station, you can see the small village of Llangower on the hillside. *Holy War* passes the tiny 14th century church of St Cywair with its massive yew tree in the churchyard before crossing the river by a two-span girder bridge and leaving the lakeside for a short distance. A deep cutting, wide enough to accommodate two standard-gauge trains, leads back to the shore, which is followed until just before the end of the journey. Before then, the track passes a small wood to Bryn Hynod Halt, a request stop serving another beach.

The open-sided carriages provide an uninterrupted kaleidoscope of idyllic lake and mountain views. Yachts and dinghies tack across the water, their sails forming ever-changing patterns in the sunshine. This is a major watersports centre, with challenging white water canoeing on the rivers nearby. Waterbirds are not deterred by all the activity and many species can be seen bobbing up and down on the waves or circling overhead.

With final views across to Bala, seen behind rows of boats on the shore, the line swings right under a bridge and into a cutting. The bridge, the third since Llangower, carries the B4403 over the line, and the cutting leads under a footbridge into Bala (Penybont) station, present terminus of the BLR. This station was intended as a temporary terminus. The BLR's aim was to continue into Bala town centre, frustratingly less than three-quarters of a kilometre (half a mile) away. A presence in the town would do much to enhance the railway's traffic prospects, but although there have been discussions on a number of possible routes, various obstacles have bedevilled the project. For now, passengers take an attractive lakeside walk into the town.

Bala pioneers

The main road bisects Bala, but the stone buildings are set back from the tree-lined thoroughfare and the atmosphere is surprisingly tranquil. However, although Bala may seem a quiet country town, it has had its fair share of contacts with the wider world.

The pioneer Welsh Methodist, Thomas Charles, whose statue stands outside the Welsh Presbyterian Church, founded the British and Foreign Bible Society. And another Bala minister, Michael Jones, emigrated in 1865 with 150 local people to establish the town of Trelew, on the windswept coast of distant Patagonia.

The Llangollen Railway

Set amid the scenic splendours of the Dee Valley, the Llangollen Railway was once part of the GWR tourist route to the Cambrian coast. After years of neglect, it has been given a new lease of life and is now the only standard-gauge steam line operating in north Wales.

There are lines with bigger and more impressive locomotive fleets; there are lines with more miles of track; there are lines which run a more intensive service. But when it comes to sheer natural beauty, the Llangollen Railway (LR) has few rivals. Located just 12.75km (eight miles) inside the Welsh border, and only a 30 minute drive from Chester, the LR rejoices in an idyllic setting beside the white water rapids of the River Dee.

The railway runs from the Eisteddfod town of Llangollen through the magnificent Berwyn Hills, the meandering river on one side and the Llangollen Canal on the other, reaching its present terminus at the village of Carrog, some 12km (7½ miles) to the west.

It would be hard to pick a more ideal setting for a steam railway, and the Flint & Deeside Railway Preservation Society (FDRPS), later renamed the Llangollen Railway Society (LRS), deserves full credit for making the choice. Unlike most preservation groups, which set out to restore a particular line, the FDRPS had an open brief to find a disused line more or less anywhere in north Wales, provided only that it could be revived as a steam railway.

A number of lines were looked at before the Society turned its attention to the former Great Western Railway (GWR) route from Ruabon to Barmouth on the Cambrian coast, which had fallen victim to the Beeching axe in January 1965.

A limited freight service from Ruabon (on the Chester–Shrewsbury mainline) had kept Llangollen on the railway map until 1968, but by 1973, when the preservationists first gazed down from the 14th century stone bridge spanning both river and railway in Llangollen town centre, the

▼ A GWR Manor class 4-6-0, No 7822 *Foxcote Manor*, passes a fixed distant beside the River Dee at Pentrefelin, where Eisteddfod excursion trains used to be berthed in special sidings. While shedded at Chester from April 1954, *Foxcote Manor* worked Wrexham to Barmouth and Chester to Pwllheli trains over the route of the Llangollen Railway.

▲ Previously on loan from the Severn Valley Railway, GWR 2-6-2T No 4566 stands at Llangollen with a demonstration goods haul. There is little in this scene to indicate that it was taken in 1992 rather than 30 years earlier, although No 4566 spent most of its life working West Country branch lines.

station had become derelict, its platforms a carpet of grass and weeds, and its overgrown trackbed devoid of any rails.

It was obvious that the task of restoration would be enormous, but there were a number of compelling reasons for taking up the challenge: the sheer beauty of the landscape; the fact that Llangollen, home of the International Musical Eisteddfod, was already an established centre of tourism; the close proximity of the A5 heritage road into Snowdonia, which gave ready access to the line; and the willingness of the local council, to which the ownership of the derelict railway had passed, to agree an initial five-year lease on the land and buildings at Llangollen and on the track bed as far as Corwen.

The preservationists took over in 1975, since when the railway has been transformed. The view from the bridge at Llangollen says it all. In place of the dilapidation originally encountered by the FDRPS, there is now a superbly restored and fully semaphore-signalled GWR station, complete with locomotive shed and workshop.

The station dates from 1860, when the then

Vale of Llangollen Railway Co. opened its line from Ruabon to the town. From here, the tracks were gradually extended, eventually reaching Bala and then Dolgellau, from where there was a Cambrian Railways connection to Barmouth.

Although there are faint hopes that one day it will be possible to reforge the link with the main-line at Ruabon, 9.5km (six miles) to the east, it is the westward section to Corwen which has been the LR's main focus of attention. So far, LR volunteers have reinstated 12km (7½ miles) of the 16km (10 mile) track, as far as Carrog.

From beside the rushing waters of the Dee – in autumn, the rapids become an arena for white water canoeing championships – the train sets off. High above it on the right is the former Llangollen goods yard – now the LR's locomotive base and engineering and carriage paint shops.

Three-quarters of a kilometre (half a mile) out from the station, the train reaches Llangollen Goods Junction, where the former GWR signalbox has been rebuilt using many of the original bricks. These were left scattered on the site after its demolition in the 1960s.

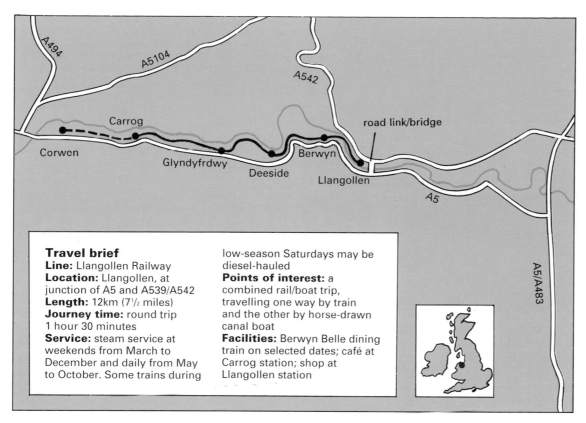

Travel brief
Line: Llangollen Railway
Location: Llangollen, at junction of A5 and A539/A542
Length: 12km (7½ miles)
Journey time: round trip 1 hour 30 minutes
Service: steam service at weekends from March to December and daily from May to October. Some trains during low-season Saturdays may be diesel-hauled
Points of interest: a combined rail/boat trip, travelling one way by train and the other by horse-drawn canal boat
Facilities: Berwyn Belle dining train on selected dates; café at Carrog station; shop at Llangollen station

It is here during busy periods that arriving and departing trains pass each other – but not until a single-line token has first been handed to or collected from the signalman. Goods Junction Signalbox – as the name suggests – also controls access to the single-line spur leading to the former goods yard.

Beyond Goods Junction, the train curves away from the canal and crosses the river by a stone and girder bridge for the stiff 1 in 80 climb up through the trees to Berwyn. On the approach to the bridge, watch out for the large expanse known as Petrefelin sidings, on the right. Originally built to berth the excursion trains arriving at Llangollen for the Eisteddfod, it is now used to stable the LR's historic collection of goods wagons, as well as locomotives awaiting their turn for restoration. A carriage and wagon museum and new restoration building is planned for this site.

Commanding heights

The delightful black and white timbered station building at Berwyn occupies what is arguably the most attractive setting on any preserved line. Perched high on a rocky ledge above the river, it affords an excellent view of the Chain Bridge – a precariously swaying suspension footbridge, now closed. Passengers often alight at Berwyn and take the short walk across the Edward VII road bridge, a little way upstream, to Horseshoe Falls, where the canal joins the river.

Leaving Berwyn behind, the train twists round a spur of rock and climbs the 1 in 80 incline up to Berwyn Tunnel – at 630m (689yd) the third longest on a preserved line. The train emerges from the tunnel and steams on through the picturesque Dee Valley to Deeside Halt where there is a passing loop and a signalbox. This

isolated halt was the temporary terminus of the line in 1990 and 1991, but the trains no longer stop here.

The route from Deeside to Glyndyfrdwy curves round beneath the vast bulk of the Pen y Garth headland, through woodland and open country. The station was reopened in 1992, after volunteers had laid 3.25km (two miles) of track in less than six months – a remarkable achievement.

The station building had been sold as a private residence so the LR imported a complete Great

▼ Hugging the course of the River Dee, a BR Class 4 2-6-0, No 76079, on loan from the East Lancashire Railway and no longer with the LR, leaves Deeside Loop on the way back to Llangollen. Few preserved railways can rival the LR for its magnificent setting.

◄BR Class 25 Bo-Bo, D7629, built in 1965, enters the loop at Glyndyfrdwy. During its days with BR, D7629 got as near to the LR as the Cambrian line to Pwllheli, on which it worked freights. Although owned by the LR, D7629 is on loan elsewhere.

forced at first to use ex-industrial locomotives and coaching stock that echoed little or nothing of its past. Gradually, however, the Great Western/BR Western Region atmosphere of the 1940s and '50s has been restored to the line.

The arrival of a GWR Manor class 4-6-0, No 7822 *Foxcote Manor*, in 1985, following a 10 year rebuild at nearby Oswestry, was a big step towards authenticity, for Manors were regularly seen on the Ruabon–Barmouth route. The rebuilding of a GWR 0-6-0 Pannier tank, No 7754, in the old goods shed at Llangollen at the end of 1992 was another significant advance towards authenticity. Also part of the locomotive stock are LMS Jinty 47298, GWR large Prairie No 4141 and LMS Black Five No 44806 *Magpie*.

A number of locomotives loaned by other railways have also helped the LR to recreate its Great Western flavour. These include GWR 0-6-2T No 5637 and 2-8-0T No 4277.

Restoration projects include an American S.160 locomotive recovered from China, large Prairie No 5199, Pannier tank No 6430 and BR standard tank No 80072.

▼ A GWR 0-6-0PT, No 7715, on loan from the Buckinghamshire Railway Centre, waits at Berwyn station. Although this engine is no longer at Llangollen, existing engine No 7754 is of the same type. With the hills providing an impressive backdrop to the viaduct and mock timber-framed station building, Berwyn is a popular alighting point for visitors to the LR.

Central Railway office building from Northwich in Cheshire. There's a manually operated level crossing gate guarding a minor road. A footbridge from Welshpool station on the Cambrian Railways' line is another feature. In 1999, the former Barmouth South signalbox was erected at the west end of the station at Railtrack's expense. It will be used as a signalling exhibition centre.

Continuing along by the river, the train soon reaches Carrog station which has been painstakingly restored from a derelict site to 1950s style. Set in a beautiful location with access to walks beside the river, this is a good place to linger and take a later train back. The village of Carrog is a 10 minute walk away.

Like many emerging railways, the LR was

Elsewhere on the railway, the period look has been enhanced by the re-erection of the former GWR signalbox from Leaton, near Shrewsbury, at Glyndyfrdwy, the inclusion of a genuine GWR pagoda waiting shelter on the platform at Deeside Halt, and the repainting of a full rake of ex-BR coaches in chocolate and cream livery.

Welshpool & Llanfair Railway

**Set amid the hills and pastures of mid-Wales,
the Welshpool & Llanfair offers a rare combination
of scenic beauty and exotic rolling stock. A former Edwardian
branch line, its locomotives now come from as far afield
as Austria, West Africa and the Caribbean.**

The rolling country of the Welsh borders is an area of great scenic charm. Small rivers wind through green valleys, pastures and woodland form a patchwork pattern and here and there a ridge of bracken-covered hills stands against the skyline. Add to this attractive prospect the fascination of a steam-worked narrow-gauge line, and it is easy to understand why a journey on the Welshpool & Llanfair Light Railway (W&LLR) in Powys has become popular with tourists and railway enthusiasts alike.

As well as its scenery and surroundings, the Welshpool & Llanfair has another attraction for steam enthusiasts; the preservation group which has run the line since 1963 operates a unique set of narrow-gauge steam engines, typical of those which British locomotive builders once exported for work on light railways all over the world.

The base for the restoration project, and the headquarters of the present-day railway, is Llanfair Caereinion, a small town in the Banwy valley. It was in 1903 that the 2ft 6in (762mm) gauge W&LLR first linked it to the bigger market town of Welshpool, 12.75km (eight miles) to the east.

End of passenger trains

The line was originally operated by the Cambrian Railways, then by the Great Western Railway (GWR) following the grouping of 1923. From its headquarters at far away Paddington, the GWR in 1931 ordained the withdrawal of the railway's passenger trains, and from then on the Welshpool & Llanfair ran only a freight service, with coal and farming sundries going up to Llanfair Cacreinion, and cattle, sheep and timber coming back.

The Western Region of British Railways closed the freight service in the autumn of 1956, and shortly afterwards the volunteer workers of the Welshpool & Llanfair Light Railway preservation group stepped in.

Although negotiations were agonizingly slow, the preservationists finally gained full powers to run the railway in 1962, but it was to be another 19 years before the line was reopened to Welshpool. Meanwhile, the enthusiasts set about restoring Llanfair Caereinion to the condition the visitor sees today.

As befitted a light railway built chiefly to carry goods and livestock, the station buildings at Llanfair were on the modest side, and the original corrugated iron booking office and waiting room have been retained for today's preservation operation. However, the picturesque signalbox at the end of the platform, despite its period Edwardian look, is a modern addition.

▶ Its smokebox surmounted by a sign commemorating the 25th anniversary of the reopening of the first section of the Welshpool & Llanfair Railway in 1963, No 2 *The Countess* heads a train across the Brynelin viaduct. *The Countess* was one of two 0-6-0 tank engines built for the line in 1902.

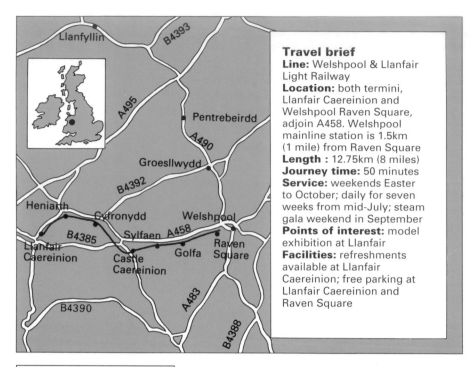

Travel brief
Line: Welshpool & Llanfair Light Railway
Location: both termini, Llanfair Caereinion and Welshpool Raven Square, adjoin A458. Welshpool mainline station is 1.5km (1 mile) from Raven Square
Length : 12.75km (8 miles)
Journey time: 50 minutes
Service: weekends Easter to October; daily for seven weeks from mid-July; steam gala weekend in September
Points of interest: model exhibition at Llanfair
Facilities: refreshments available at Llanfair Caereinion; free parking at Llanfair Caereinion and Raven Square

Troops to the rescue

On 13 December 1964, less than two years after its resurrection, the Welshpool & Llanfair was plunged into crisis. The bridge over the River Banwy was severely damaged by flooding.

With its line cut in two, the company appealed for help to the Royal Engineers, who agreed to rebuild the bridge as a training exercise. Services were resumed as far as Castle Caereinion, the then eastern terminal of the line, in August 1965, and the number of passengers carried during the year was only 540 less than in 1964, despite the setback.

Beyond the running lines at Llanfair station stand the locomotive shed and workshops. On the days when trains are operating you will probably see an engine or two getting up steam outside.

Until its closure in 1956, the Welshpool & Llanfair was remarkable for having kept running with just its two original engines, identical 0-6-0 tanks. Today, in contrast, it is the diversity of the locomotive fleet that appeals to steam connoisseurs.

Those first two engines, supplied new in 1902 ready for the opening of the W&LLR, are still active on the line. Nos 1 and 2, *The Earl* and *The Countess*, were built by the renowned

Manchester firm of Beyer, Peacock & Co. The Great Western subsequently gave them a major refit in 1929/30, from which they emerged in their present guise, sporting the copper-capped chimney and brass safety valve cover that were usual on GWR express engines more than twice their size.

Urgent priority

When the line was reopened as a passenger railway in 1963, the preservationists were faced with an urgent priority: the two Beyer Peacock 0-6-0Ts had been able to cope on their own with the fairly undemanding goods service, but now additional motive power was required.

Finding it, however, was something of a problem. Few other railways in Britain had been built to the 2ft 6in (762mm) gauge, which meant that suitable secondhand engines were not easily available in this country. On the other hand, the 2ft 6in (762mm) gauge had been popular on the Continent and in many of the British colonies, so it was here that the Welshpool & Llanfair had to look for additional engines.

The black-liveried 0-8-0T No 10 *Sir Drefaldwyn*, a stalwart of the W&LLR since 1969, is a case in point. Its profusion of domes and boiler-mounted accessories gives it a foreign look, and it comes as little surprise to find that it is a French product. It was built in 1944 and worked for a number of years on lines in southern Austria before coming to Wales.

The history of the 0-6-2 tank engine No 12 *Joan*, another well-travelled locomotive, could hardly be more different. The Stoke-on-Trent firm of Kerr, Stuart and Co. Ltd outshopped it in 1927 for work on a sugar-cane railway on Antigua in the

▶ An 0-8-0 tank engine, No 10 *Sir Drefaldwyn*, built in France in 1944 for the German military, crosses the River Banwy on the way to Llanfair Caereinion. The bridge has now been rebuilt.

▲ No 1 *The Earl*, one of the original pair of 0-6-0 tank engines which worked the Welshpool & Llanfair unaided from 1902 to 1956, heads bunker first through the gently rolling hills of mid-Wales. In 1929, the GWR fitted *The Earl* and its stable companion, *The Countess*, with new boilers and extended cabs.

together for the reopening in 1963 consisted of five bogie carriages purchased from the Admiralty. These had been used for conveying Naval personnel on the Chattenden & Upnor Railway in Kent – one of the few other lines in the UK with a 2ft 6in (762mm) gauge.

However, these provided only a short-term solution, and the line's current passenger stock, like most of its motive power, has come from overseas. The stock is of two types – a rake of modern bogie coaches from Sierra Leone and a set of smaller four-wheelers from the Zillertal railway in the Tyrol. These little Austrian coaches have open balconies at each end; ideal vantage points for enjoying the view.

Whatever is the combination of engine and coaches turned out for your journey, the scene at Llanfair station will be full of narrow-gauge atmosphere, with the engine crew loading coal up on to the locomotive's footplate a bucketful at a time, and on occasions the more energetic of the volunteer staff shunting the coaches by hand.

West Indies, and it returned to Britain for a second career on the Welshpool & Llanfair in 1971.

Another exotic acquisition is No 14, a red 2-6-2 tank engine. It was built by the Hunslet Engine Co. in Leeds for the Sierra Leone railway system in 1954, and was recovered by the W&LLR in 1975, exchanging the rainforests of West Africa for the hill country of mid-Wales.

Shortage of motive power was not the only problem faced by the preservationists. The withdrawal of the Welshpool & Llanfair passenger service in the 1930s had led to the scrapping of the line's original passenger coaches, and the train put

Bank of the Banwy

To the sound of the engine's whistle and the hissing of steam from the cylinder cocks, the train pulls slowly out of the station and sets off north-eastwards along the bank of the River Banwy.

As the loco gets into its stride, you are treated to views of unspoilt Welsh countryside at close quarters. Fronds of foliage brush past the windows and birds fly off from the undergrowth as the train steams past, the engine leaving a banner of smoke hanging in the trees in its wake.

A whistle from the locomotive soon announces the halt at Heniarth, deep in the Banwy valley and once a source of timber traffic; if no one is

◄ The 0-6-2 tank engine *Joan*, replenishing its tanks from a trackside water tower, lends an exotic touch to the W&LLR. Although built by Kerr, Stuart & Co. at Stoke-on-Trent in 1927, the locomotive spent its working life hauling sugar cane on Antigua in the West Indies. Originally equipped as an oil-burner, *Joan* was converted to burn coal and sugar waste during World War II. After a 6437.5km (4,000 mile) trans-Atlantic journey, the engine arrived at Llanfair in 1971.

waiting, the train will roll straight through at a stately 16km/h (10mph).

After a kilometre (mile) or so, the River Banwy swings off to the north and the railway has to vault the river on a plate girder viaduct of three spans before starting its climb towards Welshpool. During heavy rains in the winter of 1964, flood damage to the bridge here came close to breaching the line.

Once over the Banwy, the train is faced with a short stretch of 1 in 24 gradient along the side of the valley. As part of the Western Region in the 1950s, the W&LLR was one of the steepest sections of the BR network. You will hear a more purposeful note to the exhaust from the chimney now, as the engine toils uphill through meadows and spinneys.

The next station is Cyfronydd, built to serve a country house of that name up on the hill. Here, the train stops twice, once to be flagged across a minor road, and then again in the station itself. With such sparsely populated countryside, it is not hard to understand why the Great Western decided to abandon the passenger service in the thirties.

Magnificent views

The train steams on through open countryside, pausing briefly at the little station at Castle Caereinion, 6.5km (four miles) out from Llanfair,

and again a kilometre or so (mile) later at Sylfaen. Looking back, magnificent views open out over the rolling hills of mid-Wales.

From 1972 to 1981, when the final section of track to Welshpool was reopened, Sylfaen was the eastern terminus, and a passing loop was laid so that the locomotives could run round their trains.

Climb to the summit

Beyond Sylfaen, the engine is faced with another stiff climb through the woods to the railway's summit at a height of over 183m (600ft), before starting the steep descent down the incline known as Golfa bank to the railway's terminus at Raven Square, on the outskirts of Welshpool. In the old days, the line ran on for another kilometre or so (mile) through Welshpool town to the mainline station, a route now partially obscured by new development.

The Welshpool & Llanfair has established a fine new terminus for itself at Raven Square. The handsome station building is an authentic period piece, having been transferred from Eardisley on the Midland Railway's old Hereford, Hay & Brecon line. It was recommissioned on its new site at Welshpool in 1992, and provides a splendid backdrop as the steam engine is uncoupled from its train to replenish its tanks at the water tower, ready for the return run to Llanfair Caereinion.

▲ A young enthusiast stands close to the *The Countess* as it heads a train of mixed carriages out of Raven Square station. Like many of its engines, some of the Welshpool & Llanfair's rolling stock has come from overseas, including five vintage end-balcony coaches shipped in from Austria and four modern saloons imported from West Africa.

The Talyllyn Railway

**Opened in 1866, the narrow-gauge
Talyllyn Railway became one of the most neglected and
poverty-stricken lines in Britain. By 1950, closure seemed
inevitable. But then a group of enthusiasts stepped
in – and helped to make railway history.**

In Britain today, more than 50 preserved railways provide the welcome opportunity to ride behind a steam locomotive. New schemes are regularly proposed and this enthusiasm for recreating the past – aptly described as a second Railway Mania – is not confined to British shores. From Slovakia to New Zealand, from Switzerland to Brazil, volunteer-run railways ensure that the age of steam lives on.

Yet the first railway to be preserved and the inspiration for all that followed was one of Britain's most obscure and neglected lines. The 11.75km (7¼ mile) Talyllyn Railway (TR) opened in 1866 to transport slate from the Bryn Eglwys quarry, near Abergynolwyn, to the Cambrian Railways' mainline at Tywyn, then known as Towyn. The gauge was 2ft 3in (685mm), unusual for Britain, but shared by the Corris Railway at nearby Machynlleth.

Two locomotives were supplied by Fletcher Jennings of Whitehaven. No 1 *Talyllyn*, built in 1864 as an 0-4-0ST, was soon reconstructed as an 0-4-2ST to improve its rough ride. An 0-4-0WT, No 2 *Dolgoch*, followed in 1866. Four coaches and a brake van – all four-wheelers – along with an assortment of slate and general goods wagons, completed the TR's stock.

For 85 years, the TR led an unremarkable existence. As slate traffic declined, passenger loadings increased from the growing number of tourists in mid-Wales. In 1911, both railway and quarry were bought by local MP and landowner Henry Haydn

▼ The sylvan setting of the TR makes spring or winter an ideal season for photography, enabling the light to penetrate areas shaded by foliage in the summer. Here 0-4-2ST No 3 *Sir Haydn* hauls a train near Dolgoch. Built in 1878, the locomotive came from the neighbouring Corris Railway that ran to the slate quarries of Aberllefenni.

▲ 0-4-0WT No 6 *Douglas* stands at Tywyn station. A 1918 product of Andrew Barclay Sons & Co. in Kilmarnock, *Douglas* spent most of its pre-TR existence working the 2ft (610mm) gauge railway at RAF Calshot, near Southampton.

Jones. The quarry closed in 1947, but Haydn Jones kept the railway running. Subsidizing it out of his own pocket, he operated trains three days a week in summer until his death in 1950.

By this time, the TR was almost moribund. Virtually no maintenance had been undertaken for years. *Talyllyn* had not worked since the mid 1940s. The entire operable stock of the railway consisted of *Dolgoch* and a handful of coaches, all over 80 years old and in poor repair.

It is surprising that anyone noticed the imminent demise of this remote line. However, three enthusiasts, Bill Trinder, Tom Rolt and Jim Russell, who knew and loved the little railway, were not prepared to see it die. They called a public meeting in October 1950, which led to the formation of the Talyllyn Railway Preservation Society (TRPS).

Handover to amateurs

At the time, the idea of a railway run by amateurs with volunteer support was completely unprecedented. Nonetheless, Lady Haydn Jones handed the line over to effective TRPS control and in May 1951 the railway ran trains to Rhydyronen. The usual summer service to Abergynolwyn followed, with record passenger loadings. The tribulations of operating the delightful, if life-expired, railway are entertainingly described in Rolt's book, *Railway Adventure*.

More rolling stock was urgently required. Fortunately, the closed Corris Railway's last two locomotives survived at Machynlleth in British Railways' ownership. BR generously sold them to the Talyllyn for £25 each (plus another £25 for transport) and in March 1951 they became Nos 3 and 4 of the TR, the same numbers they had carried under Corris, Great Western and BR auspices.

The Talyllyn named No 3, an 1878 0-4-2ST

▶ One of the original locomotives of the Talyllyn Railway, No 2 *Dolgoch*, an 0-4-0WT, is seen near Nant Gwernol. Now returned to its original state, the locomotive often heads restored coaches from the closed Glyn Valley and Corris lines.

from Hughes of Loughborough, *Sir Haydn*, after the line's late owner. No 4, a 1921 Kerr Stuart 0-4-2ST, became *Edward Thomas*, after the TR's long-serving manager.

Work to make the track safer was also put in hand immediately, although the last of the old rails was only replaced in 1992. Developments and improvements continued, with more locomotives obtained, new carriages built, passing loops installed and a train control system introduced. In 1976, the TRPS extended passenger services from Abergynolwyn to Nant Gwernol along track which had carried only slate trains previously.

The TR's Tywyn Wharf terminus is a short walk from the BR station on the scenic Cambrian Coast route. Originally, Wharf – then known as King's – was only a freight yard, where slate was transhipped on to the Cambrian.

The red brick goods office forms the core of the present enlarged station building. Further down the platform is the Narrow Gauge Railway Museum, with fascinating displays about lines throughout the British Isles.

Every TR train is steam-hauled and all the original rolling stock is regularly used. If you are

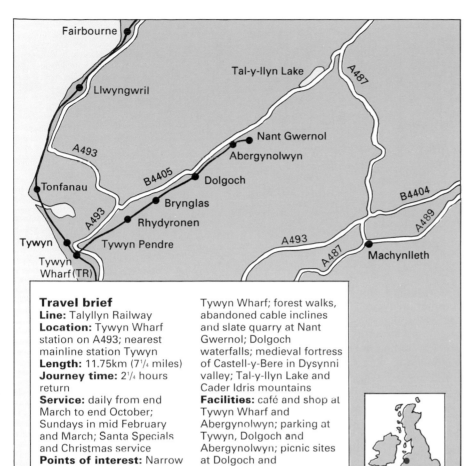

Travel brief
Line: Talyllyn Railway
Location: Tywyn Wharf station on A493; nearest mainline station Tywyn
Length: 11.75km (7¼ miles)
Journey time: 2¼ hours return
Service: daily from end March to end October; Sundays in mid February and March; Santa Specials and Christmas service
Points of interest: Narrow Gauge Railway Museum at

Faster by foot

The TR used to host a Race the Train event, and it was one of the most relaxed events on the Welsh Amateur Athletics Association's calendar. A special return train operated between Tywyn and Abergynolwyn while several hundred runners raced it over a cross-country course closely following the railway line.

The train usually took about 1¾ hours for the return journey, so many of the athletes qualified for the special certificate presented to those who managed to outpace it. Everyone taking part received a medal and all proceeds went to charity.

▶ The TR's two original locomotives – 0-4-0WT No 2 *Dolgoch* and 0-4-2ST No 1 *Talyllyn* – double-head a train west of Dolgoch. Both locomotives were built by Fletcher Jennings & Co. of Whitehaven and remained the sole motive power on the line for more than 80 years.

Pendre, the original passenger terminus and the nerve centre of the line. Carriage sheds on both sides of the track allow the TR to keep its entire stock under cover here. Inside the locomotive shed, on the right, may be 0-4-0WT No 6 *Douglas*, built by Barclay for an Admiralty 2ft (610mm) gauge line in 1918. Named after its donor, *Douglas* was given to the TR in 1953 and regauged. The railway's four small diesels can often be seen in Pendre yards.

Leaving Pendre behind, the train skirts the foot of the hills that rise to the south. To the north is the flood plain of the River Dysynni, with more low mountains beyond.

Climbing between hedges, the train passes three tiny halts before reaching Rhydyronen's slate-built station. At one time, efforts were made to promote a mineral water source here.

From Rhydyronen the railway continues along the valley of the River Fathew, a tributary of the Dysynni, with hills closing in on both sides. A long straight section gives fine views ahead of the mountain range leading up to the 893m (2930ft) Cader Idris.

Exchange of tokens

At Brynglas, the first passing loop since Pendre, *Sir Haydn*, the older of the Corris engines, may be waiting with a train for Tywyn. Tokens for the single line are exchanged before your own train pulls away again.

The valley narrows now, and the line begins to climb on to the hillside. At several places along the route the TR is enclosed by slate fences. The railway's lack of funds meant that everything was done at minimum cost and waste slate was the cheapest building material available.

Shortly after entering a pleasant wood, the line emerges on to the dramatic three-arch Dolgoch Viaduct. The gorge of the Nant Dolgoch may be glimpsed through the trees 15.25m (50ft) below. Almost immediately, Dolgoch station is reached.

lucky, *Dolgoch*, now well into its second century of service, will be working your train. Restored coaches from the closed Glyn Valley and Corris lines are often marshalled along with modern bogie vehicles, built in traditional style. Because of tight clearances under bridges, carriage doors are on the left-hand side only.

The train runs through a cutting from Wharf to

This is a charming halt delightfully set amid banks of rhododendron bushes. The open hillside rises steeply from the trackside opposite the platform.

All trains take water at Dolgoch. The original tank, now rarely used, stands on its picturesque slate plinth. Another tank, an unattractive metal structure, is located to accommodate longer trains.

It is worth breaking your journey here to visit the waterfalls in the wooded ravine. On a June weekend in 1990, the gorge became an open-air theatre for a performance of Shakespeare's *A Midsummer Night's Dream*. Transport was provided by hourly trains throughout the night, marketed as a Midsummer Night's Steam.

From Dolgoch you continue along an ever-more scenic hillside ledge, passing Quarry Siding loop by the TR's old ballast quarry. Craggy mountains, with patches of yellow gorse, rise sharply above the railway. Just before Abergynolwyn, the train passes through more woods.

Original passenger terminus

For over a century, Abergynolwyn was the TR's passenger terminus, though the present building dating from 1969 was enlarged in 1999. The long platform holds two trains simultaneously. Workings from Nant Gwernol, the upper terminus opened in 1976, arrive first, stopping at the western end where a loop allows trains from Tywyn to pass them and halt further east. Because there are no facilities at Nant Gwernol, downhill trains stop at Abergynolwyn long enough for passengers to visit the café and shop.

Heading the Tywyn train today may be 0-4-2T No 7 *Tom Rolt*. Built by Barclay in 1948 as a 3ft (914mm) gauge 0-4-0WT for Bord na Mona, the Irish Turf Board, it was regauged and completely rebuilt at Pendre, entering service in 1991.

Your train is drawn out of Abergynolwyn on to the old mineral extension, running along a precipitous ledge through dense woodland. The winding route required considerable work to make it safe for passenger trains. Above Abergynolwyn village, the line curves south into the Nant Gwernol ravine to reach the simple terminus.

A recent footbridge across the gorge provides access to a network of forest walks. You can also climb the abandoned inclines to see the remains of the Bryn Eglwys quarry at the head of the valley.

But what of the railway's namesake? The lake of Tal-y-llyn, spectacularly situated at the foot of Cader Idris, lies 5km (three miles) beyond Abergynolwyn station. The TR never reached it and was never intended to. The Act of Parliament authorizing the railway merely specified a line 'towards Talyllyn', bestowing a name on the TR almost by default.

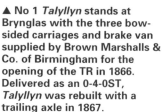

▲ No 1 *Talyllyn* stands at Brynglas with the three bow-sided carriages and brake van supplied by Brown Marshalls & Co. of Birmingham for the opening of the TR in 1866. Delivered as an 0-4-0ST, *Talyllyn* was rebuilt with a trailing axle in 1867.

Delivery to the door

Although Abergynolwyn lies about three-quarters of a kilometre (half a mile) from its station, there was once a much closer link between the TR and the village. At a point on the mineral extension where the line is 45.75m (150ft) above Abergynolwyn, a cable-operated incline allowed goods wagons to be lowered to the village.

From storage sidings at the bottom, two branches ran along the streets so that deliveries could be made by rail to the back doors of many houses and waste removed in the same way. Wagons could be pushed manually, hauled by horses or rolled along by gravity.

◄ The TR's newest locomotive, 0-4-2T No 7 *Tom Rolt*, crosses the three-arch Dolgoch Viaduct. Outshopped by Andrew Barclay in 1948, it began life as a 3ft (914mm) gauge 0-4-0WT with the Irish Turf Board. It joined the TR in the early 1970s, affectionately known as 'Irish Pete', and was given its present name in memory of the well-known writer, and one of the founders of the TR Preservation Society.

The Vale of Rheidol Railway

**For 40 years, the Vale of Rheidol Railway was
that unique entity, a narrow-gauge, steam-operated line
which was owned by British Rail. Now it is independent once
more, but still hauling tourists up to the scenic
Devil's Bridge, as it has done since 1902.**

The Vale of Rheidol Railway (VoR), like so
many other western Welsh branch lines, was
originally built to transport raw materials. In this
case it was lead ore which needed to be carried to
the coast; and, just as with its famous northerly
neighbours, the Ffestiniog and Talyllyn railways,
the mountainous countryside it had to pass through
defeated all proposals for a standard-gauge line.

A 1ft 11½in (597mm) gauge was chosen and
the 19km (11¾ mile) VoR opened in 1902. The
new railway was well aware of the economic
potential of tourism so, unlike some of the older
narrow-gauge lines, it encouraged passenger
traffic from the start. The line's mountain terminus
was deliberately located for the convenience of
visitors wishing to explore the famous Devil's
Bridge waterfalls.

The policy paid off; when the Rheidol lost its
goods traffic in the 1920s and its winter passenger
service in 1931, it continued to make money and
carry substantial numbers of passengers during
the summer months. It was so successful that it
survived up to and beyond World War II, and was
the only Welsh narrow-gauge passenger railway to
be nationalized in 1948.

Indecision by BR

Over the next 20 years the line seemed to puzzle
BR which, just when it was closing all minor
branches, standardizing locomotives and making
the decision to transform its old network into a
modern diesel and electric service, realized that it
still owned a popular, non-standard gauge railway
and three steam locomotives.

In the 1950s, BR tried to promote the VoR, but
by the 1960s it seemed determined to let the line
rot away. Popular demand kept the Rheidol
running, however, and the line survived under BR
until 1989, when it was bought by the owners of
the Brecon Mountain Railway.

In 1968, as if to atone for the years of neglect,
BR had made what was probably its most impor-
tant contribution to the future of the Vale of
Rheidol Railway. It moved the western terminus

▶ **No 7** *Owain Glyndŵr*, **currently being overhauled,
steams through one of the steep-sided rock cuttings
on the climb to Devil's Bridge. An early passenger on
the line, a colliery manager well used to deep shafts,
is said to have been so alarmed by the plunging
hillside that he sat with his head turned towards the
rock wall.**

of the line into two abandoned platforms at its main Aberystwyth station.

Although the transfer meant very little in terms of distance – the original VoR terminus was next to the mainline station – it meant that passengers now approached the VoR via an imposing building rather than the more or less open-air facilities of the old station.

These new operating headquarters of the VoR, which took over land formerly occupied by the standard-gauge Aberystwyth to Carmarthen route, also absorbed a former standard-gauge engine shed. This was large enough to house the Rheidol's locomotives and coaching stock during the closed winter season and helped to protect it from the elements.

Striking contrast

In those days, the contrast between BR's modern diesel trains and the diminutive steam locomotives of their neighbour was very much in BR's favour. Yet now, when you enter Aberystwyth station, the impression is rather different. To the left are the rusty and run-down remnants of BR's empire while to the right are the polished and brightly painted trains of the VoR. Mainline services now run only east to Shrewsbury and north to Pwllheli.

You are left in no doubt about the different scale of standard-gauge operations from those of a narrow-gauge railway. The old Cambrian Railway platforms, built at a level which allowed passengers to climb easily into their standard-gauge carriages, are much too high for their smaller VoR counterparts.

Starting the journey

A ramp leads down to the smooth trackbed surround, and from here it is easy to climb the steps of the narrow-gauge coaches. At least the high platforms provide plenty of vantage points from which you can watch and photograph the movements of the locomotive as it prepares to haul your train up the valley.

The line is worked by three 2-6-2 tank engines: No 7 *Owain Glyndŵr*, No 8 *Llewelyn* and No 9 *Prince of Wales*. On a busy day all three will be in

▲ No 8 *Llewelyn*, here bearing its former British Rail emblem and livery, heads a train out of Devil's Bridge on the nerve-tingling descent to Aberystwyth in 1971. Although the VoR has since passed to new owners, it continues to provide one of the most exciting and picturesque narrow-gauge rail journeys in Britain.

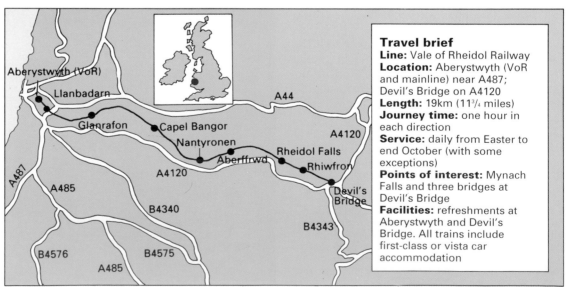

Travel brief
Line: Vale of Rheidol Railway
Location: Aberystwyth (VoR and mainline) near A487; Devil's Bridge on A4120
Length: 19km (11³/₄ miles)
Journey time: one hour in each direction
Service: daily from Easter to end October (with some exceptions)
Points of interest: Mynach Falls and three bridges at Devil's Bridge
Facilities: refreshments at Aberystwyth and Devil's Bridge. All trains include first-class or vista car accommodation

steam, two hauling trains and one as a spare. Each locomotive is 2.5m (8ft) wide and weighs more than 25 tonnes (tons), an indication of the power required for the sharp contours and gradients of the line, some of them as steep as 1 in 40.

The carriages they pull are substantial vehicles, which set new standards of narrow-gauge comfort when they were introduced just before World War II. It is not long, however, before you are given another reminder of the contrast between narrow and standard gauge.

The train steams out of Aberystwyth at the start of its hour-long journey to the top of the valley. The Vale of Rheidol and mainlines run parallel for about 2.5km (1½ miles), diverging at Llanbadarn station. From here, the mainline veers to the north, while the VoR continues eastwards along the floor of the Rheidol Valley before reaching the fast-flowing waters of the River Rheidol, which it crosses on a bridge.

As the train travels clear of urban surroundings, following the meandering course of the river along

▲ No 8 *Llewelyn* hauls a rake of GWR chocolate and cream liveried coaches out of Devil's Bridge. The locomotive bears Cambrian black livery and lettering – a reminder of the days when the Vale of Rheidol was owned by Cambrian Railways. Now it is in 1923 GWR green livery.

◀ High above the Rheidol Valley, No 7 *Owain Glyndŵr* tackles the rugged 1 in 50 approach to Devil's Bridge. No 7, undergoing a major overhaul, will return in black livery.

the valley bottom, there are tantalizing glimpses of wildlife for those with keen eyes, and tranquil oases open up between the increasingly isolated buildings.

After a while, the train begins to twist and turn along a shelf on a steep, wooded hillside, negotiating a series of sharp curves which its standard-gauge equivalent would find impassable. Here the VoR seems to enter its own little world, where modern development has yet to make its mark.

Through heavily wooded surroundings, with trees sometimes brushing the carriage windows, you catch occasional views of the steep hills on the other side of the valley and see the river swirling along its course far below.

Signposts to the past

The Vale of Rheidol Railway once boasted seven intermediate stations and halts, some serving passengers only and others catering for freight. Now hardly any signs of them remain, although occasional patches of clear ground and small signposts still mark the places where trains once stopped regularly. Passengers can still ask to be dropped or picked up at these halts.

One station that has retained its importance is Nantyronen, 61m (200ft) above sea level, where the engine pauses to take on more water before tackling the hardest part of the journey. As the line rises more than 122m (400ft) in 8km (just over five miles), the locomotive's exhaust echoes off the rocks to the right while, in places, the ground to the left drops steeply down to the valley floor. The river at this point has been dammed as part of the Cwm Rheidol hydro-electric scheme and the railway traveller can look down on the shallow lake created by the project.

On several occasions in the line's history, proposals were put forward to convert it from steam to electric working, but these were never acted on. However, the engines were converted to oil firing following the hot summer of 1976, when stray sparks threatened to start uncontrollable fires in the surrounding countryside.

Nerve-wracking experience

The next station on the line is Aberffrwd, and from here onwards the views across the valley are awesome. There is an almost sheer drop beneath the line and it is said that in the early days of its existence 'even brave men were badly shaken' by riding on it. The story has it that one railway official with a wooden leg vowed that he would rather walk back to Aberystwyth than face the return train journey.

Passing Rheidol Falls Halt, the train reaches Rhiwfron and steams under the only footbridge over the line to pull into Devil's Bridge station. Here in spring and summer the scene is almost alpine, with the carefully tended trees and shrubs blazing out in vivid colours.

The station comprises a loop and siding, and passengers can buy refreshments or browse in the souvenir shop. If you turn left out of the station and walk a few hundred metres (yards) down the road you will come to the Mynach Falls, where the Mynach River tumbles down to join the Rheidol in the valley bottom.

Opposite is the entrance to the famous Devil's Bridge itself. In fact, Devil's Bridge is three bridges, one above the other, spanning a foaming whirlpool known as the Devil's Punchbowl. The bridge attributed to the devil is the lowest and oldest of the three. According to legend, it was built by him on condition that he should have the soul of the first living thing to cross it.

This turned out to be a dog, which so disgusted the devil that he went away without claiming even the innocent canine. The actual builders of the bridge were the monks of Strata Florida Abbey, who completed it in 1087, making it one of the oldest stone bridges in the country. The centre arch was erected in 1753, while the upper one, built by Cardiganshire County Council, dates from 1901.

Such are the pleasures of a trip on the VoR – and the return journey is still to come.

New locos still going
When the GWR took over the line in 1923, the two original locomotives were worn out after some 20 years use. Approval was given to build two new locomotives at Swindon Works to an improved design with more power. These two new locomotives became No 7 *Owain Glyndwr* and No 8 *Llewelyn*. They were an immediate success. In 1924 approval was sought but not given to build a third new locomotive. Instead, GWR sanctioned a major overhaul of one of the original locomotives, *Prince of Wales*. However, Swindon Works went ahead and built a third locomotive, No 9 *Prince of Wales*, scrapping the original. These three locomotives still work the line today – over 75 years old and still going strong.

▼ A small wreath and a cynical slogan on the smokebox door of No 7 *Owain Glyndwr* mark the end of BR's 40 year stewardship of the Vale of Rheidol in 1989. *Owain Glyndwr* stands below in the former standard-gauge engine shed at Aberystwyth.

The Gwili Railway

The first standard-gauge preserved line to operate in Wales, the Gwili Railway is gradually bringing back to life part of the former Great Western route from Carmarthen to Aberystwyth. Already it offers a beguiling combination of scenic beauty and steam-era nostalgia.

In the days of steam, the British cross-country routes were a delight for the leisurely traveller and railway enthusiast alike. The Great Western Railway (GWR) line from Carmarthen to Aberystwyth never quite achieved the fame of the much-photographed Somerset & Dorset route or the fabled Carlisle–Stranraer run across Galloway, but it did possess undeniable attractions of its own.

The line ran north from Carmarthen up the green valleys of the Gwili and the Teifi and then away across the rolling Cardigan landscape past stations with names like Derry Ormond, Strata Florida and Caradog Falls Halt before reaching the shores of Cardigan Bay at Aberystwyth's imposing GWR terminus. It took three hours to cover the 96.5km (60 miles), and in the railway's latter years the motive power would have been a Manor class 4-6-0 or a Standard 2-6-4T.

As with so many of Britain's rural railways, the death knell for the Carmarthen–Aberystwyth line sounded in the 1960s. At the start of the decade, four passenger trains ran each way along the line every weekday, and the goods service was augmented by traffic from two feeder branch lines, one from Aberayron and one from Newcastle Emlyn. By early 1965, the passenger trains had gone; goods services followed in 1973. In 1975, the Gwili Railway Company was formed and two years later a short section of line was reopened.

The Gwili Railway – named after the river that runs along its length – is operated and staffed entirely by members of the Gwili Railway Preservation Society (GRPS). Lines situated near great conurbations, such as London or Birmingham, usually have plenty of volunteers to call on, but on the Gwili, which is all of 128.75km

▼ Like most preserved railways, the Gwili operates Santa Specials in December, offering photographers the opportunity to capture some winter smoke effects. Here Barclay *Rosyth No.1* runs round its train at Bronwydd Arms. In Great Western Railway days, the principal goods traffic at the station was generated by woollen mills which imported fleeces and dyes, and dispatched blankets, flannel, yarn and tweed.

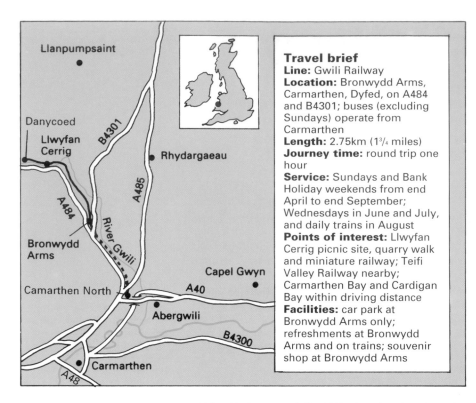

Travel brief
Line: Gwili Railway
Location: Bronwydd Arms, Carmarthen, Dyfed, on A484 and B4301; buses (excluding Sundays) operate from Carmarthen
Length: 2.75km (1¾ miles)
Journey time: round trip one hour
Service: Sundays and Bank Holiday weekends from end April to end September; Wednesdays in June and July, and daily trains in August
Points of interest: Llwyfan Cerrig picnic site, quarry walk and miniature railway; Teifi Valley Railway nearby; Carmarthen Bay and Cardigan Bay within driving distance
Facilities: car park at Bronwydd Arms only; refreshments at Bronwydd Arms and on trains; souvenir shop at Bronwydd Arms

good road access. It is on the narrow B4301 just below the point at which it branches off the main A484 from Carmarthen to Cardigan. The road crosses the railway at the bottom of a short hill, the level crossing protected by the traditional pattern of heavy, white-painted gates, complete with circular red warning target.

Next to the crossing is a 21 lever signalbox, dating from 1885. There are rambling roses round the brick base and a line of scarlet fire buckets beside the flight of steps. Visitors are encouraged to climb up and visit the signalman, who will most likely explain that the box originally stood at Llandybie station on the Central Wales line before being moved, piece by piece, to its present location in 1985.

On the other side of the line is the single platform and modest station building that now does duty as booking office, waiting room and souvenir shop. Although the original station building was demolished many years ago, the volunteers have been at pains to make the new one as authentic as possible, using materials recovered from Llandovery signalbox and Ammanford Town station. To anyone who remembers the BR Western Region country station of the 1950s, the scene will be immediately familiar: platform seats incorporating the initials GWR in their metal legs,

(80 miles) west of Cardiff, the situation is rather different. Many members of the GRPS live a long way away, so work on the line's various projects has been unavoidably slow. However, a three-quarters of a kilometre (half mile) extension to Danycoed is due to open very soon to add to the existing 2.75km (1¾ miles) of line already in use.

Bronwydd Arms station was chosen as the starting point of the restored line because of its

▼ The signalbox at Bronwydd Arms was rescued from Llandybie on the GWR section of the Central Wales line and moved to its present site piece by piece.

Late convert
The Gwili line has the unusual distinction among preserved railways of having been built originally to Brunel's broad gauge of 7ft ¼in (2.14m). Much of the early Great Western Railway (GWR) network was laid to broad gauge, which Brunel believed would allow higher speed with greater safety than the standard 4ft 8½in (1.44m) gauge adopted by other railway companies. Eventually the GWR had to change and the Gwili converted to standard gauge in 1872 – the last broad-gauge railway in Wales to do so.

◄ Barclay *Rosyth No.1* heads a three-coach train through typically lush Gwili Valley scenery near Cwmdwyfran, which means valley of the two crows, or valley of the two slopes. The River Gwili, a major attraction for anglers and canoeists, is on the other side of the railway.

trolleys loaded with milk churns and cheerful posters for seaside holiday resorts.

Like many preserved railways, the Gwili is short of covered storage for its rolling stock, and several locomotives and coaches are visible in the sidings at Bronwydd Arms undergoing rebuilding or restoration. Stroll to the top end of the platform for a view across the lines to where volunteers are busy repainting coaches or working on steam or diesel engines.

The steam locomotives on the Gwili all worked originally on industrial lines. Easy to maintain and economical to operate, they have the squat, chunky appearance typical of their kind. The two to be seen most frequently are 0-4-0ST *Olwen*, built by Robert Stephenson & Hawthorn in 1942 for use at a Berkshire power station, and *Welsh Guardsman*, an Austerity 0-6-0ST incorporating parts from locomotives built by Robert Stephenson & Hawthorn, Bagnall and Hunslet. Another 0-4-0ST, *Rosyth No.1*, was turned out by Andrew Barclay Sons & Co. in 1914 for dockyard shunting.

Coal-heaving exercise

Bronwydd Arms does not have a turntable, so most engines on the Gwili Railway face north, entering the station bunker first. Before departure, locomotives generally take water from the GWR water tower next to the platform. The coal brazier, used for keeping the water running when temperatures are below freezing, is an authentic touch. Coaling of the engine at Bronwydd Arms is arduous in the extreme, with the crew heaving coal up on to the footplate from ground level, a bucket-load at a time.

The regular Gwili passenger train is made up of several British Railways Mark I coaches from the 1950s, neatly turned out in the BR maroon livery of that period. Stepping inside, one is immediately

reintroduced to the delights of compartment travel, a thing of the past on the rail network today. A shrill whistle and wave of the flag from the guard heralds the departure of the train, hauled on this occasion by *Olwen*. The first sharp exhaust beats echo back from the engine's chimney as it tackles the 1 in 80 gradient out of the station.

The single line leads away north along the Gwili valley. Steam drifts past the coach windows

▼ Although built in 1914 for Rosyth Naval Dockyard in Scotland, *Rosyth No.1* spent much of its life in South Wales, at Pembroke Dock and at RAF St Athan. In 1973, the locomotive was bought by the Railway Club of Wales, which overhauled it before its arrival at the Gwili Railway in 1987. In the background are some of the five-plank wagons owned by the Gwili.

and the evocative smell of Welsh coal smoke permeates the corridors. The train rolls along in leisurely fashion through a landscape of meadows, rivers and wooded valleys. This is rail travel at its most relaxed.

The first stop is at Llwyfan Cerrig. Here the station, situated right next to the River Gwili, is surrounded by woodland. In former times, there was only a modest quarrymen's platform here, but the railway has built a pleasant little station with buildings brought from Felin Fach, a halt about 32km (20 miles) north on the erstwhile Aberayron to Lampeter line.

The new extension enables the journey to continue along the river bank to Danycoed but time spent at Llwyfan Cerrig is not wasted. You can look at old photographs of the line in the waiting room or inspect the various items of Gwili rolling stock on hand. Pride of place must go to the brown-painted, four-wheeled coach from the Taff Vale Railway in South Wales. Built in 1891, it was withdrawn from service in 1926 and for the next half a century languished in a Herefordshire

field, serving as a farmer's storeshed. It was restored by railway enthusiasts at Brynteg School.

North of the Llwyfan Cerrig the valley narrows. From Danycoed, the railway trackbed continues through thick woodland towards the site of Cynwyl Elfed station. The Gwili's long-term plans are to carry on re-laying the line through Cynwyl Elfed and on to the village of Llanpumpsaint. However, before that, the next extension to be tackled will be southwards from Bronwydd Arms to Carmarthen North.

On the return journey from Danycoed, the train is heading downhill, and there is less exertion from the little tank engine at the front end; in 20 minutes or so passengers are back at Bronwydd Arms station.

Regional overtones

Although the Gwili does not have any mainline locomotives of its own at present, it occasionally re-creates an authentic Western Region train by borrowing engines from other preserved lines. A particularly appropriate visitor has been Manor class 4-6-0 No 7828, sister engine to several of the type that worked the railway in the 1950s.

If the Gwili Railway is able to extend further as planned, the time may come for it to acquire some bigger engines of its own – a development that would complete the preservation picture on this engaging stretch of line.

▼ *Rosyth No.1* ambles along the Gwili Valley, recalling the days when the Carmarthen & Cardigan Railway ran a leisurely service over the line with 4-4-0 side tank engines. It was not until 1906, and the introduction by the GWR of a Carmarthen to Aberystwyth service, that the pace quickened.

The Brecon Mountain Railway

The line from Brecon to Pant was one of the most scenic in Britain, running for much of its length within the Brecon Beacons National Park. Its other attractions included a 1 in 38 gradient and the highest tunnel in Britain. Now some of these splendours can again be enjoyed.

In February 1804 history was made at Merthyr Tydfil in South Wales. A locomotive built by Richard Trevithick hauled the world's first steam train for 15.25km (9½ miles) along the old tramway from the Penydarren ironworks to the canal at Abercynon. Although the engine never entered regular service, subsequent railway development around Merthyr was swift. As the town expanded to accommodate industrial growth, major railway companies like the Great Western and London & North Western vied with fiercely independent local rivals for a share of the lucrative iron and coal traffic and the heavy passenger flows.

One of the local companies was the Brecon & Merthyr Tydfil Junction Railway (BMTJR). Although it later went on to serve the Rhymney Valley and Newport, its original mainline opened between Brecon and Pant, just north of Merthyr, in 1863, with the short extension from Pant to Dowlais Central following six years later. In 1867, however, a branch had opened from Pontsticill, 3.25km (two miles) north of Pant, following the valley of the Taf Fechan (Little Taff) to Cefn and finally reaching Merthyr in 1868.

The journey south from Brecon on the BMTJR was always a fascinating experience for, as well as the fine mountain and reservoir scenery, there was also the performance of the locomotive to admire as it struggled against the 11.25km (seven miles) of 1 in 38 gradient up to the 609m (666yd) long Torpantau Tunnel, once the highest in Britain at 400m (1312ft) above sea level.

But, sadly, revenues continued to decline, and by the end of 1962 all passenger services between Brecon and Merthyr had ceased, with goods trains withdrawn in 1964. A decade later, however, a new future dawned when an experienced steam locomotive engineer, Tony Hills, proposed the construction of a 2ft (610mm) gauge tourist line

▼ **Immaculately turned out as always, the BMR's German-built 0-6-2WT *Graf Schwerin-Löwitz*, curves away from Pant above the minor road that parallels the line. For well over a decade the engine has reliably worked almost every train on the BMR, sometimes operating with an auxiliary tender, as seen here.**

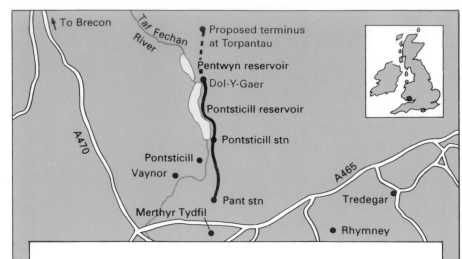

Travel brief
Line: Brecon Mountain Railway
Location: Pant station on minor roads off A465 Heads of Valleys road north of Merthyr Tydfil, Mid Glamorgan, with local buses from Merthyr to Pant cemetery
Length: 5.5km (3½ miles)
Journey time: round trip 65 minutes
Service: weekends Easter to end October, with daily trains May to August and most of September and October; a special service operates in December

Points of interest: visits to shed and works at Pant; Morlais heritage trail at Pant; remains of historic Penydarren tramroad between Merthyr and Abercynon; forest walk beside Taf Fechan reservoir; easy access by road to Pontsarn Viaduct
Facilities: free car park, café, restaurant, gift shop and picnic area at Pant; snack bar and picnic site at Pontsticill

Downhill disaster
If the BMTJR's notorious Seven Mile Bank was difficult to work for southbound trains, climbing from Talybont to Torpantau, northbound trains descending it also had their problems. Because of the 1 in 38 gradient, rigorous safety restrictions covered all aspects of operating the section. Even so, runaways did occur, the worst being in 1878 when a northbound goods of 37 vehicles, with two engines at the front and one at the back, careered downhill completely out of control. Most of the crews lost their lives in the ensuing pile-up, the result of not pinning down the wagon brakes at Torpantau as required by the rules.

▶ Coupled to a caboose built in the BMR's own workshops, *Graf Schwerin-Löwitz* drifts bunker first away from Pontsticill. When the line is extended to Torpantau, where the first sod of the original Brecon & Merthyr line was cut in 1860, trains will once again have the opportunity to pass through the highest railway tunnel in Britain.

along part of the abandoned BMTJR trackbed.

In 1976, planning permission was granted for the 8.75km (5½ mile) Pant–Torpantau route on condition that all journeys began at Pant to keep motor traffic out of the Brecon Beacons National Park. Stock began to arrive at Pontsticill, the first headquarters of the new Brecon Mountain Railway (BMR), with tracklaying around the station site following in 1978.

By the end of 1979, the line had been laid from

Pontsticill to Pant. This followed an extensive programme of repairs and refurbishments which included piping a culvert, the replacement of three bridges removed by BR and the construction of an almost 600m (1968ft) deviation at Pant, where it had been impossible to acquire the original BMTJR trackbed. The first passenger trains of the new era ran in June 1980, with most services that year worked by *Sybil*, an 0-4-0ST built by Hunslet in 1903 for the Pen-yr-Orsedd slate quarry at Nantlle near Caernarfon in North Wales.

Coming up for air
Arriving at Pant station, you will see a cylindrical brick structure by the car-park entrance. This surmounts a ventilation shaft for the tunnel on the old London & North Western Railway line from Abergavenny, which joined the BMTJR's Pontsticill–Merthyr route at Morlais Junction, near the western end of the tunnel. A second ventilation shaft stands immediately in front of the BMR's magnificent three-storey station and works building. This building, constructed in the early 1980s, incorporates a booking office, offices and workshop.

The booking office is on the ground floor and, although ticket sales are computerized, traditionalists can purchase souvenir Edmondson tickets for a nominal sum. A pleasantly spacious café is also provided, and from the concourse a ramp leads up to a mezzanine level from where you can see the engine shed and workshop and watch the process of locomotive restoration.

The workshop is comprehensively equipped, with a wheel lathe, grinding and milling machinery, a woodworking shop and a three tonne (ton) overhead travelling crane. The BMR is virtually self-sufficient for its engineering needs. The large 0-6-0 diesel standing at the far end of the shed was assembled at Pant in 1987 from a set of Baguley parts.

In previous years, two of the Vale of Rheidol

◄ *Graf Schwerin-Löwitz* receives last-minute attention before departing with a train from Pant. The station here is built on a green-field site, slightly off the route of the original Brecon & Merthyr line. The station complex is one of the best-equipped to be found on a British pleasure railway and contrasts sharply with the early days of the BMR, when facilities were provided from a portable cabin.

steam locomotives, Nos 8 and 9, have been rebuilt here, as has the Baldwin Pacific No 2, now running on the BMR. Wrecked in 1974 and subsequently purchased by Tony Hills as an insurance company write-off, this American locomotive formerly worked the Eastern Province Cement Company railway in Port Elizabeth, South Africa. The railway has plans for another ex-South African railway engine, Garratt No 77 Class NGG13, to be rebuilt in due course.

At the BMR, there is a continuous programme of carriage and wagon building. In addition to this, the construction of several new locomotives ensures a busy schedule for the BMR's engineers.

Soviet bloc survivor

Another ramp leads to the first floor of the station building, with a large covered waiting area and gift shop. Doors lead out on to a platform adorned with hanging baskets and windowboxes full of colourful flowers. At the head of the waiting train is the locomotive that has been the mainstay of the BMR from its second season, the delightful 0-6-2WT *Graf Schwerin-Löwitz*, built by Arn Jung in 1908. Although now painted in an attractive maroon livery, the engine still carries a Deutsche Reichsbahn plate as a reminder of the days when it worked on the Mecklenburg–Pommersche Schmalspurbahn network in the former German Democratic Republic.

The train consists of four wooden-seated end balcony coaches, built on South African underframes by the BMR, and a maroon caboose that was constructed at Pant in 1989. Based on a design from the long-closed Sandy River & Rangeley Lakes line in Maine, it features longitudinal

seating, a working stove and a pair of elevated seats, popular with children, which provide a high-level view from the glazed clerestory. All the views are from the left of the train and the large picture windows in the brown-liveried coaches allow them to be fully appreciated.

Punctually the train departs, passing the works yard before curving to the right above the minor road that follows the line all the way to Pontsticill. Looking back, there are good views of the weathered limestone cliffs formed by quarrying on Morlais Hill, with the gravestones of Pant cemetery sloping down one side. Further away are the freshly cut faces of the Vaynor quarries, where limestone, once used as flux in the iron industry, is still extracted, though nowadays it is used for aggregate.

Swinging back to the left along a hillside ledge, the train heads due north high above the wooded

Veteran from Germany

The original home of the BMR's German-built 0-6-2WT, *Graf Schwerin-Löwitz*, was the Mecklenburg–Pommersche Schmalspurbahn (MPSB), an extensive network of 1ft 11½in (597mm) gauge lines serving a rural area of low-lying woods and lakes in north Germany. Opening in sections between 1891 and 1928, it reached a maximum length of 217km (134¾ miles). Much of the railway closed at the end of World War II, though the route from Friedland to Anklam via Dennin lingered on until 1969.

Services were sparse, despite the fact that a maximum of 27 locomotives, 31 coaches and 768 wagons was in operation. *Graf Schwerin-Löwitz* was locomotive No 5 of the MPSB, becoming No 99.3353 of the Deutsche Reichsbahn.

▶ With the valve tower of the Pontsticill reservoir prominent in the foreground, *Graf Schwerin-Löwitz* steams past the minor road along the dam wall. The original Pentwyn reservoir attracted so many visitors that a pleasure steamer operated on it from 1866, and regular regattas were held there.

▼ The spectacular landscape of South Wales provides a marked contrast with the plains of north Germany, *Graf Schwerin-Löwitz's* original home. As the locomotive steams back towards Pant, Pontsticill village can be seen on the hillside across the Taf Fechan, while a reminder of the industrial past is provided by the quarry face on the right.

valley of the Taf Fechan. Sheep and cattle graze the steep pasture above the tree line across the river. Just after crossing an occupation bridge, the rough hillside on the right gives way to the crags of the disused Twynau Gwynion quarries, with further traces of quarrying visible towards the bottom of the valley, near a group of isolated farm buildings.

Pontsticill village is prominent on the opposite hillside, divided into three distinct sections, with the old village centre flanked by more recent housing estates. Just off to the left of the village a track leads to a whitewashed farmhouse on a plateau above the river.

The train now passes through a wood, with more remains of quarrying on the right. In summer, the bracken occasionally grows high enough to obscure the views, while the profusion of wild flowers lining the track contrasts with the gnarled trees higher up the hills.

As you cross the boundary of the Brecon Beacons National Park, the grassy dam of Pontsticill reservoir, visible for most of the way, looms ahead. The waters of the reservoir stretch away between wooded banks, with open moorland beyond. In a splendid panorama at the head of the lake are the rounded summits of the Brecon Beacons themselves, culminating in the 867.75m (2847ft) Pen-y-Fan. Directly below the train the old trackbed of the BMTJR from Merthyr can be seen as it climbs towards Pontsticill.

If you have a car, it is worth taking the minor road through Pontsticill and Vaynor on the opposite side of the valley to see the stone Pontsarn Viaduct. This and the Cefn Coed Viaduct further down towards Merthyr are the most substantial remains of the route.

As you approach Pontsticill, you look down on a small stone road bridge across the Taf Fechan, just by Welsh Water's £23 million water treatment plant. Behind it, below the dam wall, are the Taf Fechan Water Supply Board's original buildings, while the spire of the valve tower can be seen rising from the south-west corner of the reservoir.

Graf Schwerin-Löwitz hauls the train past the dam and into Pontsticill station, with the BMR's original works building on the left. The station lies on a broad hillside shelf, directly above the reservoir, with superb lake and mountain views all round.

The train continues alongside the reservoir with changing views of the mountains as it proceeds to Dol-y-Gaer. Here there is a run-round loop, but sadly lack of space means there is no platform. Passengers have to remain on the train until it arrives back at Pontsticill station.

At Pontsticill, the original BMTJR signalbox has been rebuilt and converted into self-catering holiday accommodation. Passenger facilities are provided from three converted British Rail bogie vans, with a verandah added. The 20 minute stop at Pontsticill allows time for a picnic, a short walk or a visit to the snack bar. A longer stay is rewarding, but do not forget to check the times of the trains back.

Coming soon
Just beyond Dol-y-Gaer work is in progress to extend the track a further 2.75km (1³/₄ miles) to Torpantau. This section, due to open in 2001, has tough gradients and will provide a worthy challenge for the restored South African locomotives No 2 and No 77, once it is fully operational.

Index

TELEPHONE NUMBERS/WEBSITE ADDRESSES

The Bala Lake Railway
www.bala-lake-railway.co.uk   01678 540666

Birmingham Railway Museum
www.vintagetrains.co.uk   0121 707 4696

The Bluebell Railway
www.bluebell-railway.co.uk   01825 723777

The Bodmin & Wenford Railway
members.aol.com/bodwenf   01208 73666

The Bo'ness & Kinncil Railway
www.srps.org.uk   01506 822298

The Bowes Railway
www.bowesrailway.co.uk   0191 416 1847

The Brecon Mountain Railway
n/a   01685 722988

Didcot Railway Centre
www.didcotrailwaycentre.org.uk   01235 817200

The East Anglian Railway Museum
info@earm.co.uk   01206 242524
www.btinternet.com/earm

The East Lancashire Railway
www.east-lancs-rly.co.uk   0161 764 7790

Embsay & Bolton Abbey Steam Railway
www.yorkshirenet.co.uk/embsaybasteamrailway
   01756 710614

The Ffestiniog Railway
www.festrail.co.uk   01766 512340

Great Central Railway
www.gcrailway.co.uk   01509 230726

The Gwili Railway
www.gwili-railway.co.uk   01267 230666

Isle of Man Railways
railinfo@bus-rail.gov.im   01624 663366

Isle of Wight Steam Railway
n/a   01983 882204

The Keighley & Worth Valley Railway
www.kwvr.co.uk   01535 645214

The Lakeside & Haverthwaite Railway
n/a   015395 31594

Liverpool Road Station Museum
www.edes.co.uk/mussci   0161 832 2244

The Llanberis Lake Railway
www.lake-railway.freeserve.co.uk   01286 870549

Llangollen Railway
www.joyces.demon.co.uk/llangollen   01978 860979

The Mid-Hants Railway
www.watercressline.co.uk   01962 733810

Midland Railway Centre
www.uel.ac.uk/pers/1278/rlypres/mrc   01773 747674

National Railway Museum
www.nrm.org.uk   01904 621261

The North Norfolk Railway
www.nnrail.co.uk   01263 822045

The North Yorkshire Moors Railway
www.nymr.demon.co.uk   01751 472508

Paignton & Dartmouth Railway
n/a   01803 555872

The Railway Age, Crewe
n/a   01270 212130

The Ravenglass & Eskdale Railway
www.ravenglass-railway.co.uk   01229 717171

The Romney, Hythe & Dymchurch Railway
www.rhdr.demon.co.uk   01797 362353

Severn Valley Railway
www.svr.co.uk   01299 403816

The Snowdon Mountain Railway
www.snowdonrailway.force9.co.uk   01286 870223

The South Devon Railway
www.southdevonrailway.org   01364 642338

The Strathspey Railway
www.btinternet.com/~strathspey.railway.index
   01479 810725

The Swanage Railway
www.swanrail.demon.co.uk   01929 425800

The Talyllyn Railway
www.talyllyn.co.uk   01654 710472

The Tanfield Railway
www.tanfield-railway.co.uk   0191 388 7545

The Vale of Rheidol Railway
n/a   01970 625819

The Welshpool & Llanfair Railway
Coming soon   01938 810441

West Somerset Railway
www.west-somerset-railway.co.uk   01643 704996

PICTURE ACKNOWLEDGEMENTS

Photographs: 3 Laurie Manns, 4 Peter J Stone; 5 Eric Hayman; 6-7 Robert Harding Picture Library (Roy Rainford); 8 Derek Huntriss (t); Peter J Stone (b); 9 Peter J Stone; 10 David J Holman (tc); Eaglemoss Publications (bl); 12 John Hunt (t); West Somerset Railway (Don Bishop/Steam Recreations) (b); 13 Eric Hayman; 14 John Hunt (tl); Peter J Stone (cl); 15 John Cooper-Smith; 16 Collections (Alain Le Garsmeur); 17 Mark Wilkins; 18 Collections (Alain Le Garsmeur) (tl); Millbrook House Picture Library (John S Whiteley) (tr); 19 David Rodgers (cr); Collections (Alain Le Garsmeur) (bl); 20 Mark Wilkins (t); Collections (Alain Le Garsmeur) (bl); 21 Bodmin & Wenford Railway; 22 Derek Huntriss; 23 Peter Lemmey (t); Derek Huntriss (b); 24 Derek Huntriss; 25 Geoff Silcock; 26 Geoff Silcock; 27 Peter J Stone (tl); Geoff Silcock (b); 28 John Bird; 29 Geoff Silcock; 30 Laurence Waters; 31 Laurence Waters (t); Millbrook House Picture Library (Hugh Ballantyne) (b); 32 Millbrook House Picture Library (Hugh Ballantyne) (t); Geoff Silcock (b); 33 Peter J Stone (cr); Mike Esau (b); 34 Collections (Alain Le Garsmeur) (t); Millbrook House Picture Library (John S Whiteley) (b); 35 Peter J Stone ; 36 Mike Esau (t); Collections (Alain Le Garsmeur) (b); 37 Mike Esau; 38 Geoff Silcock; 39 Mid-Hants Railway (Diana Snow) (t); Anthony Lambert (b); 40 Geoff Silcock; 41 Geoff Silcock (tr); Railways Milepost 92 1/2 (D Smith) (b); 42 Geoff Silcock; 43 Jim Winkley; 44 Anthony Lambert (t); Railways Milepost 92 1/2 (b); 46 Anthony Lambert (tl); Chris Gammell (br); 47 David Rodgers; 48 David Rodgers; 49 Peter Lemmey; 50 Laurie Manns (tl); Millbrook

House Picture Library (Gavin Morrison) (b); 51 John Everitt; 52 Jim Winkley; 53 Jim Winkley (tl); Anthony Lambert (br); 54 Neil Holmes (tl); North Norfolk Railway (br); 55 Geoff Silcock; 56 Geoff Silcock; 57 Sylvia Cordaiy Picture Library (Helga Wilcocks) (tr); Geoff Silcock (b); 58 Geoff Silcock; 59 Geoff Silcock; 60 Geoff Silcock; 61 Millbrook House Picture Library (Hugh Ballantyne); 62 Jim Winkley; 63 Jim Winkley; 64 Jim Winkley; 65 Millbrook House Picture Library; 66 Paul Stratford; 67 John Bird (t); Anthony Lambert (b); 68 Millbrook House Picture Library; 69 Jonathan Webb; 70 Millbrook House Picture Library (E talbot) (sp); David Rodgers (bl); 71 Chris Kapolka; 72 David Rodgers; 73 Millbrook House Picture Library (Hugh Ballantyne) (t), David Rodgers (c); (John S Whiteley) (b); 74 Mike Esau; 75 Geoff Silcock (bl); 76 Railways Milepost 92 1/2 (WA Sharman); 77 Railways Milepost 92 1/2 (WA Sharman) (tl); Paul Stratford (bc); 78 Railways Milepost 92 1/2 (WA Sharman); 79 Paul Stratford; 80 John Cooper-Smith; 81 Millbrook House Picture Library (Hugh Ballantyne); 82 Dr L A Nixon (tc); Laurie Manns (c); 83 Jim Winkley; 84 John Cooper-Smith; 85-87 David Rodgers; 88 David Rodgers (tl); Paul Stratford (b); 90 David Rodgers; 91 David Rodgers; 92 Museum Of Science & Industry; 93 Millbrook House Picture Library (Hugh Ballantyne); 94 Jim Winkley; 95 John A Coiley; 96 Jim Winkley (tc); Embsay & Bolton Abbey Steam Railway (bl); 97 Anthony Lambert; 98 Paul Stratford; 99 John Hunt; 100 Paul Stratford (t); David Rodgers (bl); 101 David Rodgers; 102 Anthony Lambert; 103 Collections

(Alain Le Garsmeur); 104 Collections (Alain Le Garsmeur) (t); Robert Harding Picture Library (bl); 106 David Rodgers; 107 Jim Winkley; 108 Sylvia Cordaiy Picture Library (BC); Jim Winkley (tl); 109 Jim Winkley (tr); Sylvia Cordaiy Picture Library (br); 110 Robert Harding Picture Library; 111 John Hunt; 112 John Hunt; 113 Anthony Lambert; 114 Jim Winkley; 115 Melvyn Hopwood; 116 Anthony Lambert; 117 Melvyn Hopwood (t); Anthony Lambert (b); 118, 119 Anthony Lambert; 120 Millbrook House Picture Library (Hugh Ballantyne); 121 John Hunt; 122 John Hunt (t); Millbrook House Picture Library (Hugh Ballantyne) (br); 123 John Hunt; 124 Millbrook House Picture Library (John S Whiteley); 125 Collections (Alain Le Garsmeur) (t); Dr John Sagar (bl); 126 Keighley & Worth Railway (G.Maple) (br); 127 Jim Winkley; 128 Anthony Lambert (tr); Keighley & Worth Railway (G.Maple) (b); 129 Jim Winkley; 130 Science & Society Picture Library/National Railway Museum; 131 Jim Winkley; 132-133 Science & Society Picture Library/National Railway Museum; 133 Sylvia Cordaiy Picture Library (Monika Smith); 134 Science & Society Picture Library/National Railway Museum; 135 Science & Society Picture Library/National Railway Museum; 136-137 Getty Images (Stone/C. Kapolka); 138-139 Strathspey Railway (the late Dugald Campbell) (tc); Millbrook House Picture Library (Peter J Robinson) (b); 139 Anthony Lambert; 140 Roger Bastin; 141 John Bird (tr); Anthony Lambert (b); 142 Bill Robertson Photographer; 143 Roger Bastin; 144 John Hunt; 145 Anthony Lambert; 146 John Peter (t); Anthony

Lambert (bl); 147 Dr L A Nixon; 148-149 Collections (Alain le Garsmeur); 150 John Hunt; 151 Derek Huntriss; 152 Donald Brooks; 153 Donald Brooks; 154 Donald Brooks (tl); Millbrook House Picture Library (Hugh Ballantyne) (br); 155 Anthony Lambert; 156 Donald Brooks; 157 Donald Brooks; 158 Laurie Manns; 159 Peter Johnson; 160 David Rodgers; 161 Peter Johnson; 162 David Rodgers (tr); Millbrook House Picture Library (bl); 163 Donald Brooks; 164 Laurie Manns; 165 Anthony Lambert; 166 Millbrook House Picture Library (J M Jarvis) (tl); Laurie Manns (b); 167 David Wilcock; 168 David Rodgers; 169 John Hunt; 170 John Hunt (tl); Millbrook House Picture Library (Hugh Ballantyne) (b); 171 Ralph Cartwright; 172 Millbrook House Picture Library (Hugh Ballantyne); 173 Chris Gammell (tl); Ralph Cartwright (bl); 174 Millbrook House Picture Library (Hugn Ballantyne); 175 Derek Huntriss; 176 David Rodgers; 177 Eddie Castellan; 178 Eddie Castellan; Anthony Lambert; 179 Geoff Rixon; 180 John A Coiley; 181 Anthony Lambert (tr); Derek Huntriss (bl); 182 Anthony Lambert; 183 Mike Jones; 184 Mike Jones; 185 Peter Lemmey; 186 Mike Jones; 187 C M Whitehouse; 188 Laurie Manns; 189 C M Whitehouse (t); Donald Brooks (b); 190 Donald Brooks.

All illustrations by Duncan Kitson and Paul Kellett, copyright Eaglemoss Publications, except those on pages 18, 30, 32 & 160 by Mick Gillah.

192